Life After J. E. B. Stuart

The Memoirs of His Granddaughter, Marrow Stuart Smith

Edited by
Sean M. Heuvel

HAMILTON BOOKS

A division of
ROWMAN & LITTLEFIELD PUBLISHERS, INC.
Lanham • Boulder • New York • Toronto • Plymouth, UK

Copyright © 2012 by
University Press of America,® Inc.
4501 Forbes Boulevard
Suite 200
Lanham, Maryland 20706
UPA Acquisitions Department (301) 459-3366

Estover Road
Plymouth PL6 7PY
United Kingdom

Library of Congress Control Number: 2011921893
ISBN: 978-0-7618-5463-0 (paperback : alk. paper)
eISBN: 978-0-7618-5464-7

∞™ The paper used in this publication meets the minimum
requirements of American National Standard for Information
Sciences—Permanence of Paper for Printed Library Materials,
ANSI Z39.48-1992

Contents

Contents

Foreword

My grandmother, Mary Marrow Stuart Smith, was the most interesting person I have ever known–I think you will like her story. She was eminently resourceful, seamlessly reconciling passion and practicality. She poured her heart into everything she did, to impressive effect: she was an accomplished artist, educator, naturalist, community leader, mentor and hostess. And not to be overlooked, herein we have ample evidence of her writing skill, prodigious memory and eye for detail.

Grandmother wore green sneakers, had red hair, and grew blue hydrangeas as big as platters. She had no stage fright. She had a hearty, unselfconscious and whooping laugh that belied her five-foot stature. She never owned a TV, yet stayed abreast of all news, from local to global. She could not vote until she was 31 years old, yet secured for herself an impressive amount of influence (for a woman) in the Norfolk Public School System and regional artistic circles. Collectors and curators alike prized her primitive and modern canvases and prints. I recently met a collector who has 15 of her mid-century works!

Grandmother treasured her dozens of friends and thousands of students over a 40 year career. She believed there was artistry within every young person and she worked to offer each child a range of artistic media. She accepted artistic expression where she found it and never diminished one art form over another. She was loyal, once you had earned her support, but she was no pushover. A shrewd judge of character, she was attuned to sycophancy, always observant but never cynical.

She was the eldest Stuart of her generation, and like her grandfather, Maj. Gen. J.E.B. Stuart, CSA (albeit in a different context), she understood the advantage of being a *moving target,* frustrating her critics and detractors, who could barely establish their aim. As a Stuart, she was expected to know this basic lesson, and most importantly, to personify core principles of the family: *honesty, loyalty, humility, charity, service, self-examination, gratitude, compassion and lightheartedness.*

It was my exceptional good luck to have inherited her papers, and to find a brilliant and capable editor, historian and author, Sean Heuvel. I hoped he would understand her life, which had overlapped his by only five years. I wanted someone who was familiar with our family, and a Virginian, of course. Sean was, in fact, doing research on the Stuarts when we met. He then spent hours immersed in Grandmother's writing, peppering me with insightful questions about my old family photos and about the dynamics of the Stuart clan. I found he had a familiar passion for his chosen career. He and Grandmother might be, in some respects, two peas in a pod. I am so grateful to him for his dedication to this project.

But would Grandmother have approved of my choice? I envisioned a visit between them at her beloved Drewmar, her home in Virginia Beach, Virginia. I read some of Grandmother's old letters, and felt I could "plausibly hypothesize" her account of the visit, to wit:

Dearest Sharon,
Where did you find this charming young man? He is a professor, a writer, a historian AND a researcher. So many hats! He WANTS to present my story to the world, and I think he can do it! He is clever and he has energy. He has studied our family — several generations. We are of the same mind: my story must be published for all to find whatever lesson or amusement it might offer. He is such a fine gentleman, (and you know this is of importance to me), very literary, with such a considerate manner. He was reared, as I was, to value hard work, honesty, lightheartedness, and — well, you know the rest. And he is fearless! He has brains and charm, good manners and sharp instincts. Sharon, I can work with him! We are agreed, he will be my 'emendator.' (I have a new word, use the dictionary.)

All my love, Grandma.

She was the most interesting person I have ever known, my grandmother. I think you will like her story.

Sharon Stuart McRee
Pasadena, California
September 2010

Editor's Note

The editorial goal of *Life After J.E.B. Stuart* was to write an accurate, annotated, and unabridged version of Mary Marrow Stuart Smith's original memoirs, written throughout the 1940s and early 1950s in her home (called "Drewmar") in modern-day Virginia Beach, Virginia. A secondary goal was to present the original narrative in an engaging manner that was understandable and meaningful to modern readers. The resulting book is not a literal transcription of Marrow's original 400-plus-page manuscript, as several challenges prevented an exact replication of her original words. For instance, the original version of Marrow's memoirs was a complex collection of forty-eight narrative essays that lacked formal organization. It was difficult to tell where her memoirs began and where they ended. Therefore, I consolidated her original essays as chapters that are chronologically organized, transitioning from her ancestry to her early life and later adulthood. Some of the chapter titles stem from Marrow's original writing, and I chose others to capture the theme of each respective section in the book. The book's title, *Life After J.E.B. Stuart*, is my view of the central theme of Marrow's worldview in the aftermath of her grandfather's premature death.

As an award-winning author and essayist, Marrow enjoyed writing in the genres of fiction and poetry. She included many short stories and poems as supplements to her original memoirs, including stories about her childhood dolls and poetic reflections about her home, Drewmar. Space limitations led me to omit these works from *Life After J.E.B. Stuart* since they do not directly address Marrow's life or her family's history. Also, other supplemental materials, including letters, newspaper articles, notes, and pamphlets were not included.

As I reviewed Marrow's original essays, it was also clear that she wrote them over the span of several years. Naturally, she often repeated herself and frequently discussed the same life experiences in multiple sections of the manuscript. I consolidated much of Marrow's original writing as needed to avoid unnecessary repetition and confusion. Specifically, different versions of the same story have been organized into a single account in some instances to provide greater clarity and comprehension. With the help of Marrow's granddaughter, I also rephrased some of her 19th century-era phrases and expressions into words more understandable to modern readers. These editorial decisions do not alter Marrow's original accounts in any substantive way. Rather, they retain the original flavor of her writing while helping the modern reader.

Along with consolidation of original writing, a number of changes pertaining to grammar and writing style have been made to assist readers and follow modern usage. In Marrow's original essays, there were a number of "run-on" sentences linked together by "ands" and "buts". In other places, there were sentences that contained only three or four words. Therefore, for purposes of clarity and comprehension, many of Marrow's longer sentences have been split apart while her shorter sentences have been linked together. Further, some of Marrow's original paragraphs went on for an entire page, while others were only a sentence or two long. In *Life After J.E.B. Stuart*, the paragraphs have been more uniformly proportioned. Since it varied widely in the original text, I have also made capitalization more uniform in this work.

In her original writing, Marrow made a few factual errors concerning names of people, dates, and historical events. Depending on the circumstances, I have corrected some of these errors. Others have been retained within the text but corrected in the corresponding endnotes. The names of some of her close family members have also been standardized in the book. For instance, Marrow's father (who in various outside sources is referred to as either "J.E.B. Stuart," "J.E.B. Stuart II," or "J.E.B. Stuart Jr.") is identified here as "J.E.B. Stuart II," the name preferred by Marrow as well as other members of the Stuart family. Further, Marrow's brother is identified consistently as "J.E.B. Stuart III," even though some sources occasionally refer to him as "J.E.B. Stuart Jr."

In Marrow's original memoirs, it was apparent that she had edited much of the typewritten text that was likely prepared by her husband. She sometimes crossed out entire sentences and replaced them with new ones. Marrow also frequently wrote in notes around the margins, providing more detail to a sentence or fleshing out a comment or idea. In *Life After J.E.B. Stuart*, these corrections have been incorporated into the final text and her deletions made as she probably intended. In addition, Marrow sometimes abruptly changed subjects between sections, a style that could cause confusion for modern readers. Therefore, I have added transition sentences in certain sections to make the narrative flow better. These sentences are in the third person, italicized, and contained within brackets for easy identification.

As cultural and ethnic sensitivities have evolved steadily since the mid-twentieth century, some comments in Marrow's original text now read as racially insensitive. For instance, her use of the word "Negro" would be considered inappropriate and jarring to most modern readers. However, Marrow was a product of her time, culture, and context, and such sentiments were more widely accepted during that era. While Marrow happily associated with people of many races and creeds, she used terminology that was standard during the period in which she was raised. In order to maintain historical accuracy, these comments have not been reworded or deleted. However, they do not represent the sentiments of the editor or the publisher.

There are two types of illustrations in *Life After J.E.B. Stuart*: family photographs and selected copies of Marrow's paintings. Stuart family members provided permission to use all of them in this book. Many of the family photos once belonged to Marrow, and are now in the possession of her granddaughter, Sharon Stuart McRee. Other Stuart family members, including Fred and Margaret Grover, Claudia Austin Straw, Olivia Stuart McFadden, and Col. J.E.B. Stuart IV, provided additional family photographs. Many of these photographs are being made available to the public for the first time through *Life After J.E.B. Stuart*. Sharon Stuart McRee, or her brother, Drewry M. Smith III, now own all of the paintings that are displayed in the book, and they are reproduced here with their permission.

As a family member's account, *Life After J.E.B. Stuart* provides a unique insight into Stuart family life following General Stuart's mortal wounding at Yellow Tavern in 1864. It also examines Marrow's fascinating career as an artist and educator, and reflects her opinions and judgments. Endnotes are included to help readers in identifying the politicians, educators, military leaders, actors, singers, and artists with whom Marrow associated. Since some of these individuals are little known today, short biographical summaries are provided for the readers' convenience. The endnotes are also meant to direct readers to outside sources for more information about topics mentioned by Marrow.

It is my hope that *Life After J.E.B. Stuart* assists those who are interested in Marrow's artistic achievements as well as those who are interested in Southern history, women's studies, and Stuart family history. For J.E.B. Stuart enthusiasts in particular, the book provides one of the most comprehensive genealogies of General Stuart and his direct descendants available at this time. As already noted, it is not a literal transcription of Marrow's writing. The original memoirs, along with many of Marrow's paintings and papers, are currently in possession of the Stuart family and not available to the public. However, for researchers seeking access to those original documents, efforts

are underway to eventually place them in an appropriate archival facility.
That way, they will be available for future generations of scholars who wish
to learn more about this remarkable woman and the times in which she lived.

Acknowledgments

Almost two years have passed since I first read about Mary Marrow Stuart Smith and her extraordinary life, through her own words. As the eldest surviving grandchild of the Confederate cavalry legend, Maj. Gen. J.E.B. Stuart, Marrow (as she was known to friends and family) enhanced her family's achievements as a gifted writer, artist, and educator. She also took great joy in chronicling the Stuarts' extensive contributions to the American experience. Accordingly, when her granddaughter, Sharon Stuart McRee, first shared with me Marrow's unpublished memoirs, I knew immediately that this important work must be placed in print. The resulting process of editing, annotating, and writing was an enlightening experience and a distinct pleasure.

I am immensely grateful to Sharon, my partner in this scholarly journey, for permitting me to edit this important work. She played an integral role in developing this book, and assisted with editing, photograph selection, and background research. I am also thankful for the able assistance of General Stuart's great-grandson and senior namesake, Col. J.E.B. Stuart IV, who was a key supporter of this project from the very beginning. My sincere thanks also go to J.E.B.'s wife, Mary Louise McNiel Stuart, who provided valuable background information about Marrow, with whom she was very close. Stephanie Tucker Little, who spent a great deal of time with Marrow during her childhood, was also very helpful in providing insights about Marrow's life following her retirement.

In the process of editing *Life After J.E.B. Stuart*, I was fortunate to have the support of many other members of the Stuart family nationwide. Marrow's close relatives, including Faith Samson Smith, Drewry McRee Smith III, Cathy Hodge Smith, Drewry McRee Smith IV, Galen Griepp, Ravenna Griepp, and Romy Griepp each provided encouragement for the project. Further, several more of General Stuart's direct descendants and spouses, including Thomas "Tim" Moorhead, Elizabeth "Bonnie" Hundt Moorhead, William "Brae" Hundt, John Moorhead, Col. Rorer James Grant, Helen Grant, Olivia Stuart McFadden, Laurie McFadden, Dr. J.E.B. Stuart V, Fred Grover, Margaret Grover, Flora Old Dunham, Jonathan Old, Dr. Erle Austin, Stuart Austin Nimmich, Michael Straw, and Claudia Austin Straw provided recollections, guidance, family papers, photographs, and other important information that was vital to the book's successful completion. Penny Barrott, a collateral descendant of General Stuart's wife, Flora Cooke Stuart, was also quite helpful in providing background information about Marrow's ancestors. Without the support of these individuals, *Life After J.E.B. Stuart* would not have been possible.

I am also indebted to several of my colleagues at Christopher Newport University, who were quite helpful over the course of this project. Dr. Jonathan White provided valuable insight on how to best organize Marrow's writing into publishable form. Dr. Robert Colvin, Dr. Benjamin Redekop, Dr. Elizabeth Gagnon, Dr. Phillip Hamilton, and Dr. Elizabeth Kaufer Busch each provided support and encouraged me to pursue publication for *Life After J.E.B. Stuart*. Further, my student research assistant, Caitlin "Caitie" McGeever, did a masterful job in tracking down rare historical documents about Marrow's father, J.E.B. Stuart II. I am also grateful to a host of respected historians from other institutions for their help, including Dr. Robert Kenzer from the University of Richmond and Dr. Caroline "Carrie" Janney from Purdue University. Dr. Carol Berkin from Baruch College and Dr. Catherine Clinton from Queen's University Belfast also lent their support in the book's early stages.

In the course of editing *Life After J.E.B. Stuart*, I worked with excellent research facilities at several museums, historical organizations, and educational institutions. I am grateful to library staff members at the College of William and Mary, Virginia Military Institute, the University of Virginia, and the New York Public Library for assisting me in my research. C. Waite Rawls and other staff members with the Museum of the Confederacy also provided encouragement and support for the project, while Sons of Confederate Veterans Executive Director Benjamin Sewell provided important biographical materials about J.E.B. Stuart II. My gratitude also goes to the staff of Hamilton Books and its parent company, Rowman & Littlefield Publishing Group. They were enthusiastic about *Life After J.E.B. Stuart* from the very beginning, and I am delighted that the book found a home with them. My editor, Brooke Bascietto, always answered cheerfully my endless list of questions and assisted me throughout the entire publication process, earning my sincere appreciation.

I also am indebted to my family and friends for their support and enthusiasm as I pursued publication of Marrow's memoirs. They always listened patiently as I discussed my progress with the book and often offered valuable insights and suggestions. In particular, I am grateful to my mother, Dr. Lisa Liberati Heuvel, for thoroughly editing the entire book manuscript and providing several good ideas for improvement. I also am indebted to my wife, Katey Cunningham Heuvel, who steadfastly supported this book from its earliest conceptual stages all the way through final publication as I continued to teach and pursue my doctoral studies. Katey was patient and understanding as I devoted countless hours to honoring the memory and words of this fascinating artist and educator from Norfolk. That gift of time has in turn made me a better researcher, historian, and scholar—a gift for which I will forever be grateful.

Most of all, I wish to thank the late Mary Marrow Stuart Smith herself for creating this amazing body of writing. Getting to know Marrow through her own words and helping to bring her story to life have ranked among the greatest highlights of my career. Over the course of this scholarly journey, I have made many new friends and have learned so much about art, women's studies, music, and life in post-bellum Virginia. Even twenty-five years after her death, Marrow has taught me a great deal about taking time to appreciate the beauty of the world around us, something we often forget to do in the frenzy of our modern, everyday lives. Through *Life After J.E.B. Stuart*, it is my hope that Marrow's life and legacy will continue to inspire future generations as they have inspired me.

Sean M. Heuvel
Christopher Newport University
Newport News, Virginia
November 2010

Abbreviations

AHHS—Alexander Hugh Holmes Stuart

DMS Sr.—Drewry McRee Smith Sr.

DMS Jr.—Drewry McRee Smith Jr.

DMS III—Drewry McRee Smith III

DMS IV—Drewry McRee Smith IV

ELPS—Elizabeth Letcher Pannill Stuart

FCS—Flora Cooke Stuart

JEBS I—Maj. Gen. J.E.B. Stuart, CSA

JEBS II—Capt. J.E.B. Stuart II, USA

JEBS III—J.E.B. Stuart III

JEBS IV—Col. J.E.B. Stuart IV, USA

MSS—Marrow Stuart Smith

OR—U.S. War Department. *The War of the Rebellion: A Compilation of the Official Records of the War of the Union and Confederate Armies.* 127 Vols., index, and atlas. Washington D.C., 1880-1901.

PSGC—Brig. Gen. Phillip St. George Cooke, USA

VHS—Virginia Historical Society

Introduction

Sometime in the early 1940s, Mary Marrow Stuart Smith commenced writing her memoirs at Drewmar, her quaint, waterside cottage in modern-day Virginia Beach, Virginia. Known as "Marrow" to her family, friends and colleagues, this respected artist and educator had led quite an eventful life. Born in 1889 in Staunton, Virginia, Marrow's development as an artist carried a price tag of hard work and struggle, but it was her passion and her joy. Hampton Roads, Virginia[1] became her home and the hub of her professional activities. As an artist, teacher, and educational administrator, she considered it her life's work to advance interest in art and learning, and was known widely throughout Virginia and beyond. Over the course of a forty-year career, Marrow's art studies and the exhibition of her own works took her to such varied places as Philadelphia, Washington, D.C., and New York. She interacted with some of the most prominent artists, actors, and historical figures of her day, and was known for her leadership and activism in the world of fine arts. Marrow organized countless art exhibitions and led several civic organizations over the course of her long career, leaving a lasting imprint on the art community in Virginia's Tidewater region.

As Marrow began chronicling her life experiences, she hand wrote certain sections while dictating others to her husband and accomplished typist, Drewry McRee Smith Sr. Drawing on her sharp mind and keen memory, she gradually recounted her life journey with great precision, from her earliest years all the way through adulthood. This process unfolded over nearly a decade, concluding when she was about sixty years old. As with everything else she did, Marrow pursued this project with a dogged determination, taking great care to write an interesting and compelling narrative. She eagerly wanted to retrace her life's journey and record it for posterity.

As she wrote her last chapters, Marrow was also at a major transition point in her life, which may have sparked a desire for reflection and contemplation. She had just concluded a long and eventful career as art director for the Norfolk Public School Division, and was pondering her future. Marrow had spent forty years sharing her love of art with countless students as a teacher and administrator, and wanted to find a new outlet through which to continue this work. By chronicling her story, she hoped she could continue inspiring future generations to pursue fine arts careers. Also, Marrow had just experienced her most productive and fruitful years as an artist. From the 1930s to the early 1940s, she won numerous awards for her work and achieved widespread acclaim through several media outlets. As Marrow had always hoped, she had made a name for herself in the art world, and wanted to reflect upon that success through her writing.

Along with art, family was of the utmost importance to Marrow. Born to loving and supportive parents, she also adored her brother and sisters and enjoyed spending time with several nieces, nephews, and cousins. Moreover, Marrow was descended from one of Virginia's most celebrated families. The Stuarts had been prominent in the fields of government, education, and the military since the arrival of their colonial ancestors in the early eighteenth century. As the eldest in her generation, Marrow considered it her duty to preserve this family's remarkable legacy. She had a tremendous respect for her Stuart ancestors, and always stood when she read their original letters and other historical documents to awestruck friends. During the late 1940s, Marrow had also become a grandmother. This undoubtedly fueled her desire to pass down stories and accounts of famous ancestors, such as her grandfather, Maj. Gen. J.E.B. Stuart, to the next generation of Stuarts. Aware that the world was quickly changing around her, Marrow wanted to ensure that her grandchildren, grandnieces, and grandnephews understood their family's impact on American history. These efforts prompted many admiring relatives to later label Marrow as the family's official historian.

Eventually, Marrow wrote over 400 pages of text about her ancestry, childhood, education, career, and family. Originally entitled *Early Years of a Virginia Girl*, she hoped to get this work published. Supplementing these memoirs was a rich collection of historical papers that she had accumulated tirelessly over the years, including family trees, letters, speeches, newspaper clippings, photographs, and other materials. Despite Marrow's belief that her unique memoirs would be welcomed by publishers, her first book proposal was rejected and she stopped sending submissions shortly thereafter. Thus, a publishing contract never materialized. It is difficult today to speculate why she did not find success. Perhaps the manuscript's content was too current and not "historical" enough. Or perhaps publishers then were less

Marrow with her siblings, circa 1964. Left to right (standing)—Flora Stuart Garmany and Elizabeth "Lib" Stuart James. Left to right (seated)—Josephine "Jo" Stuart Grover, J.E.B. Stuart III, and Marrow (Courtesy of Sharon Stuart McRee).

interested in women's history than they are today. Whatever the reason, Marrow eventually gave up her quest for publication in the early 1950s, placing into storage this culmination of a decade's worth of work. Consequently, her memoirs were not seen again outside the Stuart family until 2009, when her granddaughter made them available for purposes of research and publication.

The purpose of *Life After J.E.B. Stuart* is to complete the journey that Marrow began so many decades ago. It is intended to tell her story in a format as close to her original writing as possible. The edited and annotated content of Marrow's original memoirs is divided here into eight chapters. Chapter One outlines her Stuart and Cooke family ancestry from the eighteenth century through the mid-nineteenth century. It explores each family's numerous contributions to Virginia history and focuses specifically on the Civil War experiences of her paternal grandparents, Maj. Gen. J.E.B. Stuart and Flora Cooke Stuart. Chapter One also recounts General Stuart's tragic death as well as the challenges that his wife faced in the war's closing months. Chapter Two focuses on Marrow's parents, J.E.B. Stuart II and Josephine Phillips Stuart.

It relates the story of how they met and discusses their experiences and hardships as a young married couple in the 1880s. It also examines the history of Marrow's maternal ancestors and explores their deep roots in Virginia's Tidewater region. Chapter Three focuses on her childhood in Richmond, Virginia in the 1890s, as well as her father's service in the Spanish-American War. In Chapter Four, Marrow discusses her later childhood and teenage years in early 1900s Newport News, Virginia, where her father held positions with the federal government.

Encompassing Marrow's early adulthood, Chapter Five examines her financial, physical, and academic hardships in pursuing higher education at a Northern art institute in the 1910s. It also highlights her interaction with some of the most prominent actors, musicians, and artists of her day. Chapter Six focuses on Marrow's efforts to create a rich family life around World War I. Along with detailing her husband's North Carolina ancestry, it highlights her marriage to Drewry McRee Smith Sr. and the birth and early childhood of her son, Drewry McRee Smith Jr. Further, it reveals the anguish Marrow felt when her beloved grandmother, Flora Cooke Stuart, died in 1923. Chapter Seven chronicles how Marrow resumed her career in art and education while coping with the loss of her parents in the early 1930s. It also examines her struggle to support her family financially and emotionally as her husband dealt with escalating health problems. In Chapter Eight, Marrow highlights milestone events in her life through the end of the 1940s, including her son's marriage and the birth of her first grandchild. It concludes with Marrow's account of a personal tragedy that haunted her for the rest of her long life. Overall, these detailed memoirs explore nearly six decades of Marrow's life.

For reasons that are no longer known, Marrow stopped writing her memoirs around 1950, when she was about sixty-one years old. It is possible that she intended only to write about her childhood and early adult years. Certain sections of her original memoirs may have also been lost over time. Or perhaps other responsibilities drew her away from a sole focus on writing. In any case, there is no first-person account detailing the rest of Marrow's life story, which ended in 1985 with her death at age 96. The epilogue therefore provides an overview of the major events of Marrow's retirement years, drawing on family oral history and selected primary and secondary sources. However, this section of the book serves another equally important purpose. Any reader of *Life After J.E.B. Stuart* will quickly realize the importance of family in Marrow's life. In her original memoirs, she invested a great deal of time reflecting upon her pleasurable interactions with various relatives over the years. Along with her own son, daughter-in-law, and grandchildren, she enjoyed a particularly close bond with her siblings and mentioned them quite frequently.

Considering that Marrow's written memoirs appear to stop abruptly around 1950, it will naturally raise questions about her relatives' fates. What happened to her husband? What happened to her son, her daughter-in-law, and grandchildren? Where are her descendants now? What happened to Marrow's siblings and their descendants? Along with discussing the final years of Marrow's life, the Epilogue effectively answers these questions. It also examines the fate and current whereabouts of her Aunt Virginia Stuart Waller's family, with whom she was very close. Developed through months of extensive research and frequent communication with Stuart family members, the resulting biographical analysis is arguably the most comprehensive overview of General Stuart's direct descendants in existence. As with other chapters in the book, the Epilogue is enhanced by rare family photographs, which in some cases are being made available publicly for the first time. In fact, Marrow specifically mentions some of the photographs in her memoirs. Therefore, these materials, which were obtained through the help of the Stuart family, effectively supplement Marrow's original writing. Along with photographs, a few samples of Marrow's artwork, some of which are mentioned in the memoirs, are included in the book to introduce them to modern audiences. They also provide readers a look at Marrow's artistic style and commemorate the aspect of her life that she would want most remembered.

Life After J.E.B. Stuart will certainly prove interesting to any Stuart enthusiast or even a casual reader who appreciates an intriguing life story. However, it also serves significant scholarly purposes and helps to shed a new light on everyday life in a bygone era. For one, Marrow's work provides an important new resource to scholars in the realm of women's history, with a particular emphasis on the American South. In many ways, she was quite a unique individual in her time, place, and context. During an era when most women worked inside the home, Marrow staked out her own personal identity and engaged extensively with the outside world. She was quite ambitious and wanted to leave her mark on a society that by in large did not value ambition in women. From an early age, Marrow actively pursued careers in art and education and became well known in artistic circles throughout the Mid-Atlantic. Education was also very important to Marrow, and she loved to learn new things. A woman of letters, she completed advanced coursework in art, administration, and education at several colleges, universities, and institutes. Marrow later taught college-level courses at a variety of higher education institutions, ranging from the University of North Carolina—Chapel Hill, to the College of William and Mary. This was particularly impressive considering that many of her childhood female friends did not even complete high school. Moreover, Marrow successfully pursued a career while supporting a family at home, which is a challenging feat even in today's world. She was in many ways a pioneer for women in the American South and beyond.

Marrow was also unique in that she forged her own destiny in a family known for its strong and dominant males. Prior to her time, the Stuarts had been known for their leadership achievements in the realms of government and military service. One ancestor, Major Alexander Stuart, had courageously led a Virginia Militia regiment against the British during the Battle of Guilford Courthouse in March 1781. Major Stuart did not leave the field until after he had two horses shot underneath him and was himself severely wounded. He later languished as a British prisoner of war but lived to survive the conflict. Marrow's great-grandfather, Archibald Stuart, was a well-known attorney, War of 1812 veteran, and political leader who served in both houses of the Virginia General Assembly as well as in the U.S. House of Representatives. Congressman Stuart's son, Maj. Gen. J.E.B. Stuart, brought the family its greatest fame through his celebrated leadership of Confederate cavalry forces during the Civil War. Marrow's own father, J.E.B. Stuart II, followed in this military tradition by serving as a U.S. Army officer during the Spanish-American War. He later continued this tradition of service during World War I, when he was a civilian U.S. Army employee stationed in England and France.

However, Marrow charted a new course for her family's legacy by becoming a leader in the world of fine arts. Like her ancestors before her, she frequently organized large numbers of people to participate in a common cause. Her energetic efforts to establish fine arts organizations and set up art exhibitions in the Tidewater Virginia region were even discussed and celebrated well after her retirement. Instead of pursuing political prominence or military glory, Marrow's vision as a leader was to find beauty in the world around her. She loved and was mesmerized by color, and she made it her life's mission to share with the world the joy she felt around that often-overlooked element of nature. Marrow's accomplishments rivaled those of the Stuart family's other idolized female leader, her grandmother Flora Cooke Stuart. Known to the outside world as "Mrs. Gen. J.E.B. Stuart," she devoted her life following her husband's early death to rebuilding his beloved Virginia. Flora Stuart focused her efforts specifically on primary education, and spent years revitalizing a small girl's school in Staunton, Virginia. Through Marrow's efforts in the arena of fine arts, she and her grandmother demonstrated that the remarkable leadership quality long admired in the Stuart family's men was also present in its women.

Along with Marrow's personal accomplishments, *Life After J.E.B. Stuart* sheds new light on the Stuart family, and its trials and tribulations following the Civil War. It will therefore be a useful resource to Civil War historians and scholars of the postwar American South. While there are many excellent biographies on General Stuart, most of them conclude following his death after the May 1864 Battle of Yellow Tavern. However, few works examine in depth the fate of his widow and two surviving children, J.E.B. Stuart II and Virginia Stuart Waller, and hardly any discuss the fate of General Stuart's direct descendants.[2] This book picks up where others leave off by focusing on the tragedy and triumph of the General's immediate family after the war. The Civil War was devastating to the Stuarts, draining them financially, emotionally, and physically. Following the untimely death of their patriarch, the Stuarts joined the ranks of many other elite Southern families in becoming "genteel poor." Although their legendary name brought them immediate acceptance and contacts in the highest of social circles, the Stuarts struggled to get by financially in the years following the war. While they were certainly better off than the masses of former slaves and poor working-class whites throughout the region, it took the Stuarts decades to recover from the Civil War's traumatic effects. Through *Life After J.E.B. Stuart*, readers get a close look at this interesting period in the Stuart family's history through Marrow's unique perspective. While examining the challenges that the family faced during this era, the book also chronicles what it did to help rebuild the South in the decades following the war.

Life After J.E.B. Stuart also provides an interesting life story set against the backdrop of a fascinating period in American history, ranging from the Post-Reconstruction era all the way to World War II. Marrow's childhood in the 1890s occurred during a turbulent era in the American South, when the region was still recovering from the devastation of the Civil War. This was a period following the formation of the "Lost Cause" mythology, in which disappointed ex-Confederates were looking for a reason to explain their defeat and sorrow. Writers such as Edward A. Pollard,[3] Lt. Gen. Jubal Early,[4] and later Douglas Southall Freeman[5] advanced the nobility of the Confederate cause and argued that it was vanquished only because of superior Union manpower and resources. Other writers, such as Thomas Nelson Page,[6] developed the "Plantation Tradition" genre, which idealized life in the antebellum South. In both writing styles, the horrors of slavery were largely diminished while the legitimacy of secession was upheld.

During Marrow's youth in the 1890s and 1900s, the South was in what historian David W. Blight later called the "reconciliationist" phase of the Lost Cause movement, when it was "transformed into a national reunion on Southern terms."[7] During this period, Northerners were eager to put the Civil War behind them and look toward the future. Flooded with immigrants with no involvement in the war, they were tired of dealing with the enormous expense and corruption of the Reconstruction era and were ready to move on. Accordingly, they left the process of interpreting the Civil War's legacy to their white Southern neighbors. Meanwhile, white Southerners had also transitioned from attempting to explain defeat to displaying pride and nostalgia for what they viewed as a simpler and better time. Amidst the economic and social uncertainty of the period, even some Northerners began to look at the "Old South" with admiration, overlooking the brutal Jim Crow laws that permeated the region. According to Blight, "for those who needed it the Lost Cause became a tonic against fear of social change, a preventative ideological medicine for the sick souls of the Gilded Age."[8] This was the environment in which Marrow grew up, and it helped to shape her worldview as an adult.

Since Marrow was only a young child when the movement was at its peak, she did not specifically address the Lost Cause mythology in her memoirs. However, she did spend time recounting the grandeur of Confederate veterans' reunions and the unveiling of Confederate monuments, displaying a strong respect for the cause to which her illustrious grandfather sacrificed his life. She also echoed the themes of the Lost Cause's reconciliationist phase when she discussed her father's involvement in the Spanish-American War. As the first conflict in which a unified United States was engaged, it provided further opportunity for reconciliation, serving "the ends of reunion by uniting North and South against a common external foe."[9] Moreover, it allowed the sons of Civil War veterans, including her father, J.E.B. Stuart II, the opportunity to prove their manhood and self-worth.[10] However, Marrow also wrote about the turmoil felt by her grandmother, Flora Cooke Stuart, in seeing her only son fight for a government her husband opposed only a generation before. Marrow's memoirs provide a unique insight into the inner thoughts and workings of a prominent Southern family during this important period in American history.

Apart from its perspective on the post-Civil War and Reconstruction eras, Marrow's memoirs provide a fascinating look into life during the Gilded Age and the "Roaring Twenties." She took special note of the rapid rise of both consumerism and technology during this era, recalling her amazement at the development of such innovations as automobiles, telephones, and radio. Marrow also shared her delight in getting to see some of the most prominent actors and musicians of the era, including Enrico Caruso, Geraldine Farrar, Billie Burke, Edward Sothern, and Julia Marlowe. She also discussed the hardship of more challenging periods, such as the Great Depression and World War II. She wrote extensively about the difficulty of making ends meet during the 1930s with a young child and disabled husband at home. Marrow also discussed her uneasiness during the World War II era, when she worried about the prospect of her only son going off to war. Through these memoirs, Marrow recounted some of the emotional highs and lows of her long life as she experienced firsthand some of the most significant events in American history. For those interested in regional history, her rich descriptions of places and local traditions are also an invaluable resource.

Overall, *Life After J.E.B. Stuart* is an entertaining yet informative and educational book. It tells the story of a remarkable woman who set out to leave her mark on the world through her gift of art. Although Marrow did not live to complete this work herself, her style, grace, and spirit shine through in the book's print. In the end, *Life After J.E.B. Stuart* serves as a lasting legacy to Marrow and her remarkable accomplishments. Hers was a life well lived.

NOTES

1. Referring to southeastern Virginia, the terms "Hampton Roads" and "Tidewater" are used interchangeably throughout the book.

2. See Thomas D. Perry, *Ascent to Glory: The Genealogy of J.E.B. Stuart* (Ararat, VA, 2008).

3. Edward A. Pollard (1832–1872) was an outspoken secessionist and editor of the *Richmond Examiner* during the Civil War.

4. Jubal A. Early (1816–1894) served as a lieutenant general in the Confederacy's Army of Northern Virginia during the Civil War. Through his work writing for the Southern Historical Society in the 1870s, he was one of the primary proponents of the Lost Cause ideology.

5. Douglas Southall Freeman, PhD (1886–1953) was a Pulitzer Prize-winning author and longtime editor of *The Richmond News Leader*. He was best known for his multi-volume biographies of Robert E. Lee and George Washington.

6. Thomas Nelson Page (1853–1922) was also a lawyer who served as U.S. Ambassador to Italy from 1913 to 1919.

7. See David W. Blight, *Race and Reunion: The Civil War in American Memory* (Cambridge, MA, 2002), p. 265.

8. *Ibid*, p. 266.

9. *Ibid*, p. 351.

10. *Ibid*, p. 347.

Chapter One

A Noble Heritage

It was not my good fortune to know my grandfather, Maj. Gen. J.E.B. Stuart, CSA, personally. However, I have a definite image of him that has been built up by reading his letters and reports, hearing various family recollections, studying relevant biographies, and analyzing other accounts both friendly and otherwise. Growing up I especially cherished hearing my grandmother Flora Cooke Stuart's tender descriptions, remarks, and reminisces about her husband. Today, I know that I cannot look upon the commonly despised field broom straw or sedge-grass without emotion, because it often offered a bed for a few hours sleep to my weary but gallant grandfather. I often think of his great vitality, courage, spirit, resourcefulness, and magnetism. I also think about what he packed into his brief thirty-one years, and how bravely he accepted the chances of sudden death. My grandfather realized when he undertook service to his state that it could cost him his life. He seemed to shove the dark cloud back and try to offer a confident and positive approach to all matters. His faith, part of his living tissue, sustained him in extremity and helped him to endure the bitterest of circumstances.[1]

Once I was invited to talk about my grandfather at the J.E.B. Stuart Elementary School in Norfolk, Virginia that was named in his honor.[2] I was asked by one of the boys if I knew the general. As I looked into those eager young faces from multiple classes assembled in the school library, I had to say, "My father was not quite four years old when his famous father was shot at Yellow Tavern. When this happened my thirty-one-year-old grandfather was a major general who was later described as the greatest cavalry leader ever produced in America." In a pamphlet on the "Stuarts of Virginia," I read, "he was the youngest major general ever commissioned since the days of Napoleon Bonaparte. His splendid talents for cavalry command, and brilliant dashes, combined with fine social qualities, made him the idol of every household throughout Virginia... His life was more like a romance than a real existence, and his private and social character was even more admirable than his military career."[3]

My grandfather was of Scotch-Irish decent. In 1726, his great-great-grandfather Archibald Stuart[4] left Londonderry, Ireland for exile in western Pennsylvania because of his revolutionary political beliefs. He landed at Port New Castle, Delaware on a William Penn ship and went into hiding in the hills of Pennsylvania's Chester County. King George II declared amnesty seven years later, allowing Archibald to relocate to Virginia's upper Shenandoah Valley near Waynesboro. It is believed that he came to Virginia under Governor Alexander Spotswood's offer of toleration.[5] Apparently, the placid Pennsylvania Quakers and the clannish Scotch-Irish were not congenial. Archibald then sent for his wife and two sons, and eventually had another two children born in America. He gradually acquired valuable lands and property in Virginia, which he bequeathed in his will, dated November 17, 1761.[6]

One of Archibald's sons, Major Alexander Stuart, was commander of a Virginia militia regiment during the American Revolution and won high reputation for his skill and gallantry.[7] During the March 1781 Battle of Guilford Courthouse, he had two horses killed under him while leading troops under fire.[8] Alexander later became a man of wealth and influence in Virginia, serving as a patron of education and the arts. He was a founder of Liberty Hall Academy, which eventually became Washington & Lee University. Alexander and his friend Sam Houston (father of Sam Houston of Texas) each conveyed forty acres of land and made liberal contributions of money toward its erection. Meanwhile, the Major's youngest son was named Alexander in his honor. Born in Virginia[9], Alexander Jr. moved west and served the United States government as a federal judge in Illinois and Missouri. He was also speaker of the Missouri House of Representatives before returning home and serving as a member of the Virginia Executive Council.

My grandfather's father, Archibald Stuart, served as an artillery officer during the War of 1812 and was later a leading lawyer and politician. A resident of Laurel Hill in Patrick County, he was a member of the Virginia legislature and a member of Congress during the period of the Nullification Crisis. I have a very fine photograph of him—a note on the back of the photograph speaks of his splendid talents and his wonderful versatility as well as his skills as a powerful orator and advocate. It also describes him as a charming social companion, possessing wit and humor combined with a rare gift of song. My grandfather, General J.E.B. Stuart, certainly inherited many of these qualities from his father.[10]

Born in 1833, his short boyhood was spent at Laurel Hill. His mother had inherited this home from her grandfather, William Letcher, a militia officer

The Honorable Archibald Stuart (Courtesy of Sharon Stuart McRee).

who was murdered by loyalists during the Revolutionary War.[11] He left a young wife and infant daughter, Bethenia Letcher, who would later become my grandfather's grandmother. This home was on the crest of the Blue Ridge, and on a clear day commanded a magnificent view of the surrounding country for sixty miles. The home was set among a forest of oak trees and had a beautiful garden of flowers. There was a winding road down the hillside to the town of Taylorsville, now called Stuart—and the road went on to Wytheville, Abingdon, and the west. The young J.E.B. Stuart loved to explore all these roads on horseback. On one such adventure at age nine, he and his older brother William Alexander discovered a large hornet's nest. The brothers decided to knock the huge ball down and began climbing the tree. As they neared the hornets' home, some were on guard and began swarming. William Alexander got out of the way, but J.E.B. stayed until he accomplished his task of dislodging the nest. He squinted his eyes and took the stings. From then on it was conceded that my grandfather would make a good fighter and a good soldier. He had courage and persistence.

Young J.E.B. was also interested in nature and his environment, and enjoyed helping his mother with her flower garden. A few slaves helped with the maintenance of the plantation. He also loved and understood horses. The horses he rode at home were named "Duroo," "Bembo," "Roderick," "Don Quixote," "Forager," and "Jerry." On the academic front there were tutors of ability for the four boys: David, William Alexander, John, and J.E.B. When J.E.B. Stuart was thirteen years and ten months old, he was sent to school at Hillcrest, which is located between Wytheville and Pulaski. A Mr. Painter managed the school. Young J.E.B. wrote the following letter from the Hillcrest school dated December 6, 1846:[12]

My Dear Mother,

I took it upon myself to borrow a horse and come up here today (being Sunday) and here I found Uncle Jack, who expects to start for home tomorrow, and I thought I would take advantage of the opportunity to write to you, although I must confess that my conscience is in opposition with my pen, for I can't tell why you don't write to me, for you have no idea how acceptable a letter from home is of any sort, especially to me away off at a boarding school where I never hear from home or anywhere else. I have no doubt that you have all experienced this, and for that reason it appears still more astonishing why you do not have mercy on a poor little insignificant whelp away from his mammy. I hope you will not defer writing any longer, but write—write—write! I saw brother Alex in town today—he was well. I know by this time you are impatient to know something about Mr. Painter. All I have to say is simply this, that it is a first-rate place, but I had rather go to Mr. Buchanan. Tell Vic that I have got an arithmetic for her. It is a very pretty one, and if I had had any idea of Uncle Jack's being here I would have brought it. Kiss her for me and also Dave. I would also tell you to kiss Belle and Dallors, but I know you would not do that. Give my love to Papa, sisters M & C, and Vic. Give my best respects to Mr. Ayers when you see him. I wrote a long letter to him yesterday.

I ever remain your affectionate son,
J.E.B. Stuart

P.S.—I deemed it necessary to say in this that I was well, for you know I am never anything else.
J.E.B.S.

The original copy of this charming letter, written over one hundred years ago, after passing through many hands is now in the possession of Mrs. Stuart Chevalier, widow of the deceased grand-nephew of General Stuart who was a lawyer and lived at Pasadena, California.[13] My copy was made from a pen-written transcript of the letter sent to me by Miss Ellen Stuart[14] of Wytheville, a niece of the general. The "Uncle Jack" of the letter was one of the servants of the Stuart home at Laurel Hill. Bella and Dallors were young J.E.B.'s playmates. "Dave" was his brother David, who was a brilliant young man. He died of typhoid fever soon after graduating from the University of Virginia.[15] Mary, Columbia, and Victoria were his sisters, who were afterwards Mrs. Tazewell Headen, Mrs. Peter Hairston, and Mrs. Nat Boyden, respectively. Mr. Ayers was his teacher in Patrick County.

This letter is revealing to me. Clearly, my grandfather loved the freedom, security, and affection of his home life, but his mother received his chiding dissatisfaction in words away from a loved home. Further, he was very democratic and loved people, mentioning several in a short letter while not touching on other matters. Grandfather also accepted instruction at Hillcrest under Mr. Painter when he wanted to go to Mr. Buchanan's. However, he displayed great character by being fair to Mr. Painter's school. Lastly, he was loaned a horse at age thirteen to get away briefly from his studies and isolated situation, demonstrating that others placed trust in him at a young age and recognized his maturity and potential.

In 1848 when my grandfather was about fifteen years old, he went to Emory and Henry College near Abingdon, Virginia. In 1850 when not yet seventeen, he entered the U.S. Military Academy at West Point. Grandfather became a close companion of Custis Lee,[16] who was a son of West Point's superintendent, Robert E. Lee. In June 1854 he graduated thirteenth in a class of forty-six. Grandma Stuart told me that prior to graduation, my grandfather stood sixth from the top of his class, which would have placed him among the first group of graduates drafted for the elite artillery or engineering divisions. Therefore, he apparently "eased up" in his studies until he was sure his average would place him in the cavalry division. At the academy, Grandfather was noted for his skill as a horseman.

After my grandfather's graduation, he was commissioned a 2nd lieutenant in a regiment of mounted riflemen who patrolled the wild and remote regions of western Texas. This was excellent training for his future duties and career. He was at Fort Clay[17] in December 1854 in an expedition against Apache Indians and was later stationed at Fort Riley in Kansas, where he participated in raids against Indians who had attacked the white settlers. In May 1855, Grandfather was transferred to the 1st Cavalry regiment as a 2nd lieutenant and ordered to proceed to Fort Leavenworth, Kansas. It was there that he met and later married my grandmother, the daughter of the post commander, Lt. Col. Philip St. George Cooke. The wedding took place at the Cooke home on November 14, 1855. With this union, the Stuart family was linked with another old Virginia family of distinguished lineage.

It is recorded that the Cookes came to America at an unknown date from Herefordshire, England, and that they had a coat-of-arms and belonged to the gentry.[18] The first Cooke I can find living in America is (John) Nathaniel Cooke and he was a wealthy ship owner in Philadelphia. His will is recorded in Philadelphia's City Hall, and he left land on Cherry Street. Nathaniel married a Miss McPherson, and they had an only son, Stephen. Stephen Cooke was later sent by his father to a university in England to be educated as a doctor. He completed his studies, and was returning to take part in the war between England and America. The British captured him at sea and took him as a prisoner to Bermuda.[19] While on parole there he met and married Catherine Esten, daughter of the Honorable John Esten, who was governor of Bermuda.[20] Catherine's mother was Rebecca Spofforth Esten, a lady of distinguished English lineage.

Their first child was Dr. John Esten Cooke, and he became a noted physician in Virginia and Kentucky. He was born in Boston, Massachusetts on March 2, 1783 while Catherine was visiting her father-in-law, Nathaniel Cooke. There were altogether six sons and two daughters from this marriage, and several were born in Bermuda. The daughter, Catherine, died unmarried but five others married and had descendants. Dr. Stephen Cooke continued to reside and practice medicine in Bermuda until 1791. He then moved to Alexandria, Virginia, and shortly afterwards settled upon a plantation called "Glengarry" near Leesburg in Loudon County, Virginia, where he died in 1816. The youngest member of this family was my great-grandfather, Philip St. George Cooke, who was born there on June 13, 1809. After studying at the academy of Martinsburg, Virginia, he entered West Point in 1823 and graduated in 1827. Cooke was then assigned to the Sixth Infantry regiment and was stationed for many years on the frontier. Those were the days of "do without" and "struggle" and Major Bennett in his "Journal and Reports" of that time recorded that "Philip St. George Cooke seemed to be made of iron."[21]

Meanwhile, one Abram Wilt came from Germany to Philadelphia in 1743 and married a Miss Danner. They had four children, the second of which, Catherine Wilt, married Joseph Hertzog. Their third child, Rachael Wilt Hertzog, married Philip St. George Cooke on October 25, 1831. Rachael met Philip while visiting her sister Mary at Fort Leavenworth. Mary was married to Major John Dougherty, who at that time was the government agent for all of the Indians west of the Missouri. The subsequent union of Philip and Rachael brought about a blend of German and English strains. Following his marriage to Rachael, Philip moved to Fort Riley and served with the Second Dragoons. He became a 1st lieutenant in March 1833 and was promoted to captain in May 1835. My great-grandfather went up to the rank of major in February 1847 and was brevetted lieutenant colonel the same month. He was engaged in various Indian expeditions and became a colonel in 1858.

Averam B. Bender wrote in "The March of Empire"[22] that as a lieutenant colonel serving under Col. Stephen W. Kearny, my great-grandfather
conducted the second expedition to California. In 1829 and again in 1843
he commanded military escorts protecting Santa Fe traders, also serving in
the Black Hawk War. In the 1830s, Cooke made visits to the villages of the
Oto, Omaha, and Pawnee Pict tribes, and in 1848 he accompanied Colonel
Kearny on his famous expedition to the South Pass. Between expeditions he
was stationed at Jefferson Barracks, and at Forts Crawford, Snelling, Leavenworth, Gibson, and Wayne. In October 1846, Colonel Kearny placed him
in charge of the Mormon Battalion, with orders to open a 2,000-mile wagon
trail from St. Louis to California by Santa Fe. Cooke's problems seemed in-
surmountable, because the members of the group assigned to the undertaking
were too old, too young, or too feeble. Many women were also included. The
train left Santa Fe and moved down the Valley of the Rio Grande to Rincon,
New Mexico with a long string of ox and mule-drawn wagons carrying the
rations. Also included were a herd of cattle and a flock of sheep that hindered
the march.

On they struggled by foot southwest to Ojo de Vaca, or Cow Spring, and
on over the mountains to the San Pedro River. Discipline was difficult, food
became scarce, sickness was prevalent, and many men did not have sufficient
clothing. However, the group became happy and lively when trading with the
Pima Indians on the Gila. The weary train reached San Diego on January 29,
1847. Cooke had accomplished his mission without any loss of life. Thus, they
had opened the first wagon trail through the Southwest to California. Much
later, a Los Angeles newspaper dated July 16, 1957 hailed the march as a feat
"unequaled in the annals of American history."[23] In later years, the Mormons
recognized Cooke's service and thought so highly of him that they built a
monument to him and wanted him to be buried on their soil. I am fortunate to
know my great-grandfather through the pages of history and records. He was
a superb soldier who loved his country and served faithfully. Cooke was also
scholarly and witty, and even published a book on cavalry tactics in 1860.

[*While Marrow's great-grandfather was successfully advancing his antebellum army career, his son-in-law was just beginning his.*] J.E.B. Stuart,
who had been promoted to the rank of 1st lieutenant, was stationed at Fort
Leavenworth in 1856-57. Here he was involved in many skirmishes and local raids. In 1857, Grandfather entered upon another Indian war against the
Cheyenne warriors who were attacking western settlers. In the chief battle of
this campaign the Indians were routed, but Stuart was wounded while rescu-
ing a fellow officer. A two-wheeled ambulance drawn by three mules took
him back to a camp hospital. The story of the encounter was given in a letter
to his wife dated July 30, 1857:[24]

Very few of the company horses were fleet enough after the march, besides my own brave Dan, to keep in reach of the Indians mounted on fresh ponies. . . . As long as Dan held out I was foremost, but after a chase of five miles he failed and I had to mount a private's horse and continue the pursuit. When I took the rear of the enemy again, I found Lomax[25] in danger from an Indian who was on foot and in the act of shooting him. I rushed to the rescue, and succeeded in firing at him in time, wounding him in the thigh. He fired at me in return with an Allen's revolver, but missed. My shots were now exhausted, and I called on men approaching to rush up with their pistols and kill him. They rushed up but fired without hitting.

About this time I observed Stanley and McIntyre[26] close by. The former said 'Wait! I'll fetch him' and dismounted from his horse so as to aim deliberately; but in dismounting, his pistol accidentally discharged the last load he had. He began, however, to snap the empty barrel at the Indian who was walking deliberately up to him with the pistol pointed. I could not stand that, and drawing my saber, rushed on the monster, inflicting a severe wound across his head that I think would have severed any other man's, but simultaneous with that he fired his barrel within a foot of me, the ball taking effect in the breast, but by the mercy of God, glancing to the left and lodging so far inside that it could not be felt. I rejoice to inform you that it is not regarded as at all fatal or dangerous, though I may be confined to my bed for weeks. . . .

Some lull in these raids followed, and my grandfather found time at Fort Riley to perfect an invention he had conceived at West Point. He obtained a leave of absence to visit Washington D.C. and negotiate with the government about his patented invention of a saber attachment.[27]

It was on the night of October 16th, 1859 that a band of twenty men seized the United States arsenal at Harper's Ferry. John Brown was the fanatical leader who believed that all slaves should be set free, and he had previously made disturbances in Kansas. He sent out men and arrested about sixty prominent citizens, who were subsequently locked up in an engine house. However, his attempt to call to arms the slaves of surrounding plantations failed completely. Brown and his followers then took refuge in the engine house and released all but ten of the citizens. Grandfather was sent on a secret mission to assist Lt. Col. Robert E. Lee, his old superintendent from West Point, and he volunteered to act as Lee's aide-de-camp after Lee was assigned command of a U.S. Marine contingent ordered to suppress the insurrection.

Colonel Lee placed the marines around the engine house and sent Stuart to demand surrender. Lee's aim was to avoid bloodshed, and ensure protection from the angry citizens until the insurrectionists could be placed safely under federal custody. Grandfather later wrote, "I approached the door in the presence of 2,000 spectators."[28] He stood at the door that was then opened by Brown four or five inches. Placing his body against the door, Brown held a loaded carbine and could have easily wiped my grandfather out. The parley was a long one. The terms of surrender were scorned, and Grandfather then waved his hat above his head as a pre-arranged signal. The marines quickly pounded away at the doors and killed ten men and wounded others. John Brown and seven of his men were tried for treason, found guilty, and later hanged. That same day, Colonel Lee sent my grandfather to a farm Brown had rented, and the result of this mission was that a number of pikes were brought back that Brown had intended to use in arming the slaves. This John Brown raid cast a gloom over the country.

Although my grandfather was promoted to captain in the months following the Harper's Ferry incident, the need to defend his state made him resign from the army after it seceded in April 1861. Casting his fate with the Southern cause, Grandfather went to see Jefferson Davis and enlisted in the Virginia militia. On May 10, 1861 he was commissioned a lieutenant colonel of infantry in the Provisional Army of Virginia[29] and quickly reported to Colonel Thomas J. Jackson at Harper's Ferry. Grandfather then organized several troops of cavalry to assist the infantry, and was later transferred to the cavalry under Gen. Joseph E. Johnston. Initially, this cavalry unit had 21 officers and 313 enlisted men who were all good huntsmen, using their own guns without any military training.

[*Meanwhile, Marrow's great-grandfather, Philip St. George Cooke, decided to pursue a different route of service.*] Caught between his U.S. Army affiliation and Virginia connections, he had to think out his decision. In June 1861, Colonel Cooke published a letter in which he declared that he owed allegiance to the federal government rather than to his native state of Virginia. He was subsequently promoted to brigadier general in November 1861. This decision was difficult, as two of his sons-in-law cast their lot with the Confederate cause. J.E.B. Stuart was to become a major general and key Confederate cavalry commander while Dr. Charles Brewer, married to his daughter Maria, was to become a Confederate surgeon general. Further, Cooke's only son, Harvard graduate John Rogers Cooke, would also go on to serve the Confederate Army as a brigadier general. Conversely, another son-in-law named Jacob Sharpe, who was married to Cooke's daughter Julia, would eventually become a Union Army general.[30] These divisions caused the family to suffer great anguish.

[*While General Cooke made his way in the growing Union Army, his son-in-law J.E.B. Stuart rose quickly through the ranks of the Confederate Army.*] Following his initial appointment as a lieutenant colonel of infantry, my grandfather was commissioned as a full colonel in June 1861, when he organized the 1st Virginia Cavalry Regiment. In July 1861, he was present at the Battle of Bull Run and was promoted to brigadier general two months

Brig. Gen. Philip St. George Cooke, USA.

later. Grandfather was then made a major general in July 1862 at age twenty-nine, and placed in command of all cavalry in the Army of Northern Virginia. Grandma Stuart was proud of her husband's record and wanted her children and grandchildren to know the facts. Accordingly, she maintained meticulous records of her husband's rapid ascension through the Confederate ranks.

What did the chief of cavalry and the commander of the famous Stuart horse artillery accomplish? Lt. Col. W.W. Blackford[31] in his book, *War Years with J.E.B. Stuart*, stated it splendidly:[32]

1. He served as the eyes and ears of Generals Lee and Jackson. He also kept them informed about location and movements of the federals and spied out their secrets.
2. He screened the location of the Confederate troops.
3. He felt the way for the army.
4. He protected the flank and the rear when the army was on the march – and worried the enemy's flank.
5. He made quick raids into the Union territory or around their army to secure supplies or information.

6. He engaged in small but severe battles and skirmishes – in which the army did not take part.
7. He tore up enemy communications and destroyed their depots.
8. He contributed and developed new cavalry tactics – a very heavy responsibility rested on the cavalry.

I liked this book immensely because Colonel Blackford and my grandfather were friends and they lived together through that day-to-day existence on the march or in camp. Also, Blackford had direct knowledge of the adventure, perils, social life, and of course many of Grandfather's secret plans as an aide on his staff. Blackford also admired the fine integrity of my grandfather, and there was a mutual trust. As such, Blackford went on many secret missions and his judgment was trusted completely. At one point, my grandfather presented "to my esteemed friend Colonel Blackford" a paperback book of *Napoleon's Maxims,*[33] which later got into my possession. I knew Blackford's grandson, Frank Blackford, who was married to one of my most talented art students, Norfolk native Polly Baldwin. Although I cherished the little volume I gave it to Frank with a little message and signature.

When I look over the military books my grandfather possessed and studied, I know he was serious about his profession. He was conscientious, prompt about his duties, and deeply respected his men. Although he expected much from them, my grandfather's men would follow him on the long marches and into battle, always giving their best. Sometimes they would say, "General we are exhausted and must rest." Then my grandfather would say, "drop out of line and rest or nap, and then join the ranks later." General Stuart's endurance was phenomenal. He had Scottish endurance and could ride for fifty hours at a time. Such a feat was recorded during the Chambersburg Raid, when he rode 90 miles in 36 hours in October 1862. My grandfather could relax on his trusted horse, and keep up the march for days in some of his most famous raids: the Chickahominy Raid and the Chambersburg Raid. Sometimes for recreation there were social parties with creative charades, dancing, singing, and music between these long marches. "The Bower," which was the Dandridge family home, was a favorite place to set up camp so the evening could be enjoyed with good company.[34] The Bower was located eight miles from Martinsburg and ten miles from Charleston, West Virginia.

The duty of the Confederate cavalry was to mislead the enemy. So when marching, if the Union enemy were camped nearby or on the look-out, the flying dust from horses' hoofs would allow an estimate of the Confederate force's size. Therefore, my grandfather quite often resorted to deception, ordering his men to stir up dust with pine branches after he and his command passed to make it appear as if a large cavalry unit was passing down the road.

I love the story Colonel Blackford told of the raid into Pennsylvania, north-ward to Chambersburg. The force assembled at Darkesville and camped that night above Williamsport, planning to cross at McCoy's Ford.[35]

On this raid my grandfather planned to take nothing but horses, since there were many heavy Conestogas in the region that were good for moving artillery. The day was cloudy and the farmers were thrashing wheat. Horses were taken out of barns and led off by Confederate forces. Meanwhile, a very genteel old lady came out and requested that the Confederates allow her to keep her old driving horse, which she said was thirty-five years old. She had owned him since he was a colt. It was a handsome, dark-brown horse with head up and fine eyes. However, upon closer inspection, gray hairs could be seen over the glossy hide. Colonel Blackford opened the horse's mouth and confirmed that the lady had told the truth, since the horse's teeth were worn off level with its gums. Of course my grandfather did not take her horse! In the end, the column of 12-15,000 captured horses was about five miles long, and the terrible night watch and march home started. It must have taken endurance to march all night. Many men reportedly went to sleep on their horses. Finally, the column reached Hyattsville, Maryland after marching sixty-five miles from Chambersburg in twenty hours!

On October 8, 1862, a dance and charades were given to the young ladies at The Bower. After the dance, which ended at 11pm, a young adjutant named Lt. Channing Price[36] presented papers and letters to my grandfather for approval and signature. The Confederates were compelled to act quickly if they were to cross before the mountain streams brought high waters and encircle General McClellan's army. My grandfather and his staff used the few hours left to sleep in a haystack in an open field. On October 9th at 4am, all forces assembled at Darkesville in a heavy fog without fires. General Lee had ordered a cavalry detachment to march to the rear of Chambersburg and endeavor to destroy the Cumberland Valley railroad bridge. That would leave the Federals with only the Baltimore & Ohio railroad to move men and sup-plies in that region. They were also to secure information about the Federals as to position, force, and intention, and to secure provisions and horses for the Confederate forces. Eighteen hundred handpicked cavalrymen did not know where they were going, but they trusted their commander. There were six hundred men from each brigade, under Wade Hampton, Rooney Lee, and William E. Jones respectively.[37] There were also four guns from the horse artillery. Grandfather told the men that this enterprise demanded "coolness, decision, bravery, implicit obedience, and strictest order and sobriety on the march and on the bivouac."[38]

Embarking upon the mission, they reached the Potomac after dark and crossed at McCoy's Ford. The next morning there was a heavy fog that hid

them from the Union infantry. General Logan[39] spread news of approaching
enemy troops, but he waited to react. With the Federals alerted to their raid,
the Stuart cavalry reached Chambersburg under a cold, drizzling rain. On the
farms all suitable horses were seized, but each owner was given a receipt.
With Lieutenant Thomas and nine men demanding the town surrender, there
was no resistance, and Union property was seized or destroyed. During
the night rain poured on the weary and hungry Confederate soldiers. My
grandfather and his staff officers did not rest or sleep since every ford of the
Potomac was guarded by Union troops. Hurriedly and eagerly, the soldiers
bought articles at the stores in Chambersburg. Grandma Stuart had written
a list of much-needed articles to use in sewing. She asked for needles and
dress goods, as well as sewing silk. My grandfather bought some of these
items for her, especially handsome pieces of cloth. Discipline was strict since
the provost guard would arrest soldiers if they took personal property from
the stores. Later, Capt. Calbraith Butler[40] of South Carolina set a fuse to the
ordnance storehouse and it went in a blaze.

At the break of day they set out and passed Cashtown and Fairfield, and
then went south toward Emmitsburg in Maryland. The people there gave a
warm welcome, but haste was necessary. Grandfather captured a courier and
learned that Union forces were after him. They had plans of attack, but were
not sure where he was. Meanwhile, he was aimed for the Potomac. The tired
men and horses marched all night, and by daylight on October 13th they
reached Hyattstown. Now there were 5,000 Federals guarding the fords, so
Grandfather rushed on to Poolesville, where there was unexpectedly a resist-
ing body of Union cavalry. In response, he turned into the woods and after
about two miles came out upon a road where they encountered another Union
column. Grandfather ordered a charge and drove the Federals back, moving on to cross Whites' Ford. There, they ran into a Union commander, but
General Fitz Lee[41] bluffed or frightened him into a retreat and once more my
grandfather slipped through the Union lines.

This Confederate raid on Chambersburg was one of the most remarkable
in history. In thirty-six hours, General Stuart and his forces rode completely
around the Union Army. Hundreds of horses were captured, and the Confederate cavalry crossed the Potomac in the face of vastly superior enemy forces.
Within the Confederate ranks, only one man was wounded. My grandfather's
sagacity, boldness, and quickness were taxed to the utmost.

Colonel Blackford recalled in his book, *War Years with Stuart*, "General
Stuart was always dressed well, and was well mounted, and he liked his staff
to do the same. In our gray uniform, cocked felt hat, long black plumes, top
boots, and polished accoutrements, mounted on superb horses, the general
and his staff certainly presented a dashing appearance."[42] Apparently, Grand-

father's brother, William Alexander Stuart, kept on the lookout for splendid, blooded creatures like "Star of the East" from Fauquier, "Skylark" from Maryland, "Lady Margrave", and "Dan". The faithful "Tony" carried him on cavalry excursions at West Point and was condemned by a board of officers as unfit when Grandfather graduated. Colonel Blackford also wrote "Jackson and Stuart were the only two men I ever knew whom I thought unconscious of the feeling of fear. It was in action that Stuart showed to the greatest advantage. I have never seen his superior on the battlefield."[43] When Grandfather was driving Patterson[44] off, Gen. Joseph E. Johnston said of Grandfather, "he is a rare man – wonderfully endowed by nature… calm, firm, acute, active, and enterprising."[45]

[*While Marrow's grandfather was performing valiant service for the Confederate cause, her grandmother was acting just as nobly on the home front.*] She carried on her role as an army wife, following her daring husband in his cavalry exploits and battles. There were also two small children to keep her occupied. Grandma kept informed of all battles and results and made her children's clothes along with seeing to her husband's clothing and needs. She moved her lodging constantly to be near the battlefields. First, she started forth living in one room with her two children at Warrenton. Grandma

Maj. Gen. J.E.B. Stuart, CSA.

adapted herself to various conditions to be had when her husband could leave the battles long enough to have the company of his family. Grandfather was never happier than when he was with his wife and children.

After Warrenton, there was the airy room in a spacious house known as "Machen's" near Fairfax Courthouse, then near Orange Courthouse. Later, Grandma lived in the Duval and Brewer residences in Richmond, the bare, bleak Mellon home at Centerville, and the Fontaine home near Beaver Dam. General Hill, General Longstreet, or some other person of prestige would suggest a place after they found it worthy and Grandma would move there to be near the battleground. While staying in Lynchburg the baby Virginia Pelham Stuart was born October 9, 1863, joining her three-year-old brother, J.E.B. Stuart II. This child was named "Virginia" in honor of Grandfather's beloved state and "Pelham" in memory of the gallant young leader of the Stuart horse artillery.[46] My grandparent's eldest daughter, little Flora, had died on November 3, 1862 from diphtheria. Unfortunately, Grandfather could not leave the battlefield at the time to give comfort or see his darling golden-haired child. Both parents cherished her memory forever.

[*In the war's later stages, Marrow's grandfather was in Virginia leading his men and fighting desperately against Maj. Gen. Philip Sheridan's Union cavalry.*] He sent in a last report on May 11, 1864 at 6:30am stating, "my men and horses are tired, hungry, and jaded, but *all right*."[47] This was at Yellow Tavern in between Richmond and the Union lines. Grandfather beat the Federals in getting to Richmond, but was highly exposed leading his men in battle. Consequently, a Union sharpshooter named Pvt. John Huff found himself with a clear shot at the general. Reportedly, Huff approached his commanding officer Col. Russell Alger[48] and asked, "I can shoot General Stuart. . . . shall I?" The order was "yes."[49] Grandfather received a mortal wound just above his sword belt in his liver. He turned to his men, every inch the general, and gave a last command: "Go back! Go back and do your duty as I have done mine—and our country will be safe! Go back! Go back! I had rather die than be whipped!"[50]

Captain Dorsey[51] held Grandfather on his horse, guiding him out of harm's way. Then, helped by cavalry troopers, the wounded general was eased from his horse to a tree. Private Wheatley then took charge and procured an ambulance. Dr. John Fontaine and two aides, Venable and Hullihen,[52] came up and took Grandfather to his brother-in-law Dr. Charles Brewer's home on 210 East Grace Street in Richmond. On May 12, 1864, the young major general came to his end. Grandma made every effort to get to her wounded husband, but was not informed of his wounding until it was too late. She was staying with her friends the Fontaines at Beaver Dam, and telegram wires along the

Virginia Central Railroad had been cut, so there were consequently many relays of the message to her.

To complicate matters, Union forces guarded all roads leading to Richmond and Grandma's friend Edward Fontaine kept the tragic message in his pocket until she had eaten her lunch. Presumably, he wanted to work out a method of transportation before informing her of the sad news. After learning of Grandfather's condition, a wounded officer offered his own ambulance to transport Grandma rapidly to Richmond. Thus, she started out in the army ambulance drawn by two mules, with her three-year-old son, J.E.B. "Jimmy" Stuart II, and the seven-months-old Virginia Stuart, along with a nurse named Tilda and the Reverend Woodbridge[53] as escort. The ambulance had to take a roundabout way on minor roads, little traveled by-ways, and back roads. Between prayers, she wondered in suspense, as the ambulance bumped over the ruts, if she could reach the bedside of her wounded husband in time. A sudden halt and a shot went over the vehicle, which jolted to a stop! Fortunately for them, it was not the enemy but friendly Confederates.

Meanwhile, a terrible thunderstorm was raging. They came to a swollen stream and endeavored to cross with a Confederate officer guiding them. Grandma told me that the water came in over the floor of the wagon, and it tilted forward and to the side. The small son and his sister (my father and aunt) slept on with a blanket over the hard wooden side-seat while Grandma sat nervously forward with her gold watch in her hand, riding courageously into the dark unknown. With a vivid flash of lightning, the watch recorded 2am. That was the hour in which my grandfather breathed his last. Grandma arrived at the Brewer home too late to say her goodbye. Later, the gold watch she carried that night became Grandma's cherished possession. The watch and Grandfather's precious West Point ring had been gifts to her from her husband. She later willed the watch to her namesake, my sister Flora Stuart Garmany, and the ring to my brother, J.E.B. Stuart III.

Years after her husband's death, Grandma told me the following story that is not recorded: A few years after the war, she went to visit her parents, General Philip St. George Cooke and Rachael Cooke at their home in Detroit, Michigan. There was an afternoon tea served and Colonel Alger (who had later become a general) called. When he was introduced to my grandmother he said, "Mrs. Stuart, I am sure you would rather not meet me, as I am responsible for all of your tragedy and sorrow. It was I who gave the order to a sharpshooter to shoot General Stuart." Grandma turned away in her fresh grief. She had been a devoted wife to the plumed cavalier for about nine years. Paradoxically, she was also the daughter of a Union leader who eventually became a major general in the federal army. Now this was all over.

She was a widow with two small children, and her future mission was the rehabilitation of a ravaged Virginia. She could not bring herself to reply to his confession.

Immediately after the death of her beloved soldier husband, Grandma gathered her two children and her few personal possessions and went to Saltville, Virginia. "Brother Alex" (William Alexander Stuart) had promised his young warrior brother that if anything happened to him, he would look out for his widow. This promise was later fulfilled and Alex insisted on Grandmother making her home with him at the Ellwood Farm near Saltville. His first wife, Mary Carter Stuart, had died in 1862 and left three sons – Henry Carter Stuart (who later became governor of Virginia), Dale Stuart, and John Stuart. Shortly thereafter, Alex married a widow named Ellen Spiller Brown with whom he started a second family.

Alex Stuart was a successful businessman and lawyer. First, he was deputy clerk in Giles County and then deputy clerk in Wythe County's circuit court. He also owned a dry-goods store and was a bank cashier in Wytheville when the Civil War broke out in 1861. Early in summer 1861, Alex became a partner in the firm of Stuart, Buchanan, & Co., which leased the celebrated Preston Salt Works. These salt mines supplied the Confederates with salt during the war and caused a good deal of litigation. However, due to his energy and sharp legal mind, Alex won his legal battles and established his claims to the property. [*However, the salt mines were also the source of a terrifying experience for Marrow's grandmother in the war's closing months. She wrote about it years later for a Norfolk, Virginia newspaper in 1906:*][54]

I recall the December of 1864 with a shudder because of the visitations of a large body of the Union army coming in upon us from Tennessee, and during their stay we had one of the most fearful storms of snow and wind I have ever seen in Virginia. My home after May of that year was at the "Salt Works," in Washington County, a section of the state greatly valued by the South, and as greatly coveted by the North. It was in this little village, nestled among the mountains of southwest Virginia, that a large proportion of the salt needed for our army was made. A Union effort was made in October 1864 to gain possession of these works, but it proved a signal failure. About the middle of December there came to us a rumor that General Stoneman,[55] with a large force, was making his way toward our section. Their approach became a certainty as the days passed, and on the 21st our "home guard," a small body of poorly armed elderly men assembled, determined to hold the invaders in check as long as possible.

The Union army came over the mountains east of the Salt Works Valley, having had quite a severe fight near Wytheville, in which they were severely worsted. All day long our people held the enemy in check, and not until nightfall did they retire, seeing that the federal force was so strong that they must necessarily evacuate the valley under cover of night they left us going we knew not where, and leaving us, a party of women and children, under one roof, a mile or more beyond the works.

At bedtime, the heavens were illuminated by the burning of a mill, and slowly the Union troops came in, driving away their fears by the use of a torch. No sleep came to us unprotected ones that night, and by seven o'clock the next morning, we found the house surrounded by a Union regiment who demanded a hot breakfast. This home in which I, with others, found a refuge had been the home some years before of the Hon. William C. Preston,[56] but was then occupied by Mr. Palmer, the manager of the salt works. Eight ladies and six children were there housed, with no protection but that offered by three or four Negro servants, and but for them we would have suffered for food. They were kept steadily at work cooking for the Union soldiers camped about the house.

At about noon a storm of wind and snow began, and with intense cold. Very soon all who could crowded into the house occupying several rooms on the first floor but one that was needed and locked. In it had been placed the few trunks we had hurriedly packed when we came from our own home, because of its exposed position near the salt works and furnaces. After a demand from the Union troops came for the key, our friend Mrs. Palmer asked me what could be done. I was fearful that my trunks might be searched and the contents possibly taken from me. I offered to go and see about it, hoping in some way to save my possessions if trouble came.

The Union regiment's colonel stood by to see the trunks brought out and carried to another room when his attention was attracted by the initials on mine: "J.E.B.S." He turned to me and said, "Whose trunk is that?" I replied as quietly as my excessive agitation would permit, and said, "It is mine and it contains my husband's uniform and letters. Shall I unlock it so you may examine the contents?" Then in a manner most manly and dignified, he asked, "Are you the widow of General Stuart?"

"Yes," I replied. He then turned to me, saying, "madam, there are some gentlemen in the Federal Army," and immediately directed the men to take the trunk upstairs. I felt I had a friend in this man, which was proven afterwards. He was a colonel from Kentucky.

Night came on again, which was spent watching and wondering what was to follow. The 23rd dawned upon us, the storm still continuing unabated. But through it all the Union Army's errand was being effected – the destruction of the salt wells, salt warehouses, and furnaces. Fortunately, there was no large supply of salt on hand. What there was they threw out to be destroyed by the weather. Their efforts to burn the long shed-like buildings, called furnaces, were to some extent a failure, as all the older ones were so impregnated by the salt vapors that the torch had little effect. The large iron kettles, in which the soiled water was boiled and the salt thus formed, were broken or made useless, large sledge hammers being used for the purpose, these having been brought with them. This work of destruction continued all day and night, and, although we were a mile away, the noise was distinctly heard.

*A warehouse, stored with ammunition, was set on fire (the enemy not knowing
its contents), and for a time one could imagine a battle was in progress. Now
and then a shell would burst through the heavy brick walls, terrifying all who
saw it. We had lived in this anxious, unhappy condition until the morning of the
24th broke upon us, when we observed a restless moving in the different camps.
It was not long before we knew the cause—the command was making prepara-
tions to retire and soon we learned from the man in charge of a small mill, in
which grain was crushed for the cattle that the mill was to be burned. We were
horrified, for with the wind blowing as it did the fire would inevitably spread to
barns, stables, and the house.*

*When told of this I determined to appeal to General Stoneman, who had been
an acquaintance in other days. The note was carried to him by the miller, but
no answer came back except a verbal message, "Orders have to be obeyed; all
mills destroyed."*

*One more effort had to be made to save us from impending danger and this
time we turned to "the gentleman in the Federal Army." He saw at once the
folly of carrying out such an order, and said, "I command the rear guard, and
will see that you are not exposed to such danger." He was true to his word, for
as the troops passed out through the gap in the mountains his command was
the last to leave—and the mill was not fired. We heard afterwards that he was
the last man to go out.*

*Thus after three nights and days, spent in the greatest suspense and anxiety,
we were at last free from the pleasure of a bitter and vindictive foe. To encourage and cheer, the storm soon began to abate, and in a few hours the sun, in
great glory, burst through the clouds as though sent by a loving father to comfort us after the trials through which we had passed.*

*December 25th, a day usually kept with feasting and rejoicing, found us in
our home once more, and though surrounded by many signs of vandalism and
destruction, we sat down to our Christmas dinner of bacon and cornbread with
grateful hearts—we had our loved ones again with us.*

*Thousands of our Southern women suffered more severely and we ask,
"why?" God only knows. We bow to his will and dare not to question.*

Mrs. J.E.B. Stuart

[*Following the war, Marrow's grandmother continued to work hard at
Brother Alex's home.*] As William Alexander's family increased and his home
became congested, Grandma Stuart was given a small house in Saltville for
herself and two children. Columbia Boyden, the daughter of General Stuart's
deceased sister, Victoria Stuart Boyden, also lived there. Grandma had a small
colored boy who helped with the work. She now worked diligently. There was
the necessary cultivation of a garden, canning of fruits and vegetables, helping
with the numerous children of the two households, sewing clothes, and making
tallow candles—all necessary for survival in the lean post-war years.

Later Grandma secured for herself a teaching position in Richmond, where she taught English and Music one year in Mrs. Carrington's private school. Then she taught at Richmond's Powell Seminary. During this time my father was placed at Norton's School outside Richmond. He was probably about age ten. Next Grandma served as an assistant principal at a Lutheran School in Staunton. The Church Board of V.F.I.[57] subsequently asked her to take over the principalship of the Episcopal V.F.I., as Mr. Phillips was not succeeding in his management and the school needed to be reorganized. So Grandmother went to V.F.I. and worked intensely making over the devastated school. Grandma told me she received *only board* for herself and daughter Virginia for five years while she paid Mr. Minor, the mathematics professor, a good salary.

For nineteen years Grandma gave her best efforts to this important undertaking—educating Southern girls. Over the years she made a great success of the school yet educated many who were unable to pay after the war. She told me she gave thousands of dollars in scholarships to worthy young Southern women who could not afford the cost of tuition or other expenses. She educated all of her brother[58] John Rogers Cooke's girls: Mercer, Rachael,

Flora Cooke Stuart (Courtesy of Sharon Stuart McRee).

Hailey, and Nannie: and all of her sister's daughters—the Brewer girls—
Maria, Flora, Wirt, Rosalie, and Rachael. Grandma also educated her nieces
the Duvals—Cousin Kate, Cousin Di, Cousin Florence, and Cousin Esten.
There were also many daughters of Episcopal clergymen and many others
who knew her generosity. These bills had to be absorbed out of Grandma's
profits. Cousin Ellen Stuart, her niece, was given a position to teach art in the
school, and Cousin Esten Duval and Cousin Di Duval were given positions
after they received their education.

What were Grandma's duties? Hours and hours of letter writing by hand to
prospective students, supervising meals for all, supervising the cleaning, having furniture repaired as needed, conducting religious services, having pianos
tuned, overseeing the course of study, holding teachers meetings and receiving parents and visitors. When I was a small child, I would visit V.F.I. (later
renamed Stuart Hall Academy in Grandma's honor) in the summer when the
school session was over, and it was almost impossible to get a glimpse of
Grandmother. There were sessions with the serving woman or seamstress,
curtains were made, and sheets were hemmed—each marked with the date
purchased on each sheet by Grandmother herself. Then, the long morning
sessions with letter writing and in the afternoon callers. At night we gathered
for musical games and sometimes sang our favorite hymns or songs. We were
all saddened by the singing of "Rock of Ages" because it recalled the dying
moments of our great General Stuart.

Mother gave me ten pieces of walnut furniture that had belonged to
Grandma when I was married. Among the collection was her walnut writing desk, which she had a Staunton man make with a hidden slide across the
front, allowing her to tuck out of sight the letter she was writing when inter-
ruptions occurred. This desk was slightly damaged in our fire of November
1948, and I gave it to Olivia Stuart,[59] my niece who had attended Stuart Hall,
and my sisters had it repaired for her.

So we may conclude Grandma's life is definitely divided into four periods,
and in each entirely different developments took place. First were her nineteen girlhood years (1836–1855) at her military father's home at army posts
and at the frontier forts - at Jefferson Barracks, at Fort Leavenworth, at Fort
Riley, and at Fort Gibson (Indian Territory). Secondly came her romantic
marriage in 1855 and nine years of devotion to her soldier husband and her
children living under trying conditions at Fort Riley and near Confederate
battlefields. This meant constant moving and preparedness, and adaptabil-
ity–and in the end acceptance of her husband's heroic sacrifice of his life in
May 1864.

The third phase of her life involved her acceptance of her great sorrow and
her sincere service to the Commonwealth of Virginia and to the entire South
in making education possible for young women of the South. She herself

had been born in the West (at Jefferson Barracks[60]) and had been trained or educated almost entirely at Army posts and in St. Louis. But she undertook to help rebuild a ravaged civilization in the South. The fourth period of her life brought about a giving up of public life in 1899 and a loving acceptance of the care of her grandchildren following the death of her precious daughter, Virginia. Grandma retreated into an intimate life with these children and received her friends and relatives into the Waller home, and she became a great force in the lives of her grandchildren, keeping up with their interests. I am one who has felt her inspiration, generosity, unselfishness, guidance, and devoted love. I think my grandmother was the grandest and finest woman I have ever known, and it is my duty to proclaim this tribute to her to the world. These are my people, my noble heritage.

NOTES

1. MSS was born in 1889, twenty-five years after General Stuart's death.

2. Opened in 1920, J.E.B. Stuart Elementary School was paired with Granby Elementary School in 1971, with Granby serving grades K-2 and Stuart serving grades 3-6. Stuart Elementary was later redeveloped as a gifted student center in 1986.

3. The pamphlet to which MSS is referring is likely "Stuarts of Virginia" written by Walter P. Stuart in 1965.

4. Archibald Stuart was born in Ireland in about 1697.

5. The Honorable Alexander Spotswood (1676–1740) served as lieutenant governor of Virginia from 1710 to 1722. This would possibly make the MSS account inaccurate since Archibald Stuart would not have arrived in Virginia until the 1730s–years after Governor Spotswood was out of office.

6. For a more thorough background of Archibald Stuart written by his descendent AHHS, see Hugh Blair Grigsby and Robert Alonzo Brock, *The History of the Virginia Federal Convention of 1788* (Richmond, Va., 1891), pp. 379–393.

7. As executive officer, Maj. Alexander Stuart took temporary command of his Virginia militia regiment after his commanding officer, Col. Samuel McDowell, was taken ill with malaria.

8. For further information about Maj. Alexander Stuart's Revolutionary War service, see Lawrence B. Babits and Joshua B. Howard, *Long, Obstinate, and Bloody: The Battle of Guilford Courthouse* (Chapel Hill, NC, 2009), pp. 67, 127, 129–30, 133–35, 139–40, 171, 176–77, 209, 220, 224–25.

9. Alexander Stuart Jr. was born in 1770 and died in 1832.

10. After winning election to the Virginia House of Delegates in 1819 and 1831, Archibald Stuart (1795–1855) served in the U.S. House of Representatives from 1837 to 1839 and the Virginia Senate from 1852 to 1854.

11. William Letcher (1750–1780), listed as either a Virginia militia captain or colonel in various historical sources, was active in recruiting soldiers for Continental Army service prior to his murder.

12. JEBS I to ELPS, 6th Dec. 1846, in Adele H. Mitchell (ed.), *The Letters of General J.E.B. Stuart* (N.p.: Stuart-Mosby Historical Society, 1990), pp. 4–5.

13. James A. Stuart Chevalier (1879-1956) of California was a grandson of General Stuart's sister, Bethenia Pannill Stuart (1819-1910), who married Rev. Nicholas Chevalier in 1842. He was a prominent attorney and author.

14. Ellen Stuart was the daughter of JEBS I's brother, John Dabney Stuart (1828–1877).

15. David Stuart's death occurred in 1845.

16. Maj. Gen. George Washington Custis Lee, CSA (1832–1913) of Virginia, who would later serve as president of Washington & Lee University from 1871 to 1897.

17. Fort Clay was located near present-day Evansville, Wyoming.

18. For a more thorough background on the Cooke ancestry, see John O. Beaty, *John Esten Cooke, Virginian* (New York, NY, 1922), pp. 2-6.

19. One source contradicts the MSS account and indicates that Dr. Stephen Cooke saw actual service as a surgeon in the Continental Army during the war. See Beaty, *John Esten Cooke, Virginian*, p. 2.

20. The Honorable John Esten was actually president of the Bermuda Assembly and would often govern in the absence of the official royal governor. Therefore, he was regarded as a *de facto* governor and addressed as such.

21. This source has not been clearly identified at the time of this writing.

22. See Averam Burton Bender, *The March of Empire: Frontier Defense in the Southwest, 1848-1860* (Lawrence, KS, 1952).

23. This source has not been clearly identified at the time of this writing.

24. JEBS I to FCS, 30th July 1857, in Mitchell (ed.), *The Letters of General J.E.B. Stuart*, pp. 166-67.

25. Maj. Gen. Lunsford Lindsay Lomax, CSA (1835-1913) of Virginia. For a more detailed account of this episode, see Jeffry D. Wert, *Cavalryman of the Lost Cause: A Biography of J.E.B. Stuart* (New York, NY, 2008), pp.33–34.

26. Lt. David S. Stanley, USA of Ohio and Lt. James B. McIntyre, USA of Tennessee. Stanley would go on to serve as a major general in the Union Army during the Civil War and was awarded the Medal of Honor for his service at the Battle of Franklin. McIntyre served as a Union Army major and brevet colonel during the Civil War.

27. This invention, a saber hook meant to improve the attachment of sabers to belts, received a U.S. Patent (number 25,684) on 4th Oct. 1859. The U.S. Government also paid JEBS I $5,000 for a "right to use" license.

28. JEBS I to ELPS, 31st Jan. 1860, in Mitchell (ed.), *The Letters of General J.E.B. Stuart*, p. 186.

29. JEBS I to FCS, 9th May 1861, in Mitchell (ed.), *The Letters of General J.E.B. Stuart*, p. 199.

30. Col. Jacob Sharpe, USA of Michigan served as a brevet brigadier general.

31. Lt. Col. William Willis Blackford, CSA (1831–1905). He served on JEBS I's staff during the Civil War.

32. See W.W. Blackford, *War Years with Jeb Stuart* (New York, NY, 1946).

33. See Napoleon I, *Napoleon's Maxims of War* (New York, NY, 1861). Multiple versions of this book have been published since the 1820s.

34. "The Bower" was owned by Adam Stephen Dandridge and his wife, Serena. It was used by JEBS I as both a headquarters and venue for social events.

35. McCoy's Ford is located in western Maryland.

36. Lt. R. Channing Price, CSA of Virginia was a cousin of JEBS I who served on his staff. Price later became a major.

37. Brig. Gen. Wade Hampton III, CSA (1818–1902) of South Carolina, Brig. Gen. William H.F. "Rooney" Lee, CSA (1837–1891) of Virginia, and Brig. Gen. William E. "Grumble" Jones, CSA (1824–1864) of Virginia. Hampton would later become a lieutenant general and Lee a major general. Jones was killed in battle in June 1864.

38. *OR*, v. 19, pt. 2, pp. 55–56.

39. MSS refers here to Hugh Logan, who was a trusted guide and scout for JEBS I. It is unclear why she refers to him as "general."

40. Col. Matthew Calbraith Butler, CSA (1836–1909) of South Carolina. While MSS refers to him as a captain in her writing, he was colonel of the 2nd South Carolina Cavalry by October 1862. He later reached the rank of major general in the Confederate Army. After the war, he served as a U.S. senator and U.S. Army major general during the Spanish-American War.

41. Brig. Gen. Fitzhugh Lee, CSA (1835–1905) of Virginia. A nephew of Robert E. Lee, he was later a major general in the Confederate Army and served as governor of Virginia after the war.

42. See Blackford, *War Years with Jeb Stuart*, p. 93.

43. See Blackford, *War Years with Jeb Stuart*, p. 79.

44. Maj. Gen. Robert Patterson, USA (1792–1881) of Pennsylvania.

45. Joseph E. Johnston to Jefferson Davis, 10th Aug. 1861, *OR*, v. 5, p. 777.

46. Maj. John Pelham (1838–1863) of Alabama.

47. JEBS I to Braxton Bragg, 11th May, 1864, in Mitchell (ed.), *The Letters of J.E.B. Stuart*, p. 392.

48. Col. Russell A. Alger, USA (1836–1907) of Michigan commanded the 5th Michigan Cavalry during the Battle of Yellow Tavern in May 1864. Following the war, he was brevetted a brigadier general and then major general of volunteers, and later served as governor of Michigan, U.S. senator, and as U.S. secretary of war in the McKinley Administration.

49. For Colonel Alger's description of the event, see *OR*, v. 36, pt. 1, p. 828; Some modern historians, including Jeffry Wert, have challenged this interpretation, claiming that Private Huff was nowhere near JEBS I during the battle. For Wert's interpretation, see Wert, *Cavalryman of the Lost Cause*, p.357.

50. H.B. McClellan to FCS, 16th Oct. 1864, Stuart Papers, VHS.

51. Capt. Gustavus W. Dorsey, CSA of Virginia.

52. Capt. Andrew R. Venable, CSA and Lt. Walter Q. Hullihen, CSA of Virginia.

53. The Reverend Dr. George Woodbridge.

54. This account was written as part of a series about Southern women for the *Virginian-Pilot*. A woman who saved a clipping of the original 1906 article gave it to MSS many years later. The newspaper clipping was so badly deteriorated that MSS had to transcribe the account by hand.

55. Maj. Gen. George Stoneman Jr., USA (1822–1894) of New York. He served as governor of California after the war.

56. William C. Preston (1794–1860) of South Carolina was a U.S. senator who had briefly lived in Virginia during an earlier stage in his career.

57. Virginia Female Institute (later renamed Stuart Hall Academy), located in Staunton, Virginia.

58. Brig. Gen. John Rogers Cooke, CSA (1833–1891) of Virginia.

59. Olivia Stuart (B. 1931) is the daughter of JEBS III (1897–1990) and sister of JEBS IV (B. 1935). She later married Keith G. McFadden (1927–2006) and settled in Arizona.

60. Jefferson Barracks Military Post was located in LeMay, Missouri, just south of St. Louis. It was an active U.S. Army installation from 1826 to 1946.

Chapter Two

My Parents' Story

If I were allowed four words to describe my father, I would say *honest* to the nth degree; *restless* with energy and desire for adventure; full of *zest* for life; and *military*. He was generous and a good provider. Very strict with us girls, he bought our shoes and schoolbooks, encouraging us to do our best in the classroom. When we were sick, he was solicitous and full of tenderness. Mother was always his queen, and he took the responsibility of family life with great pride. Father had individuality, loved freedom, and possessed great vitality. He was also frank, and at times blunt. A Norfolk newspaper wrote, "Captain Stuart was known as a man of rugged and sterling qualities, and of adventurous, fearless, and enterprising disposition."[1]

J.E.B. Stuart II was born at the U.S. Army post Fort Riley in Kansas on June 26, 1860 and for his entire life loved the military. His father, then-Lt. J.E.B. Stuart, became involved in the great struggle of the War Between the States, resigning his U.S. Army commission to offer his services to his native Virginia. He would go on to achieve great fame as a cavalry commander in the Confederacy's Army of Northern Virginia. My father knew his father for only three and a half years, and during those years his mother lived near the various battlefields. The constant shooting of guns and the jerky life of surprise and attack, with occasional short intervals of rest, seemed to have created restlessness in my father's disposition. Lt. Col. Heros Von Borcke, who served on my grandfather's staff, once mentioned in his memoirs[2] about the war how "little Jemmy" (as he was called) was taken into the lines with his mother on a visit to his famous father.[3]

The last temporary home for this family group was, as Grandma expressed it, "with my dear friends the Fontaines at Beaver Dam, Virginia". General Stuart, then stationed at nearby Hanover Court House, dashed up and checked on the safety of his family, consisting of his wife, his son J.E.B. II, and his infant daughter, Virginia Pelham Stuart. During the brief visit, Little Jemmy was hoisted up to kiss his father "farewell"—forever. The May 11, 1864 Battle of Yellow Tavern quickly followed, leading to the death of the brave cavalryman. After that, his surviving family had to endure the ensuing dark days of sorrow and the reconstruction of Virginia and the other Southern states.

Following Grandfather's death, Grandma took her two small children to Saltville, Virginia, and was welcomed into the home of "Brother Alex" Stuart, who at that time had three children by his first wife. My sister, Jo Stuart Grover, has a book of my father's from Saltville that is dated June 18, 1872. It was presented to him for proficiency in natural philosophy and history. Father was next placed out in the country at the Norwood School, while Grandma taught at the Carrington and Powell Schools in Richmond. He was less than thirteen years old and on his own. Next, Father was at the Episcopal High School in Alexandria, Virginia from 1875 through 1877, before enrolling in Virginia Military Institute (V.M.I.).

On August 10, 1879, Father had his picture taken in his V.M.I. uniform and presented it to his mother. He looked neat and alert, as well as youthfully handsome. Around this time, he also visited his grandparents in Detroit, Michigan. This grandfather was Virginia native General Philip St. George Cooke, who served in the Union Army during the Civil War. My father had been named after him at first, but when General Cooke defied his native state to continue service in the Union Army, and when General Stuart was mortally wounded in battle, my father was renamed "J.E.B. Stuart II" after his illustrious father. Evidently, by this time the breach in the family had been healed, but years earlier, at the outbreak of war, General Cooke had spoken of "those two mad boys," referring to his own son and his son-in-law, J.E.B. Stuart, who both became generals and served the Confederate cause. Remaining with the Union Army, General Cooke wrote of himself, "I have served too long in the Army of the United States. . . . I cannot abandon the standard now."[4] I learned that the years 1878 to 1880 found Father at V.M.I., being hazed, doing drills, and studying Latin and Algebra. "Uncle Alex" Stuart was backing Father in his V.M.I. schooling. But something happened, and the whole class walked out. The authorities said that the students could be reinstated if each person would apologize, but Father said he had done nothing wrong and therefore refused to apologize. Consequently, he did not graduate from V.M.I.—much to Uncle Alex's disgust. [*However, Marrow's father would soon move on to other adventures.*]

A loving letter to his mother at Staunton, dated September 22, 1881, from Windsor Shades, showed that while Father was in camp and had an engineering job, he was also homesick and had a bad cold.[5] Shortly thereafter, a December 23, 1881 letter to his mother placed him in Newport News, working for the C & O Railway as an eager young engineer.[6] In this capacity, Father directed the construction of the railroad from Richmond to Newport News and worked on planning the town of Newport News, even laying out some of its streets. These were also courtship days, and he used Sundays for horse and buggy trips to travel about seven miles into Warwick County in order to see my mother, Josephine Phillips.[7] Known as the "Belle of Warwick County," she descended from an old English family that had lived on the Virginia Peninsula for generations.

When England and Ireland were seething with wars and political feuds, two lads by the name of Marrow, each younger than twenty, were put in the care of a servant and supplied with a generous purse of money for passage to America.[8] They settled in Virginia's Warwick County on land that was granted to them by the King of England. These aristocratic youths wore lockets around their necks and were shortly thereafter married to two sisters by the name of Garrow. Later, my great-great grandfather, William Marrow, (who was one of the two youths) built a homestead.[9] I have in mind certain cherished memories of this place and a love for it conveyed by my mother. The house was painted white to be distinguished at a great distance, and the lane leading to the house was one mile long, with a cedar tree and a holly tree alternating every few feet apart, which were all planted by slaves. There was an outside kitchen, a well, a smokehouse, a carriage house, a stable and barn, and a backhouse, or "garden house," as it was called. Along with slave quarters behind the house, there was all the requisite equipment for a colonial plantation life.

In the vicinity of the plantation was Warwick County Court House, or a building where the county records were stored safely. Such records included deeds of property, wills, marriage records, and birth records—but chiefly papers dealing with transactions in land. Therefore, there was a need for lawyers. During the Civil War, this Warwick Courthouse was burned, but some of the records were previously moved to Richmond. Also located near the Marrow Plantation was a cemetery lot, enclosed with an iron fence, and set some distance from the house. My great-great grandfather, William Marrow, along with his wife and a few others were buried there. There was also a small schoolhouse, and my grandmother, Mary Marrow Phillips, taught there for many years. My mother also taught there for one winter to make money for her trousseau.

I gathered from Mother that life there was quite pleasant and elegant at the old Warwick County home under "Grandpa's" (William Marrow's) roof, with his valued guidance and bountiful providing. He had been an active plantation owner, living life as an English squire, and had been a man of prominence in that part of the country. Sometimes he would be called on to guarantee some

*Mary Marrow Phillips, circa 1855
(Courtesy of Sharon Stuart McRee).*

friend's note, and if the friend did not pay a piece of the Marrow land was consequently sold to meet the obligation. The years added to this patriarch's dignity and standing. He found time to relax after the mid-day meal, and he took his nap in man fashion on a day bed (it was really like a Roman couch), which was placed in a corner of the dining room. The old English silver gleamed from the sideboard. The servants gathered the wood on the place and kept the fires burning brightly. Mother spoke of the hog-killing time in the late fall and the delicious meat. Hickory was the wood used for smoking the hams. Black walnuts and some thin-shelled scaly-barks[10] were plentiful from native trees. Mother made candles and cakes from these with the assistance of young, Negro helpers. Chickens, milk, and green vegetables were also plentiful. Mother said the various boys of the family often whittled on the chairs or nailed their projects on these fine old chairs. Many were imported from England and made after Hepplewhite or Chippendale designs. The early slaves on the place made other chairs of walnut. The latter were simple and strong, put together with dowels and not with glue.

One night, someone carelessly put the hot ashes against the side of the house, and during the night there was a blaze. The occupants in the house barely escaped. Practically nothing was saved. Someone pulled out the old organ my mother played, and two elegant old decanters were brought out in someone's hands. Aunt Mamie's trunk was also pulled out. That was all—only a graceful Davenport sofa with black horse-hair covering happened to be in some slave's quarters to be repaired, and that was saved, and later inherited by my sister Jo. Six birds-eye maple-dining chairs that had been lent to Daniel Marrow (my great-uncle) of Hampton, Virginia, were also safe. Cousin Mary Marrow lent the chairs to Cousin Lizzie Ivy, who afterwards had it written in her will that the chairs would go back to Cousin Mary. The decanters graced Mother's sideboard for years, and Dr. George Ben Johnson of Richmond later begged my mother to sell them to him for $100. Mother ultimately gave them to her nephew, along with a book of letters. The land remained in the family, and old "Aunt Columbia" and "Uncle Washington" (freed house slaves) lived on the land as caretakers.

After the Civil War, the slaves belonging to my grandfather, Col. Jo Phillips, CSA, were freed, but they continued to live upon that land. In fact, Colonel Phillips had inherited these slaves and had planned to give them their freedom. Ironically, the war upset his plans. He was called to Confederate military service and did not return, killed in a skirmish near Donaldsonville, Louisiana in 1863.[11] He was quickly buried and the exact location of his grave remains unknown. There have been hundreds of letters written to find out, but without success. One of the most magical memories I can recall from my childhood is seeing "Aunt Columbia" and "Uncle Washington" sitting on an old hand-made wooden cart drawn by a mule. They proceeded to stop in front of our home and hop down off the cart to give us Christmas goodies. They brought popcorn and a large cloth bag of black walnuts to us, and some choice pig meat to Mother. They also brought a Christmas wreath of holly or cedar, some fresh eggs, and another small bag of hickory nuts. These two were the soul of goodness and we adored them.

We return to 1881 and Mother and Father. I understand that their courtship, engagement, and planning for the future took five years. My mother went on having her friends and admirers around her and kept her engagement secret. Then my father inherited from a cousin a small fortune for those days, and he and Mother were married in Old St. John's Church at Hampton, Virginia on July 21, 1886.[12] The bride wore green, and years later Mother would laughingly quote to us the old saying, "married in green, shame to be seen." Shortly thereafter, Father bought a small farm in Kansas and the newlyweds headed west to the prairie. I wish I could write, "and they lived happily ever after." Years later I tried to patch out that story. Where was the farm? I went to the various relatives in the family and asked among others Aunt Lou and Great Aunt Maria of Hampton. They did not know exactly but said, "it was near Kansas City—it was a terribly raw place—a rough place—it nearly killed your mother." This was all interesting information but too vague to offer a complete understanding of what transpired. Finally, I asked Cousin Mary Marrow Blackiston of Hampton. She said, "Your mother and father had a wheat farm at Larned, Kansas." That was apparently a short distance (about five miles) from Kansas City. She had visited Mother there at one point, but volunteered no additional information. However, from conversations with other relatives, I was able to piece together what happened to Mother and Father on the prairie.

Problems with the new venture began immediately. Perhaps Kansas had once offered Father a happy home life and he thought with his energy he could live and succeed in the great stretches of plains and see the prosperous West open up and develop. However, he had accounted only for himself and not for his delicate and refined wife. She could not stand the rugged existence without near neighbors or comforts or some help from servants. Simply put, my mother had been gently reared, and the hard pioneer life of those days was cruel. My mother did not complain, but I have heard her tell of the cold nights when the wind howled around the farmhouse and every available piece of clothing was piled upon the beds to keep them warm. Once in the middle of the night, Mother had to dress and go to the barn while Father held the mouth of a steer open and my mother poured oil down the throat of the suffering, cholera-ridden beast.

There was no domestic help then. Mother had been reared on the elegant Marrow Plantation, where the devoted slaves, even though freed, stayed and looked out for the mistress and her children. For instance, Mother said that Old Aunt Columbia washed her hair, manicured her fingernails, and kept her wardrobe pressed and laundered—all for her "honey chile." In Kansas, washing clothes was beyond my mother's strength, and I doubt if she had ever attended to those things. My father went from scattered house to house, offering pay for a "washer woman." These big strong women offered to help for the time being, but said they could not accept money. In fact, they did leave their own duties to come and help. However, actual domestic servants were not to be found in pioneer Kansas.

After many months of isolation on a not too thriving farm, and trying to plant and keep things going, my mother was expecting a little one. So now, with the developing new life coming, my mother became even more help-less. With no available long-term domestic help, Father wrote East and asked Mother's cousin, Elizabeth "Lizzie" Ivy, to come and visit, give companion-ship, and take some of the strains off Mother. Cousin Lizzie told me that the nights were cold, and the rushing, howling winds swept across the prairies and penetrated the house. There were never enough blankets or enough heat, and dust storms were frequent. The people were kind, but were absorbed in their own struggles—all hard working individuals. Cousin Lizzie also said that Mother never uttered a complaint. After an exhaustive stay, Cousin Lizzie left and my mother's sister, Mamie, came. However, Aunt Mamie quickly left and died from typhoid fever back in Warwick County. The heat of that summer was unbearable and few neighbors called. The little one was born on September 10, 1887, and was named J.E.B. Stuart III. My mother knew little to do for a baby, and any kind of doctor was hard to find. The little baby changed all life for his parents. They could not find any food that agreed with him. He suffered from diarrhea and consequently became weaker and weaker. So my father, with fatherhood strongest in him, pitched up his farm, sold it on the spur of the moment at auction for practically nothing, and moved his wife and ill baby back East to Virginia.

Many, many years later (in March 1945) in Norfolk, as I was driving with my husband on Monticello Avenue, I saw a vital young sailor who made a gesture for a ride. We picked him up and, to make conversation, I asked him from what part of the country he hailed. It has been my experience that these soldiers and sailors always respond to such a question. They love to tell you where they originally lived or where they are native. This young man said that he was from Kansas City. I then said, "Maybe you can tell me where would be a little town called Larned? I have not been able to find it on any map I have looked at, and I am very much interested because my mother and father used to live there." He said, "Larned—well that is right where I live, or rather, near there. It is a thriving town with an insane asylum and a boys reformatory." He further mentioned that it was a few miles southwest of Kansas City. I then asked, "This is in the rich wheat country, isn't it?" He answered that, "Yes, it is a wonderful wheat country. My father farms four square miles of wheat fields." A look of longing for the waving wheat and the mighty tractors seemed to come across the handsome man's face. Then, I meditated on how different my life would be if my mother and father had continued to live in Kansas and raise wheat.

Upon returning home to Virginia, Father and his young family turned to his mother in Staunton for help. These were among the lean years after the Civil War, and business was moving slowly in a devastated South. My grandmother, Mrs. J.E.B. Stuart, was now succeeding with her school where she was putting her best energies. She had taken over the old Virginia Female Institute (V.F.I.), which had been run by a Mr. Phillips.[13] He was dissipated, and the school had gone down. Consequently, my grandmother was invited to come in and take charge as principal. For years, she was only able to earn money for her board (and that of her young daughter) from the undertaking, while she had to pay a good salary to Mr. Minor, the mathematics teacher. However, as the years went on my grandmother gained prestige in the community, and the outstanding qualities of her character and the standing of her school became well known to Southerners. Therefore, she eventually began to make money. My grandmother was also influential in helping establish Emmanuel Episcopal Church across from the school.[14] This happened because she and other Episcopalians did not feel that the old church, Trinity (under Mr. Houlihen), followed the ritual correctly. Thus, the V.F.I. girls attended Emmanuel Church.

So my father at this point brought his family and interests to Staunton, where my grandmother was by then well known. He started to work as a clerk in the Staunton Bank. My mother and her little son boarded at the old Trout house on Augusta Street. Not any place in the world could have been more elegant, with old China, old furniture, treasured possessions, and gentle manners. Several Trout ladies lived there, including Miss Louise Trout, Miss Hattie Trout, and Miss Gay Trout. The home was made of old stone, and one stepped from a stone porch to a stone-paved entrance bridge to the street. Only an iron fence on a stone wall separated the street from the lower yard. This substantial stone house was two stories high from the front and three from the back, and had rooms balanced on a center hall. Miss Louise kept house and directed the large black cook who made marvelous hot rolls. Miss Hattie taught and Miss Gay worked for over forty years as a teacher at the Staunton Deaf and Dumb Asylum.[15]

My mother lived with this thoughtful family and tried to rear her first-born. However, he ultimately succumbed to a bowel complaint in July 1888, when he was less than a year old. When he left this world, the medicine shelves were loaded with his medicines. Poor little J.E.B.—at rest in beautiful Hollywood Cemetery in Richmond—near the great Confederate cavalry general and beside the General's little Flora. My mother now tried to find herself. She was happy in her marriage, but she had been uprooted from the Tidewater and taken to the isolated Kansas farm. Then her only sister, Mamie, had died. Then back to the mountains of Virginia, to bear another great grief in the loss of her little son. She spent her hours of confinement embroidering, making scallops on small petticoats and creating small flowers on dainty dresses.

On May 28, 1889, I was born at the beautiful Trout home at No. 9 North Augusta Street in Staunton, Virginia. I like to think now that the great Woodrow Wilson had been born at the Presbyterian Mansion in Staunton, not too far away. Staunton—beautiful Staunton—looking out to Betsy Bell Hill and to the Blue Ridge Mountains. The people tell you about Betsy Bell, the lovely young girl who went out to drive the cows to the meadow and disappeared in some strange manner on this hill. She was never heard from again and her name became a legend. Betsy Bell Hill also has a companion hill called Anne Gray. Staunton is made of up hills and down hills, looking into the green cup of the fertile valley—and sometimes wistful and tearful, sometimes very spiritual—tender greens disappearing into soft clear blues, misty blues, dark, threatening looking, purple blues—with glistening radiant parents in the sun—with dark foreboding in a storm—with dramatic power and promise when emerging from a storm. Beautiful Staunton in the Blue Ridge and Shenandoah Valley—here I started to grow my roots—which were hard growing at first.

My mother was very ill and very nervous–so I was taken away from her to save her life. My two grandmothers were there to assist. A fine old colored mammy was also procured for me. She gave me a little whiskey with water to keep me alive. I cried all night because I was hungry, and slept in the daytime from sheer exhaustion. Next the doctors and the loving group of watchers—Grandma Stuart, Grandma Phillips, the good Trout ladies, interested cousins, and the mammy—watched and waited and tried various foods, rocked me to and fro, and walked the floors with me. At that time the care of a new baby was an unknown science. My insistent hunger made me unruly–I needed a mama. Next, a wet nurse was secured and she came to offer me nature's own nourishment. My colics and hunger continued and I was put on a barley-water diet. This kept me alive and hollow-eyed, and made the doctor remark, "She has persistence—a most remarkable persistence. She will be a president's wife yet!"

Then it happened that my wonderful Grandmother Stuart knew Mrs. William Miller who had her first-born, Janet, and a surplus of milk. So my grandmother worked out a plan—she bought a gentle white horse and a buggy—and I—the little bawling bit of humanity who wanted to live so insistently–traveled with my grandmother twice a day to the Millers, on the hilltop, to borrow some of Janet's birthright and be Mrs. Miller's foster child. I received the real mothering at last and started to grow into a wistful childhood. The persistence, insistence, and tenacity of life never cease to seem a great miracle. Finally thriving, I was later christened at Old St. John's Church in Hampton, Virginia.

My father was ambitious and venturesome, coming from army people on both sides of his family, so it seemed for him time to progress to a better position. He moved his family–consisting now of my mother, her mother, and myself–to Lexington, Virginia, where he secured a position at the Rockbridge National Bank. There, my sister Flora was born on June 16, 1890, exactly thirteen months after my birthday. My memory of Lexington is very nebulous, but I remember years later going to Mother and describing two dramatic scenes that happened. Mother said, "Maybe you have heard us talk about this." So, she questioned me carefully. She was convinced that these two scenes were riveted into my memory when I was around two years old.

The first scene was in a bedroom, and my mother and grandmother were both amazed how a rat could have carried off stockings down a rat hole. Here Mother, Grandmother, and I stood, the two of them talking as I gazed down the hole. Always with an immense imagination, I envisioned some monster making away with our personal belongings. I was tempted to borrow something like Alice's vial to make myself small enough to explore the rat's dark gallery.

Scene two was my daily promenade, walking beside the colored nurse who pushed the carriage, which held my infant sister, Flora. In great solemnity we encircled the recumbent statue of General Robert E. Lee at Washington and Lee University.[16] We did not talk while we reverently circled the sarcophagus several times. Repetition and solemnity made a vivid impression on my memory. After only a short stay in Lexington, my father was ready to move on to his next adventure. He continued his trek across Virginia while my mother patiently followed, falling in with the ever-changing pattern of his life. They eventually ended up in the small industrial town of Buena Vista in 1892. Father began working in a local bank while the family settled in to a large, rambling, white frame house with a large yard with a white fence on the hillside.

J.E.B. Stuart II and Josephine "Jo" Phillips Stuart with their children, Mary Marrow Stuart (right) and Flora Stuart, circa 1892 (Courtesy of Sharon Stuart McRee).

I have vivid impressions of my life there even though I was only three years old. My mother was not so well, as she was waiting for little Jo to arrive. I was an energetic, bright child with not enough to keep me busy and I craved companionship. My little sister Flora was only a toddling baby and failed to satisfy me, so I ran away daily for adventure. It was quite a distance away to play with the Richardson children. There were ten children in this family, and I found three or four who were quite congenial. Mother would send out searching parties for me after I had not been seen for two hours and the front gate, down the sloping yard, was left wide open. There were no footprints, but my flights were always to the Richardson home, which was the nearest house despite its considerable distance from my own. I was fascinated by color, and here I could live in a world of color. Buena Vista was noted for its glass manufacture, and broken glass bits were strewn about. These odd-shaped bits could be gathered into my little apron and then arranged in a sequence on the ground around the Richardson well or into a mosaic under a tree. Oh, such heavenly bliss to work in iridescent color and manipulate it into patterns of orderly color arrangement! The same colored glass had indefinite possibilities. Then came Belle to snatch me cruelly away and say, "You bad child—your Mama is nearly crazy worrying about you! What makes you do as you do? You are certainly going to get a spanking!" Oh, the disgrace of all this exposure. I went sorrowfully home and got "the spanking". The next day I went again to the magic colors with the magnetic pull. This spiritual romance became more and more necessary for me.

I often wonder what I would have done with a paint box, or some colored chalks or a few crayons—or what they could have done to me. However, such things did not exist in 1892. Already I was a persistent child and I knew what I needed—color. I was creative and determined, and even though I was a very shy child and afraid of a physical encounter along the way, I went out to satisfy this great longing. I was repeatedly punished and I repeatedly insisted, so my parents worked out a plan to keep me at home. They bought a better lock for the gate and placed it so high that I could hardly reach it, and they bought me a little wooly lamb to divert and amuse me. I tried to love the little creature. I tried to convey how lonely I was in that big yard set on a large, lonely hill. However, the creature just butted me down and I cried. I tried again to embrace the soft little baby and again it butted me down. Giving up, I then stood at the fence and looked through the palings. I had a great resentment over my confinement, which restricted my development, so I ended up picking on my little sister. I pushed her around, and one day, as she sat in her carriage, I pushed the carriage forward. Mother came and caught Flora in her arms, and the carriage bumped down some ten steps. Then I found Mother's old gingham house apron and a pair of scissors. Hiding under a table, I ended up gouging holes in the apron. The little lamb was later sent away.

By this point I was three years old and Mother was still waiting for Baby Jo to come. She would lie in the afternoon hours stretched out on a sofa by the window. Flora would climb around on the sofa and I would generally be cutting out pictures under the table or somewhere. Flora had much exuberance on that hot August day—she jumped from the sofa out the window and fell ten feet below on the soft grass. Mother was wild with fear that she had injured herself and sent for a doctor. The doctor assured Mother that no bones were broken, and Flora was not hurt in any way. Jo was born on August 9, 1892. There is another story from our life in Buena Vista that I clearly remember. Mother's cousin, Elizabeth Ivy, came to visit us again. We called her "Aunt Lizzie" because she had been reared by my Grandmother Phillips exactly as my mother. Grandmother had reared her sister's children when their mother died, and had reared her brother's three children when Grand Uncle Daniel Marrow's wife died, along with her own children—making nine children in all.

We all went for a walk, which took us to the beautiful Natural Bridge. Mother and her three children rested on a log in the shade or on some rocks in the sun, but Father and Aunt Lizzie went on and on, jumping from rock to rock. Finding a foothold on the slippery rocks was exciting. Then, what time was it? Father had lost his famous father's gold watch. Gold watches were scarce anyway, but this was one handed in trust to my father after he was old enough to realize that it had been worn near his father's heart. So a depression was felt, and Aunt Lizzie and Father, with faint hopes of finding it, started to retrace their path on the rocks. Perhaps a little prayer was also uttered. Then, Aunt Lizzie saw the watch hanging on a small twig just above the rushing waters. I have begged to hear this story over and over because Mother told it as she lived it—and the watch could have fallen on rocks or into the whirling waters—but it did not. On another occasion, we awoke and found a deep, glistening snow covering all. We quickly discovered that huge bear tracks were impressed in this snow in our backyard—the poor bruin was likely nonchalantly looking for food. We felt we were near to the great American wilderness and that we were pioneers. [*However, the family's wilderness experience quickly came to an end as Marrow's father was already planning for their next adventure in Richmond.*]

NOTES

1. This source has not been clearly identified at the time of this writing.
2. See H. Von Borcke, *Memoirs of the Confederate War for Independence* (Edinburgh, Scotland, 1866).

3. General Stuart's son was known by several nicknames, including "Jimmy" and "Little Jemmy." As an adult, he was referred to as "J.E.B. Stuart," "J.E.B. Stuart Jr.", or "J.E.B. Stuart II."

4. See Cooke Family Papers, 1855–1871. Accession 23896. Personal Papers Collection, The Library of Virginia, Richmond, Virginia.

5. MSS may have been referring to the historic home, "Windsor Shades," located on the Pamunkey River in King William County, Virginia.

6. MSS refers here to the Chesapeake & Ohio Railroad.

7. Warwick County, Virginia was later annexed by the City of Newport News in 1958.

8. Relatively little is known about the Marrow family in Virginia. Several sources indicate that they have resided in Virginia's Tidewater region since at least the 18th century.

9. Though unconfirmed, some sources say that the Marrow Plantation (known as "Oakville") was located somewhere near modern-day Marrow Drive in Newport News.

10. Scaly-bark looks like a type of hickory nut.

11. A veteran of the Battle of First Manassas, Col. Jo (short for "Joseph") Phillips (1831–1863) commanded the 3rd Texas/Arizona Cavalry Brigade following his service in Virginia. During his Civil War career, Phillips served under Confederate generals John B. Magruder (1807–1871) and Richard "Dick" Taylor (1826–1879).

12. Established in 1610 in present-day Hampton, Virginia, St. John's Episcopal Church is the oldest English-speaking parish in the United States.

13. Later renamed Stuart Hall School, Virginia Female Institute was founded in 1844 and is considered one of the oldest Episcopal schools in Virginia.

14. Emmanuel Episcopal Church was founded in 1893.

15. This school was later renamed the Virginia School for the Deaf and the Blind.

16. Established in 1749, General Robert E. Lee served as president of then Washington College from 1865 to 1870. The institution was later renamed Washington & Lee University in his honor. General Lee is buried in the Lee Chapel on the university's campus.

Chapter Three

A Richmond Childhood

My mother and father were now ready for another move. The little five-member family went to Richmond and we lived there for six years-from 1893 to 1899. Father worked in Mr. John Branch's bank—the First National Bank of Richmond—where he was a note teller. I remember Father was at work at nine in the morning. Dinner was served there at three o'clock after the bank hours, and was part of the pay. Then the accounts were balanced, and Father came home in time for supper. All very confining, but refined work. We lived in a rented house on Clay Street, near the old armory. I have two or three vivid impressions of my short stay there. Flora and I slept in a little trundle bed that was pushed out at night, but during the day was concealed under the big bed. This old house had been papered and papered, and was infested with bugs that made our life miserable. Finally, we had to leave.

Mother kept a cook and a nurse to help with us children. She came from the country, and one day she promised to take us to gather chinquapins[1] when they were ripe. We took our baths and were dressed in white starched dresses. I was ready first and was told to wait and not go outside the gate. I waited and waited but we did not start, so I opened the gate and walked down the block a short distance. When I came back I was told I had disobeyed and I could not go. I was heartbroken. Flora, Jo and the colored girl got on the streetcar and went to the country, and left me boohooing and bellowing. I held on to my little lard bucket and cried my eyes red and was sent to the bedroom. To this day, I cannot forget the sting of that disappointment. At dark the three returned, laughing and loaded with the shining black nuts. The next day they were cooked and strung, and I made a long string that went around my neck three times. As I wore the strand of beads I suffered, and as I ate them one by one I did my penitence. I really felt there was a great blank in my life because I did not go chinquapin hunting on that perfect day.

48

On Sundays I was often sent alone to the Sunday school at St. James Church at Fifth and Marshall. In those days it was not an unusual sight to see cattle being driven from the country through the streets for slaughter purposes. As I was winding my way to Sunday school, I saw a great drove of cattle suddenly descend upon me. I ran screaming into a Negro man's arms, crying "save me!" He laughed and composedly opened a gate and guided me up on the porch and closed the gate. From this vantage point I enjoyed watching the steer pass. Around this time, Father was tired of old houses so we bought a new home in a new development at No. 9 North Harvie Street. We had a long backyard there, which gave us three little girls plenty of room to run. My mother was friendly with neighbors wherever she moved, but she had a decided English background and English ideas, along with a certain reticence about disclosing one's personal affairs to others. Therefore, her code of manners and behavior was very strict. She would sometimes say to us, "You are entitled to go with the best people, but you do not have to tell them everything you know." Conversely, Father and Grandma Stuart were wonderfully democratic! Father learned in the West to respect any worthy man. Grandma Stuart had had struggle in her life, so for her, every teacher, student, and helper at her school had integrity and counted in God's scheme.

In the brick house next door on our left lived Mr. and Mrs. Jeter Jones—an old couple—and next to them lived their son with his three children (a boy and two girls). These two brick houses formed with ours a group of houses bounded by alleyways on each side, making a "U" shape. Then beyond the alley lived old Mrs. Shepard with her numerous old maid daughters. On our right, backyards ran toward the alley that adjoined our property on the long side. These houses faced Floyd Avenue. We faced the Little Sisters of the Poor garden and buildings on Harvie Street.[2] Our curiosity was forever piqued to understand the mysteries that went on over there. The queer costumes of the Sisters fascinated us as we would catch glimpses of them meditating and walking in that garden. Occasionally, through the shrubbery, we could see a statue of the Virgin, and sometimes the chanting of music drifted our way, but we never explored the secrets over there. The stone wall and iron fence forbade any intimacies.

Mother did call on Mrs. Shepard and we three children often ran down there. They liked children and often invited us up to a sewing room or bedroom upstairs. I chatted, and on one occasion I found the ladies making a bed quilt of calico pieces. I was fascinated with the dark-red and dark-blue squares. My color sense dominated over my morals. I coveted these alluring colors. Consequently, when the ladies went into the next room for a moment, I hurriedly stuffed the pieces in my belt and on into my drawers, and then made a quick getaway. But alas! I trailed these pieces all the way from that room to my home. When I got home I gloated over these colors, then tucked them into my bureau drawer for further enjoyment and contemplation. Shortly thereafter, I heard Mrs. Shepard's voice and she said, "Mrs. Stuart, I would not tell everybody, but I am telling you because I know you want your girls to grow up right."

Then Mrs. Shepard left and Mother found me in the nursery I shared with Flora and Jo. Each of us had a separate bed and a separate bureau drawer with our name on it. I was sent to bed right then and there, and had only bread and water for supper. However, I did not mind that as long as the beautiful colors hidden in my bureau drawers were not taken away from me. I was willing to make a sacrifice for color any day. No one tried to analyze my case. Here I was running away from home for color, stealing for color, and exerting persistence beyond my years when I modeled in mud—all aesthetic leanings! Later I took these scraps to Staunton when we visited Grandma Stuart. She did not know about the stealing and unwittingly added to my collection of bed-quilt squares, also teaching me how to sew them together and arrange them in blocks. Later, I heard Mother remark, "All children steal until taught right from wrong."

We were rather discouraged from playing with other children. Therefore, Flora, Jo, and I found our simple pleasures in that backyard. We were also very shy, and spent our time playing with mud pies, climbing the back fence, or watching the Catholic schoolboys play for hours at a time. Sometimes we talked to Millard Jones through the fence. We also had a large cherry tree for shade, along with a hammock. One time, Jo caught her curl papers in the hammock and hung screaming, by her hair, which ripped from her head! Each afternoon we went in to take a bath and dress in a lovely, white starched dress and wear a large ribbon bow of white or pale blue or Nile green. I enjoyed selecting the colors and sometimes wore a flowered ribbon. The afternoons afforded us a walk to the park with the nurse, or just a chance to stay clean and play on the front porch.

On rare occasions we enjoyed our lovely shoebox lanterns, and Mother or some older person was there to see that we had no accident when we lighted them. We spent the morning cutting crescents, moons, flowers, stars, diamonds, and various shapes in the four sides of a shoebox turned upright, and then made an opening at the top. We sat on the front porch and used many colors of tissue paper that we pasted inside. We then fastened a candle to the bottom and attached a string at the top. What a sight—lovely little girls swinging magical lanterns in their hands! Fairyland held no more magic—the blue night was best for them. I always had the prettiest lantern because I used my hands well and worked harder over the shapes and finding colors to blend.

Sunday was always an eventful day. We had waffles or Sally Lunn bread and syrup—sometimes maple syrup—for breakfast, and could eat with Father. On weekdays, our breakfast consisted of milk, roe herrings, batter bread or cornbread, and sometimes black molasses to finish the meal. We each had a silver cup for the milk as well as our own silverware. We would then attend services at Holy Trinity Church at Monroe Park, where Mr. John Gravatt Sr. was rector. Father taught Bible class and sometimes went ahead of us. We went to Sunday school, trudging along Floyd Avenue those ten or fifteen blocks and returning the same way, because Father disapproved of our riding on streetcars on Sunday. He thought that the poor motorman and conductor should rest on the Sabbath day.

On festive days and at Christmas time, teasing bad boys behind fences would throw firecrackers at my feet. I suffered excruciating terror at this performance, and I know I must have pleaded with Mother to let me stay at home. I tried to anticipate the agony before I was in it, and therefore hung back and dashed through and skirted the curbing trying to avoid it. We stayed through the long church service and behaved. Poor little baby Jo was the only one who broke the behavior code. She crawled under the pew and dissected a prayer book on one occasion when Mr. Gravatt preached too long for a child. Praying and standing to sing did allow some change in the span of interest. Although we did not understand what was said, Mother thought we should get into the church habit. After dinner, Father and Mother took us for an afternoon walk. We generally walked out Monument Avenue into the country, or sometimes visited the beautiful Hollywood Cemetery. We would then return weary from the long strolls. Somewhere during this period Father also taught on Sunday afternoons at the Richmond Penitentiary. He gave his Sundays faithfully to these religious and civic matters.

During this time, Grandma Stuart made periodic visits to see her only son and his family. She slept in our best spare room, where the lovely pillow shams lifted on frames at night and hung with fluted ruffles covering the pillows during the day. A water pitcher was set and accessories were arranged on the marble washstand with a screen, even though the bathroom was next door and the imposing marble-top bureau with empty drawers was available. A closet was made in the corner with curtains hanging from a triangular shelf, and a nice green and tan Brussels carpet was over the floor. This room seemed far away because we children were kept out of it.

Grandma Stuart generally came in the summertime, which I think she did because she was free from her principal duties then. She immediately rented a Victoria,[3] with cabman, and took us for a long drive each afternoon through beautiful Richmond. Mother and Grandma faced front, and we three little girls sat backwards. Ginter Park was often the destination of the drive. Grandma wore black gloves and used a fascinating little sun parasol—all black—with ruffles and piqueted edges and a handle that folded.[4] We spent a

Brig. Gen. John Rogers Cooke, CSA.

good part of the drive watching her grace in using the queer little parasol. She wore a bonnet with flowing crape from the back and white edging at the face, and dressed in the best quality heavy black silk or faille—stiff but dignified and proper. She also wore black moiré cloth for house occasions. In winter she wore a black astrakhan fur coat. We always felt uplifted from these visits from Grandma. She had sincerity, understanding, and parental love. She was of course strict and religious. While we knelt around the table after breakfast, she conducted our morning prayers and seemed to put more variety in the prayers than Father, who usually said the same prayers each day.

During these stays, Grandma also visited the family of her brother (and my great uncle), former Confederate Brig. Gen. John Rogers Cooke. Uncle John and his wife, Nannie Patton Cooke (of aristocratic Virginia standing), also lived in Richmond.[5] Defying his father who remained in the Union Army, Uncle John had fought with my Grandpa Stuart during the great War Between the States.[6] Following the war, he fell on hard times. Although he was an 1855 Harvard graduate and former army general, Uncle John was forced in the lean postwar years to clerk in a grocery store on Main Street to make ends meet. He had eight children and a wife to support, so he put his pride behind him and met the situation with all of the true fitness that was his. He later died from his wartime wounds in 1891. As with Uncle John, other returning soldiers found civilian living altogether disorganized, so I was told. Uncle John and Aunt Nannie had a large family. There was Cousin Mercer Cooke, Cousin Rachael, Cousin Hallie, and Cousin Nannie (who we called "Little Aunt Nannie"). Those were just the cousins who stood out most in definite memory. There was also Cousin John Cooke, the oldest, who was by then a private in the U.S. Army. Further, there was Cousin Philip St. George Cooke, whom we seldom saw, who worked as a clubman. Along with Cousins Stuart Cooke and Fairlie Cooke, there were also twins who died in infancy.

We loved to go to see Great Aunt Nannie at No. 7 Third Street. For three cents we would ride there on the streetcars from Main and Harvie to Main and Third. Mother let us go and spend Saturdays there. We climbed ten or more steps and pulled a glistening metal doorbell that tinkled in the basement kitchen. After some time, the maid let us into a hall, where two lovely parlors were located. We would then go upstairs, where "Big Aunt Nannie" would kiss us. Cousin Mercer, Cousin Hallie, Cousin Rachael, and "Little Aunt Nannie" also kissed us in cousinly fashion. Aunt Nannie was a little deaf, so the girls talked loudly so she could hear. We took off our hats and talked a little, where the usual polite questions were exchanged. We then explored the basement, yard, or the four-story house itself. On occasion, we went to Chimborazo Park for a slide down the hill. We later had a fine, hot dinner in the basement dining room that was served by a colored maid. Aunt Nannie talked a great deal and told us how after the Civil War they were so poor that butter could only be served once a day in her house. After midday dinner, the girls undressed, slipped into gowns, and took a nap.

We always enjoyed our time at Aunt Nannie's house. The romance of the basement, the beauty of the heavy iron porch railing, the wonder of being on our own, and the warm welcome! We stood on the elevated veranda and surveyed the neighborhood of old Richmond—the magnolia trees, gray classical buildings, and red brick buildings with heavy iron trimmings. As an adult, I later learned the real story of how Aunt Nannie obtained this fine home. Because Grandma Stuart and her brother were so close, she worried in the years following the war about how he was so poor and how his family had so little. Consequently, she wrote to her father (General Philip St. George Cooke) in Detroit and asked him for help. Shortly thereafter, the general bought the lovely and large Victorian home at No. 7 Third Street for his son and family. They all lived there until all four daughters married and their parents died and the family scattered.

Father seemed to enjoy his family and often took all of us children and Mother on picnics. I remember especially one of these occasions. We three little girls were nicely dressed in white dresses and Mother in a white waist and dark skirt. After the basket was packed we took the trolley to Ginter Park. No homes were there then—just large trees. It was a large, expansive park with a few benches, tables, maybe a spring, and the old Ginter Residence. We ate our enjoyable lunch and were exploring the nooks and corners of the park and walking along the edge of the lake. Father stopped and called to us to come see a hornets' nest. He had found it on the ground and thought it was abandoned. So he poked and punched it—and Jo, about five years old, was bending directly over it—when all of a sudden the angry insects began pouring forth. Father grabbed Jo with his left hand and started batting with his new Panama hat in his right hand while he took off running. At the end of the race the hornets flew off, but not until Father was exhausted and his hat in shreds. Fortunately, Jo was not harmed!

Meanwhile, Mother carried on her social duties during this period and made calls regularly. Visiting cards left by callers were checked each week, and calls that should be returned in the week were noted. White gloves had to be worn, and they always had to be pristine white. Since cleaning establishments did not exist then, Mother usually took her gloves to the bathroom, shut the door, opened the window, and then cleaned them with naphthalene. Mother and Father also had friends come regularly to play duplicate whist in the evenings. Mr. and Mrs. Christian lived around the corner on Floyd Avenue and often played cards at our house. Mr. and Mrs. West came sometimes, and Mr. and Mrs. Winn came one week and then Mother and Father went to their home the following week. This provided us with considerable social interest. Often, we children were called into the room to speak to the guests, or we went in to kiss our parents good night and then went on upstairs—for we could not enter into that adult world.

One Easter Aunt Lizzie came to visit us. I think she had been studying at Farmville Normal School[7] and wanted to visit Mother. She brought us some candy Easter rabbits and I promptly ate mine up. Conversely, little Flora went to sleep loving her rabbit. After she went to sleep beside me I ate hers, too! In the morning, Flora woke up and noticing her present missing asked, "Where is my rabbit?" I promptly told her that I had eaten it. Flora then turned reproachfully to me and said simply, "Now, Mary, you ought not to have eaten my rabbit." This was typical of Flora—always good-natured!

When I was seven years old, my parents made arrangements to send me to a private school, and I ended up enrolling at Miss Lizzie Robinson's school. Although Miss Lizzie was a kind person, I can honestly say that I learned nothing at her school. Although I was successful in learning a few French phrases, I could not find my bearings and did not know what it was all about. However, when recess came I became a vital person. We went to a large vacant lot to play and I always had fun there. I quickly discovered that I could run faster and jump rope longer than any other girl at the school. This pleased me so to be able to excel. Back in the classroom, I continued to struggle during each afternoon session. Situated in a study group with twins, the three of us participated in spelling recitation. For purposes of expediency, I tried to only pick out every third word to study and recite, but discovered that if one of the twins missed a word, it threw me all out of whack. I felt that I was engulfed in dumbness! My father soon discovered that I was not learning anything and that his money was being wasted, so much against his principles, I was sent to a public school on Main Street (near Harvie). Flora went with me. Prior to our enrollment, Father took us to Dr. George Ben Johnston's office and had us vaccinated. We were then tested in school and were both placed in second grade since Father wanted us to be together. We thereafter went all through school together. I often explained to people that I had lost a year starting to school because I had been ill as an infant.

In 1897, Richmond had a terrible blizzard and snowstorm, and snow was piled in drifts higher than a child was tall, and communication lines were devastated. Men dug channels for pedestrians to walk through. Despite all of the snow, Mother sent Flora and me to school. We trudged between high banks of snow on each side of us. Only a handful of kids went to school that day, so they were later sent home. However, despite the occasional weather problems, we did well in this new academic environment. Prompted by a hard, plain teacher named Miss Pilgrim, Flora and I learned the multiplication tables backward and forward. In class, we used a slate bound by red felt to protect the desk. A little Jewish boy passed the bucket of water and each child dipped his or her sponge into that bucket, which was very unsanitary. Sometimes, Miss Pilgrim took a leather strap that had been made of four or five strips and lashed some boy. Although there were over forty children in that class, Miss Pilgrim made them behave. I shudder now when I reflect on some of those scenes. But Flora and I talked it over and decided to endure all things and learn.

Christmas was coming and I wanted a large doll—a real doll. So, when Mother began to take inventory to find out what each child wanted, I said, "I don't want anything but one great big doll—so tall!" I then held my hands out three feet from the floor. Somehow, Mother managed this expensive request. She asked the relatives to give her money as my gift, so she could buy a large doll. She then went to Thalheimer's and bought a slightly worn window shop doll, and put it in a large trunk in the servants' hall. This hall separated our part of the house from the servants' room over the kitchen and had steps that led down to the butler's pantry and into the kitchen. For some reason, she did not lock the trunk. Christmas was coming and I was an insistent child. When Mother was at church, I put in a search to see if there was a doll around the house. I found it and it was so large it took my breath. I carefully took the doll out of the trunk and played with it. I watched the clock and put the doll back before Mother returned from church. I then bore the secret in my heart.

Christmas Eve came and I was so excited that I could not sleep. Finally, I put on my wrapper and crocheted slippers and slipped down the dark steps into the sitting room that adjoined the parlor. A soft glow from the Latrobe was the only light. I quickly found the doll, fully dressed, stretched out on a cold, marble-top walnut table. Around the doll were seven games besides. I was overjoyed over the doll! I sat by the Latrobe and warmed the doll and loved her passionately. Never was a cold piece of material loved more - I sat there for hours. However, daylight was coming and I had to get back to bed before the others awakened. I did not want to lose that doll by any punishment. The next morning I dressed with the others and rushed excitely to see my gifts, as if I was surprised. I named her Margaret Randolph—because I loved the name Margaret—and because Mother had a friend named Mrs. Randolph. She was mine!

My lovely brown-eyed doll could shut and open her eyes. I played with her and loved her dearly. One day her head drooped and wobbled around. I ran to tell Mother and sobbed. She hardly knew what to do. My grief was intense, so Mother said, "We will find a doll doctor. I am sure he can mend your doll." Se we dressed immediately and started to a doll store on Broad Street. We walked over to Broad Street, boarded the mule car and dropped our three pennies in the box. I sobbed softly and held my doll. When we went into the store, the doll man told Mother how a hook in the neck had become disjointed, and he instructed us what to do if it happened again. My doll was all right! We thanked the man and went home. Later on Mother took her tangled wig and had the hair steamed and curled. Today, I still possess my beautiful Margaret Randolph![8]

In the fall or the winter I suffered from terrible earaches, which may have come from the nurse letting me sit on the damp ground in the park. Mother would put salt in a biscuit pan and heat it in an oven and pour it into a large, black stocking kept for that purpose. I cannot count how many times I fell asleep on the soothing salt bag. On one occasion we girls got the measles with a vengeance. Flora and I had them first before Jo was also infected. We were moved into the large front room and a large hammock was hung across the room, making it dark. Mother nursed us and amused us. She sat in the light outside the door and made us rag dolls out of old sheets all day long. I had ten such babies made for me of all sizes and

Mother marked the faces on the dolls with pen and ink while sewing arms on each side–crude affairs.

Mother had two servants and was free to enjoy some social pleasures, and she considered it extremely important to carry on her duties as a wife as well as a mother. I have often suspected that she rated being a wife as the most important of obligations. For his part, Father surely wanted a male heir. However, it was not until I was eight years old that such an event occurred.

As a general rule, Father did not allow us to chew gum, because he thought it was unladylike. However, now that we were sick with the measles, he broke all rules and bought us every variety of gum available—pepsin, spearmint, Sen-Sen, etc.—by the dozen packages. We thought it a wonderful lark! Towards the end of our confinement our eyes hurt and were red. Flora and I recovered and nursed Jo at the final stages, thus relieving Mother. Father praised us, and I remember he rewarded me with a lovely blue bathrobe and a tall green bottle of perfume.

I believe it was at this time that I boldly marched up to Dr. George Ben Johnston and said, "Doctor, please bring me a baby brother." He said, "Be a good girl and I will try to find you a baby brother." I didn't think he sounded very sure. Shortly thereafter, on July 8, 1897, a baby brother came and I took possession of him. I called him "my baby," since I was the one who had asked for him! I slaved for him and never thought any duty related to him was anything less than heavenly. J.E.B. Stuart III he was, because that name must go on. He was a large, healthy, blonde baby who weighed eight pounds when born. Mother had a white nurse named Connie, who devoted her time to him. However, I was often allowed to help and to hold the darling child. He was nearly as large as I was, and my lap was small. One day I was sitting in a child's chair holding him and he wiggled off my lap and hit the floor with a thump. Mother came running upstairs and scolded me. It was unavoidable. I felt disgraced, but my tenderness toward this youngster grew.

In 1898, America declared war on Spain. People talked and letters were written as excitement swept old Confederate Richmond. Father was a military man in every sense of the word. He had a father who was educated at West Point and who had also given his life for his country. His mother was the daughter of another West Point graduate, General Philip St. George Cooke, who had served in the Union Army during the Civil War. Before that the Stuarts had served in the Revolutionary War and before that had fled Scotland, and then Ireland in search of liberty. So my father hoisted a large United States flag over our house. Volunteers were called for, and Father volunteered. His country was calling! Grandma Stuart wrote a heartfelt letter to him, saying "but, dear son, you did not need to volunteer." She still found it hard to recognize the new flag; because all of the brave Confederate blood

*Capt. J.E.B. Stuart II, U.S. Army
Volunteers (Courtesy of Sharon
Stuart McRee).*

had been poured out under the Confederate symbol. She had passed through
the War Between the States and lost nearly all that was dear to her. The dark-
ness of her life had unfolded under the stars of the Union flag. For sixty years
she lived on afterwards with these touching, sacred memories of sorrow.
Now, here was her only son flaunting a large United States flag—and he was
proud of that new flag! What kind of world was this?

Father was made a captain in the Commissary Department, U.S. Army,
1st Brigade, 1st Division, VII Corps, under Brig. Gen. Loyd Wheaton.[9] One
beautiful day in March—I think—Father put on a dark blue uniform and
we all went to the boat to see him off. We sobbed and sobbed and kissed
him goodbye. I was convinced in my childish mind that it was the end of
all things. I never expected to see him again. Sorrowfully we went home—
emptiness filled our house—a gloom settled on our spirits. I sobbed out of my
loneliness for many nights on my pillow because I might not see my father
again. Then the gay letters came—adventure after adventure—telling of the
beauties of semi-tropical places where the army settled. We longed for the
sunshine of Charleston, Savannah, Jacksonville, St. Augustine, Tallahassee,
Miami, Key West, Tampa, and Havana, Cuba. These exotic locales were all
on his itinerary.[10] Pictures came from beautiful Savannah, Georgia, showing

palm trees waving in the breeze, blue waters, sunny skies, sandy shores, little tents in a row, and Father standing with other officers in importance.[11] And the wonderful menus! Steaks every day, guava jelly, coconuts, and tropical fruits just to name a few. Father was rid of the confining bank. His tales of the tropical country took the sting out of the separation, but Mother carried on alone.

One late night the doorbell rang. What should we do? There was a chain lock on the door, but it would never do to open the door. Mother was really frightened. She called from the window but received no answer. She then flung open the blinds on the alley side and yelled for Mr. Hill, who lived in a back room with the Christians in the third house from the corner. Finally, Mr. Hill answered and came over, ultimately facing the intruder. It was a telegram! The delivery boy did not understand why he had caused such a furor. The message read: "Congratulations on our wedding anniversary—J.E.B. Stuart—July 21st, 1898." The next day, all of the nearby neighbors came and laughed. Poor Mother—she could not laugh!

Mother was fond of dressing Flora and me and sending us forth to make calls on adult relatives and friends. Was she proud of our manners? Did she wish to have a rest from us and our energetic ways? Did we really bring forth a friendly response that helped to promote the Stuart family? I wonder. One time, Flora and I were dressed and sent to call at Bishop Gibson's home, which was near Holy Trinity Church. We were shy and dreaded the approach, but Cousin Lucy Gibson was there. She had red hair, a lovely and kind face, and always put us at ease, bringing out our conversational interests. Cousin Mary Gibson was very nice, too. They had a brother, Rev. Churchill Gibson, who was minister at Old St. James Church on Franklin Street. In the parlor of these Gibson cousins I enjoyed sitting on a golden chair that had a magical music box that operated when one was seated! So Cousin Lucy asked about our "Papa." That was all we needed. I launched forth about Father, stating that, "Mother received a postcard from Father this morning and he said the fare is fine: he had whale on toast for breakfast." Of course, I should have said, "quail on toast," but my listeners were elegant Virginia ladies, and they laughed quietly and went on with the conversation. I innocently rejoiced that I had entertained them! I did not know of my blunder until years later when Mother told me.

Once or twice Mother trusted us to go see the Mariott twins who I had met at Miss Robinson's school. We also went to visit Cousin Bethenia, a niece of Grandpa Stuart and daughter of Rev. Nicholas Chevalier.[12] She gave me an old-fashioned coral breast-pin and string of coral beads on one of these visits. On other occasions, we went to spend the day with old Mrs. Day, who was the grandmother of Mary Day Winn and Elizabeth Winn. I adored Mary

Day Winn—she was a kindred spirit. Flora played with Elizabeth. Years later Mary Day went to Vassar, and Elizabeth went to Stuart Hall around the time that Flora and I attended. Moreover, she took studio artwork as I did. However, by that time the romance of childhood friendship was gone.

During this period, a Confederate Reunion came to Richmond. The papers were full of the glory of it. Bunting was hung on every house as the veterans in gray began to arrive. To commemorate the occasion, Grandma Stuart made for her three little granddaughters three little cotton Confederate flags—all by hand. They were each bright red, blue, and white, and included the thirteen stars crossing on a red band on a blue field—I still have mine today![13] Excited about our gifts, we stood on our terrace on the big day and waved these flags as the passing marching band played "Dixie" with spirit. The veterans in gray finally marched again! They waved at us as they passed our house. I think it must have been planned that these veterans come up Main Street and pass in front of our home on their way out to the Lee monument. The Stuart monument had not yet been erected. Did they know they were passing the Stuart home? Over the course of the reunion, there were houseguests and many large receptions—the heart of the South was throbbing. The excitement of that occasion swept me into ecstasy. As the reunion came to a close, I watched the gray fade away, and heard the drum beats finally fade into eternity.

Since Richmond was in the midst of a hot and busy summer, Staunton in the Shenandoah Valley was a peaceful place to go. We had our bags packed and waiting. Mother and her family of four children, and the white nurse, Connie, were waiting for the carriage or hack to take us to the station. Grandma Phillips was coming from Hampton to join us at Staunton. At first the excitement of the journey was thrilling, but we began to count the long hours of that trip. We could look out the window, play games, get a drink of ice water from the cooler, and walk up the aisle occasionally. Finally, we reached Gordonsville with its noted fried chicken. Voluptuous Negro girls gracefully tilted trays on their heads. For twenty-five cents, a crisp, brown breast of chicken was yours. Now we felt better. The heavier engine was pulling us into cooler air—Charlottesville—and then the conductor said, "Tunnel ahead," and the porter shut all windows and turned on the electric lights. The tunnel was somewhat frightening but the porter came and brushed the cinders off us and paid much attention to Mother's little family.

Now Staunton and the Blue Ridge! Grandma Stuart had sent Tom, the colored man, to meet us in the carriage. It felt good to stretch and touch the ground. Tom made a big fuss over us—and he had real enthusiasm. We drove directly to the Virginia Female Institute (now called Stuart Hall in my grandmother's honor). Grandma Stuart gave us all a devoted kiss and caress, as well as a warm reception. Supper was soon served in the large dining room, which in the winter was gay with the voices of eighty or one hundred girls. I was ravenously hungry. I had been taking iron, and the crisp mountain air was a tonic and the cooking was delicious. Brown, hot turnovers with homemade butter, cold beef, milk, some of Tom's homegrown tomatoes in a saucer with dressing, and homemade preserves were among the items on the menu. The adults drank iced tea.

Eight o'clock was our bed hour in Staunton. We were usually ready after a long day of play and exploration at the school. The music hall with all the little rooms with a piano in each room was a fascinating place. The tennis courts and Tom's garden were interesting, but the flowers were Tom's special pride. We could spend hours enjoying the fountain splashing into a circular pool, bordered by nasturtiums. The robins were so tame and came so near. They were fat with good eating. We could sit on a bench quite near and watch them bathe. We could also take a leaf and then puff it up and make a frog's stomach. Around the front veranda was every variety of fuchsia—dear little velvet bells. I loved the rich red violets and blue violets and would not hurt them. How did Tom raise them? They were potted and grown in a small greenhouse with steam pipes running from the institute. Tom had the "growing hand." In the summer these beauties flaunted their splendor. Even today I get hungry to see a fuchsia—they bring such lovely memories. I have never seen so many fuchsias and so many different kinds. Did Grandma Stuart love them like I did?

How I loved to walk around in that garden. The schoolgirls called one section "paradise." They were allowed to stroll there on Saturdays and Sundays. In this section were gorgeously strong horse chestnuts, and the blossoms were fragrant, and the shiny black nuts could be picked up on the ground— "buckeyes" we called them. Here the squirrels came to play their games or to get their food. The squirrels and robins were a continuing drama - and the restoring, invigorating air and beautiful nature were there – shadows and sunshine and bubbling waters, and quiet except for a robin's splash or pit-patter spray from the iron fountain.

We arose at some time between six and seven o'clock in the morning, had a bath, and then dressed. We assembled in Grandma Phillips' room, where she helped us learn a verse from a psalm each morning. At breakfast and after prayers, we recited this verse in unison with the Waller children—our first cousins, Flora and Matt (Cousin Virginia was not born yet). My aunt, Virginia Waller (Father's sister), was there and taught her little ones at her end of the house. We learned the 23rd Psalm verse by verse. It has since stood me in good stead: "Yea, though I walk through the Valley of the Shadow of Death—I will fear no evil. For Thou art with me, Thy rod and Thy staff they comfort me. Thou preparest a table before me in the presence of my enemies." Such comforting words—I know Grandma Stuart found supreme comfort in this Psalm and wanted us to know it.

We had breakfast at eight and afterwards Grandma Stuart conducted our prayers. Grandma directed the servants, went to the bank occasionally, supervised a colored sewing woman (who made Flora and me several blue seersucker dresses), and wrote letters and letters. She was always busy with a long list of activities. Various rooms were overhauled and laundry had to be checked. After supper we gathered in a parlor and Aunt Virginia played games with us, and we often sang hymns. One game we played was, "This is the way we comb our hair, this is the way we brush our teeth, this is the way we wash our clothes, etc." We formed a circle, sang, and made motions to correspond with the words. Our favorite hymns were, "Now the day is over, night is drawing nigh; Shadows of the evening, steal across the sky," and "rock of the ages, cleft for me, let myself hide in thee." This hymn we felt belonged to Grandpa Stuart because in his last hours he requested that it be sung. "Lead, kindly light" was another favorite, and "I need Thee every hour."

The afternoons afforded some lovely drives and Tom drove the horses. He was a favorite servant—where did Grandma find him? He could raise vegetables, flowers, milk the cows, manage the horses, keep the grounds, keep the furnace in the winter, meet all arrivals, and do many other things. Tom's manners were always correct, and he had the dignity of life. He was lean and wiry, with medium tan colored skin and graying hair. Overall, Tom was dependable. However, August was nearly gone and the school was getting ready for the return of the girls. Our lovely visit was coming to an end. Every moment had been pure happiness. Grandma Phillips had helped us in dressing, and had almost constantly coached us in proper manners. She wanted us to measure up to the highest standard of behavior, and we did. Nevertheless, we had to leave and go back to Richmond and the long backyard. We had to leave the robins, the bright nasturtiums, the velvety fuchsias, the poetry of the mountains, and the uplifting Blue Ridge. Most of all, we had to leave dear good Grandma Stuart and Tom, who really loved children and showed us so many interesting things.

Back in Richmond, our lives went on without Father. We had the comforts of life and found interests of various kinds. Richmond was hot in the summer, so after Mother brought us from Staunton we went in the country about twenty miles outside of the city to Forest Hill. Mother found board for us at a reasonable rate, and several Richmond families were also boarding there. A fresh water spring was not too far distant, and water was stored in bottles and later hauled to Richmond. Around the house ran ditches to take the slop water off from the house. I may have played around these ditches on a few occasions. Anyway, I contracted a fever—an intermittent fever as Dr. Johnston called it. Consequently, Mother rushed us back to Richmond. I was so ill that Dr. Johnston stayed at my bedside and watched over me carefully. I had hemorrhages and sinking spells. My bed head posts had bricks under them to prop me up. I made a gallant fight to get well—a pale, weak, and wistful little thing. Unfortunately, my hair began to fall out. Mother consulted the barber and he said I must have my head shaved, but I refused. I had two long braids of thick vermilion or red-orange hair. I was very sensitive over having red hair. Often, I had wondered why I had been made so different from other children. Father and Mother had never showed any partiality about us three little girls. I was the oldest and had more responsibility put on me, but at the same time I was allowed first choice. Father would say, "Mary is the oldest – let her pick the ribbon first." Or when he divided a stick of peppermint candy, I was allowed to help myself first. Father generally made a great ceremony over measuring and cutting with a knife a stick of candy into thirds. When he got it divided the parts were equal, but so often I heard, "Mary is the oldest—she must set a good example."

Well, Mother decided my tresses must be cut off. More than that, she and the barber decided my head must be shaved. They told me if I allowed the barber, "to shave my head backwards," my hair would come out curly. I said, "No—I cannot bear to not have any hair." But my hair by that time was coming out in handfuls, so I concluded that I would be baldheaded anyway—and maybe always bald. The barber also assured Mother again that if I had my head shaved, I would have new and curly hair. So I therefore consented. When the barber came to the house Mother decided to have Flora and Jo's hair cut short as well in order to make their hair thicker. So I went through the ordeal and wept in private after what had happened to me. I did not ever think I had any good looks, and now I was baldheaded and my freckles looked very pronounced.

Mother made me a black cap with an elastic band. After about three weeks a bristly red hair crop grew out very straight. But, worse than this, as soon as I discarded the cap, Mother had pictures of us taken in the back yard. One picture was of us three girls standing beside a large dry goods box, which was our dollhouse. Another picture showed our baby brother chewing on a clothespin while Mother was in her housedress and gingham apron standing with us girls. I always hated that picture. Father must have been sent one, because when he came home he said, "I left little girls when I went away; now I come home and find that I have little boys!" These were cruel words to my sensitive nature. I never wanted to be a little boy—and I knew that I was homely. My bright red braids had given me a certain distinction—and I had tried to make my manners approve reproach. Mother had often said,

Marrow with her mother and siblings, circa 1898. From left to right—Flora Stuart, Marrow, J.E.B. Stuart III, and their mother, Josephine "Jo" Phillips Stuart. Marrow's sister, Josephine "Jo" Stuart, is standing below (Courtesy of Sharon Stuart McRee).

"pretty is as pretty does," and I understood that it would be a very fair world if I behaved. I include this sketch of myself because it is typical of me—sensitive—having pride—cooperating—with good manners—reasoning out reactions—why did I get sick? How did Mother and Father feel about this dreadful thing that had happened to me? Why was I born with freckles and red hair—such an ugly duckling!

[*Unfortunately, Marrow was not the only sick member of her family during this time.*] Upon Father's return home from the war, he was sick and yellow with jaundice. At home on temporary furlough, he was now eager for his permanent release from military duties. After finally resigning his captaincy, it took him months to get well. Father had so much to tell us—especially geography. Trunks came and we sat around in the back parlor or sitting room and let Father unpack the specimens. Shells from Florida and every kind of coral were the first items to leave the trunk. Father also showed us coconuts and sawed some of them in cross sections so we could understand. Palm leaves, photographs of avenues in Havana, and guava jelly from Cuba were also available in abundance.

We also heard the story of the Spanish teapot. Here was this lovely, thin, and nearly global pot on three simple feet with a graceful handle and spout. Father had seen three pieces in an old junk shop in Havana, Cuba. He could have bought all three pieces (the tea pot, a coffee urn, and a little hot water pot) for five dollars. "Well," Father said, "they looked like junk—they were so black." Therefore, he only bought the smallest pot for one dollar and a quarter. He later had his orderly clean it with brick dust. Here it was—an old Spanish heirloom that was so light, so exquisitely etched, with a mono-gram! Mother was wild over it. She asked Father why he had not given her the whole set instead of that duck-handled black silk umbrella for which he paid five dollars. Father sat down and wrote to a friend in Cuba and tried to describe the shop, urn, and little pot. However, he never did find the compan-ions to this little hot water pot. He later took the gem to a Richmond jeweler to have a knob made. The jeweler then put a modern, ornate pansy knob on the piece—a terrible sacrilege. Afterwards I think it was changed to a plain knob, and Flora later inherited this exquisite little pot. I could have had it and in fact longed for it, since I loved its romance.

Years later when Mother divided the family silver, I had first pick and took the old Sheffield candlesticks that had been in the Stuart family for five generations. These pieces had graced the mantle in the home of General Stu-art's mother, and had also belonged to his Grandmother Pannill. After all, the candlesticks did proclaim the distinction of any family able to own Sheffield plate in the early days of the country. They were also a part of my heritage, and I am glad I was able to choose them. Maybe on the second round of pick-ing I might have chosen the little Spanish silver pot. However, Flora had good judgment and snapped it up. She also received the two silver water goblets that were marked "P.W.H. to Flora." Cousin Peter Hairston had given these to Grandma Stuart as her wedding gift. Since they had "Flora" engraved upon them, Mother said that they should go to my sister Flora.

Back to the trunk and geography lesson we must come. The floor of our home was literally covered with tropical materials. We used them to live over the moments of the war with Father. The Spanish-American War seemed to be a lovely experience in a tropical land. Father also had a glass with a pic-ture of the beautiful battleship *USS Maine*. It had an inscription that read, "I am going to war with Spain for blowing up the *Maine*." Today, we really do not think as that glass was designed to make us think! It was just a bit of war propaganda. I think it has been proven when the ship was investigated that there was an internal explosion, or that it hit a mine—always a mystery. Father had bought a phonograph and we now had an entire collection of records. They included the "El Capitan March," "Flee as a Bird to Yonder Mountain," "Jerusalem," "Hosanna in the Highest," "Beulah Land, Sweet Beulah Land," and William J. Bryan's "Cross of Silver and Crown of Thorns" speech. He played them over and over until we knew them by heart. After a few months, Father was getting well and he was getting restless. The bank was so confining and there was little room for advancement. Soon we would move to Newport News, Virginia.

NOTES

1. Chinquapins are a type of nut.

2. Little Sisters of the Poor is a Catholic mission that provides assistance to the elderly poor. In 1874, six of the Little Sisters originally established the mission in Richmond. They later moved to the location mentioned by MSS in 1877, before moving again to their current location (now called St. Joseph's Home for the Aged) in western Henrico County in 1976.

3. A Victoria was a one-horse carriage with a front-facing bench seat. Popular among wealthy families, it was particularly fashionable with ladies for riding in the park. The name was later applied to the Ford Crown Victoria automobile.

4. For the rest of her life, Flora Cooke Stuart wore only black to mourn her husband following his death in 1864.

5. Anne Gordon Patton Cooke (1844–1914) was a great-granddaughter of Brig. Gen. Hugh Mercer (1726–1777) of the Continental Army, who was mortally wounded during the Battle of Princeton in 1777. Her grandparents, Robert Patton and Anne Mercer Patton, were also direct ancestors of Gen. George S. Patton of World War II fame.

6. John Rogers Cooke (1833–1891) served as colonel of the 27th North Carolina Infantry before commanding a brigade in Lt. Gen. A.P. Hill's corps. He was wounded seven times during the Civil War.

7. The Farmville Normal School later evolved into Longwood University.

8. The doll is now owned by MSS's granddaughter, Sharon Stuart McRee.

9. A Michigan native, Brig. Gen. Loyd Wheaton (1838–1918) had been awarded the Medal of Honor for his service in the 8th Illinois Infantry during the Civil War. Ohio native Maj Gen. Joseph Warren Keifer (1836-1932) commanded the 1st Division. A Union Army officer during the Civil War, Keifer later served in the U.S. Congress and was Speaker of the House from 1881 to 1883. Maj. Gen. Fitzhugh Lee (1835–1905), an ex-Confederate general and nephew of Robert E. Lee, commanded the VII Corps. Lee had also served as governor of Virginia from 1886–1890.

10. There is debate within the Stuart family as to whether JEBS II actually served in Cuba during the war. He may have visited the island on brief wartime trips, but it is

unlikely he was stationed there during the actual fighting. The VII Corps spent the entire war encamped in various parts of Florida. As such, the 1st Brigade was stationed in Miami during the fighting. While it had trained for combat duty, the war ended before its service in that area was needed. Thus, it only served in Cuba for postwar occupation duty, and that is likely when JEBS II spent time there.

11. The VII Corps was transferred from Camp Cuba Libre in Jacksonville, Florida to a camp in Savannah, Georgia in October 1898.

12. Bethenia P. Chevalier (b. 1844) was the daughter of Rev. Nicholas Chevalier (1810–1866) and Bethenia Frances Stuart (1819–1910). Bethenia Frances Stuart was a sister of JEBS I.

13. The flag is now owned by MSS's granddaughter, Sharon Stuart McRee.

Chapter Four

Life in Newport News

Newport News—on Hampton Roads and at the mouth of the James River—a town of big open spaces. With the deepest harbor on the Atlantic seaboard, it has become a thriving town with overnight growth. As an industrial town, Newport News is a paradise for both the skilled and unskilled laboring man. With its great shipyard and two of the largest dry docks, the town produces the finest battleships and giant ocean liners.[1] It is amazing to think that they all start as a sketch on paper in some naval architect's office. Newport News also brings to mind images of large grain elevators as well as foreign ships coming and going, with brusque sea captains walking around the docks. Only one railroad—the terminal of the Chesapeake & Ohio—services this thriving area.[2]

When I think of my young life in Newport News, I do not recall the steel and ships, but I do envision the rich, virgin earth. I also reflect on my tramps over fields of sweet potatoes and turnips, and skipping along a railroad track to the woods where the largest pansy violets grew. I think of the steady stream of shipyard workers carrying their lunch pails and walking briskly to or from work. I think of standing waiting for a trolley car after the tired men had occupied the seats on every available trolley for hours, and of my parents' warning to "get home before the shipyard rush." I remember the surging crowds at a ship launching, and even now hear in my imagination the blows of hammers and the pegs being knocked from under the ships. First a volume of rhythmic sound, and then finally a scattered worker giving the last single thrust at the dramatic last minute—then the weary wanderings in black cinder paths to the big gate. In contrast to a launching scene, I can remember the poetic beauty of the peaceful James River at sunset or under the glory of moonlight.

No wonder Father was attracted to this magnet of a town to find work and opportunity, and to cast his lot for his fortune and for the future of his family.

Mother seemed to be glad to be moving. She had many relatives and friends at the adjoining old town of Hampton, and her old Warwick County home had been near—only seven miles from Newport News. Her own mother, Mary Marrow Phillips, now lived at Marrow Point in Hampton with her brother, Daniel Marrow, and his daughter, Mary Marrow Blackiston. Great Uncle Clay Marrow and his wife, Maria, also lived in Hampton in a small cottage on Queen Street near the bridge. We children were more than delighted with the adventure and were eager for something new. We thought to live by the sea would be wonderful. Father left Richmond in March 1899 and stayed at Aunt Lou Phillips' home until September. Once during that time Mother went to visit him. She brought her two babies, little Jo and Jebby, and the nurse Connie. Mother and Father went to the Chamberlain Hotel at Old Point for an outing, I happen to know.[3]

Flora and I were left with Grandma Phillips and the servant at Richmond. In order to get Grandma Phillips to Richmond, the yellow fever blockade had to be run. This was the time when yellow fever broke out at the Old Soldiers' Home in Hampton. There was a fine oyster shell road connecting Hampton and Newport News, and one streetcar line also connecting the two towns. During the epidemic, travel between the two places was restricted and the passes were few. Cars ran to the edge of Hampton, and then a person could only enter the boundaries of Newport News with special permission. So Father went with horse and buggy to the Hampton line, marked by a group of pine trees. There, he met Grandma Phillips and got her through the lines, so she could board the C & O train to Richmond.

These were exciting times. Prominent citizens were organized into the Vigilantes or Vigilant Guard. This was to keep the old soldiers or any others from landing or slipping from rowboats into the town along the extensive seacoast. The town of Newport News provided my father, now called "Captain Stuart," with a horse to assist in this effort. All during the night, he guarded that part of the waterfront boulevard that skirted Hampton Roads from the East End, or from the Chestnut Avenue side. In the dead of night, as he passed Aunt Lou's house he would give a war-whoop call. In the daytime, he slept at Aunt Lou's and the horse slept in the stable there. The water frontage Father patrolled is now called Stuart Gardens, where twelve hundred war-workers' homes were located. During World War I, it was called "Camp J.E.B. Stuart"—named after my grandfather.[4] I like this story of Father riding in the night because it so characterizes him. He loved adventure and freedom, and he was truly of the bold pioneer type in spirit and manners. Father had the zest for life as well as courage, and in this episode I could see him dramatizing the night raiding of his own father, the famous Confederate cavalry leader.

Finally, the peril of the yellow fever died out as suddenly as it came. No doubt these citizens were thankful, because some remembered the drastic devastation of the yellow-fever epidemic in Norfolk and its surrounding places in the post-Civil War years. With the crisis over, the citizens who had fled to old Yorktown returned. In the fall of 1899 the Stuart family left Richmond. At first we visited Mother's brother, Uncle Edwin Phillips, who had a large, rambling house at Chestnut and 21st Streets. His beautiful wife, Aunt Lou, was eleven years younger than he. She was the former Miss Louise Sinclair, and had distinguished lineage. Her mother was a Catlett from Gloucester County.[5] Aunt Lou had dark-gray eyes and straight black hair, with clear olive skin. Since her marriage she had allowed herself to get somewhat stout.

There were only two boys in the family at that time—Edwin Keith (named after Uncle Edwin and after Aunt Lou's brother Keith), and Joe Phillips, who was named after his late grandfather who had served as a colonel in the Confederate Army. Sinclair and Daniel were not yet born. My cousin Martha was born the following fall on November 20, 1899, and she was the excuse that prevented Aunt Lou from fleeing to Yorktown during the yellow fever scare. Edwin, the eldest child, was practical and had a sixth sense for business. He helped his father at the large coal yard on Saturdays and after school hours. At Aunt Lou's my chief diversion was going to the store to buy some candy. I seemed to have plenty of nickels and dimes given me, and would walk three blocks to a store, or farther on to another store, and buy an assortment of candy. I would then eat it from the bag as I walked nonchalantly back to Aunt Lou's. This was a bad habit, and I had never been allowed to dissipate in such an orgy of sweets–and between meals too! However, I was so restless—and it offered an adventure in buying and trading. I doubt if Mother or Father knew what I was doing.

Aunt Lou kept an open house and neighbors came and went all day. Some came to borrow since she had rural inclinations and raised chickens. Aunt Lou generally had two or three cows that afforded fresh milk for the table and allowed the boys to make pocket money. Edwin milked the cows and Joe delivered the milk to the numerous neighborhood customers before breakfast. Therefore, these boys were coming and going all day, occupied with their business. Martha, who had been born in November, now became part of the family group. She was the only girl and was accepted by all as the little queen. She was always being petted or fed by her "Bam-ma," the old, delicate Mrs. Sinclair, who managed to cling to life for many years even though she had a bad cough and was bent over nearly double. This entire set-up at Aunt Lou's expressed confusion, and there was not a single corner where I could find repose or go and think and create. I did watch and study the gray Plymouth Rock chickens and I did go see the cows but was dreadfully afraid of the beasts. Consequently, I walked to the candy store constantly—sometimes I made five or six trips a day. Unfortunately, I would then suffer from an upset stomach!

Aunt Lou was motherly and approachable, and she thought that we were so well mannered. She has since told me how Father did not want us calling out what we wanted at the table. Instead, she said, I would pull Father towards me and whisper in his ear what I wanted. Our bedtime hour was immediately after supper. Always by eight o'clock we were out of the way and Mother and Father were free from us unless we had croup. But not so with Aunt Lou's brood. They sat around in rockers or on someone's lap and blinked, and one by one they dozed off. Finally, Uncle Edwin would gather up one child, Aunt Lou would gather up one, and Mrs. Sinclair had her Martha. Then, Uncle Edwin would put himself to bed, for he had such an early morning schedule. There were no reading lamps or card games.

There were daytime activities of cows, chickens, vegetable gardens, and sometimes ducks and pigs. In other words, a small farm on the outskirts of town. Mother and my Grandma Phillips sewed and mended, and chatted with Mrs. Sinclair while also receiving callers. Aunt Lou's sister, Mrs. Andrews, would drop in to chat in the morning and then return in the afternoon. She never seemed to bother about her own housekeeping, her three boys, or her husband. Instead, she had a servant and let that person manage the house and household affairs. A capable cook prepared the cooking at Aunt Lou's. Negro or white peddlers brought fish and oysters to the door, and Aunt Lou's brother (Keith Sinclair) would come in from the country about once a week with gifts including lamb, potatoes, and turnips. The items all came from his fine farm on Back River, near Hampton. He would send one (and during the war two) barrels of flour on the streetcar, and the conductor would put them off at Aunt Lou's door. In those days, flour came by the barrel—biscuits and rolls were made every day—and Aunt Lou had an abundance of eggs, chickens, and milk on the place. We lived sumptuously.

It was certainly hospitable of Aunt Lou and Uncle Edwin to invite us there and say, "Stay with us until you get located." We did stay for three or four weeks, and then Father rented a house for us at 23rd and Chestnut. He also went into the real estate business with Mr. Howard Collier as his partner. We moved into this house and the wet plaster gave us all bad colds. Little J.E.B. III was quite seriously ill while we were there. Meanwhile, the workmen came and went, trying to fix the house for us. Grandma Phillips was there to help Mother, and we had a cook. We went to the only available school - the Thomas Jefferson School on 28th Street—that was so far away. Father would have to put Flora and me in the buggy and drive us there each day. We did not stay in this house more than six months, and Father bought a larger and fairly comfortable house on 29th Street that was closer to the school we attended. We lived on 29th Street for four or five years.

There is an old saying that "three moves are as good as a fire." No doubt our furniture got banged up with each move. I wonder how Father's old walnut desk that he inherited came through these numerous vicissitudes. This old desk had stood for fifty years in one corner without being moved. Then my father inherited this beautiful old early American treasure piece and it subsequently traveled with us Stuarts. Father had the Old Dutch legs sawn off and casters put on. On the back of the desk was written in large letters, "J.E.B. Stuart," and it was put on freight trains without even being crated—but no doubt someone always said, "Be careful with this desk!" It was the pride of our family, particularly for Father, and Grandma Phillips loved to take a red flannel rag and rub those solid brass Chippendale handles. We also rubbed in bees wax melted in turpentine to bring out more shine in the already glowing wood. The desk is now my proudest material possession![6]

[*Along with the relocation of Marrow's family to Virginia's Tidewater region, her Grandma Stuart also moved to the area.*] When I say Grandma was selfless, I have in mind her giving up her duties as principal and director of Stuart Hall at Staunton, Virginia, when the school was paying, and going to Norfolk to take care of her motherless, one-month old grandchild, Virginia Waller, and keeping house for Uncle Page Waller.[7] Aunt Virginia died on September 9th, 1898, and Grandmother took the month-old infant to Staunton and had a fine nurse to give every attention to the baby for that session. Then she ended her career and went to Norfolk in 1899. Uncle Page gave Grandma a definite amount for the housekeeping expenses. There were three Waller children, Uncle Page, Grandma Stuart, and two servants, and of course quite often houseguests. When the cost of living went up and guests came Grandma went into her own purse to buy the extra ducks or a homemade cake or other choice delicacies from the Woman's Exchange. Grandma went to market on Saturdays and brought some things back in a basket on the trolley, and had other things sent. During the week she could order over the telephone from a reliable butcher. Fanny was the excellent cook, and she was taught to make delicious chicken gumbo soup or vegetable soup for the first course of dinner—and sugar cookies for "Tea" from Grandma's old Virginia recipes. This Fanny served faithfully as cook for twenty or more years.

Each summer when Father was living in Newport News, Flora and I were invited to visit Grandma in Norfolk for a week. This could have been in July, as we were on vacation and Grandma always went away in August with the three Waller children to the Warm Springs or the White Sulphur Springs, sometimes adding a visit to Stuart relatives in Abingdon or Wytheville.

Virginia Stuart Waller, circa 1887 (Courtesy of Sharon Stuart McRee).

Uncle Page owned a substantial three-story brick house on Pembroke and Warren Crescent near The Hague, where he could reach his launch easily. Grandma had given Aunt Virginia a lot adjoining the home on Warren Crescent. In spite of the breezes coming over the waterside, the summers were sultry and hot. Often the afternoons were devoted to boat rides in Uncle Page's launch. If Matt was home he took charge of running the engine, and he became quite "bossy." He loved to tinker with the engine. But these excursions were delightful! I can remember the fine Ocean View spots fish that Fanny cooked and Uncle Page liked so well. One day two little ducks were served at the two o'clock dinner. Uncle Page, after expertly carving, asked me if I would have white meat or dark meat. I hesitated a minute and said, "a little of both, please." Virginia and Flora Waller gave a war whoop and Uncle Page cunningly said, "sorry, there is no white meat to a duck." Virginia and Flora also chimed in, saying, "there is no white meat to a duck!" These meals were always elegant and served with dignity and style. We were not allowed to pass anything, and Grandma pressed her foot on a floor button to summon the maid to pass dishes.

After the eight o'clock breakfast meal was completed, there were short readings from the Gospels, and prayers were conducted by Grandma. Breakfast was always leisurely, as Uncle Page did not work. He had an income from various investments he had made from an inheritance from his Aunt Sally Tazewell's estate, and he had sold his mill at a good profit. Flora and Virginia went to a private school–the Phillips-West School of Norfolk. Virginia then attended Stuart Hall and focused on music, and then studied music at Peabody in Baltimore, where she graduated. Matt attended the Julia Smith private school for boys at York and Duke Streets, Norfolk. Then, he was sent to Woodbury Forest in Orange County, Virginia, followed by one year at V.P.I. in Blacksburg, Virginia. Matt liked machinery, and not things in a book![8] Virginia gave a recital at the Norfolk Society of Arts and played beautifully. She stopped playing after that. I always felt that she featured her music to please Grandma. When we were visiting Grandma, certain interests were provided to keep us busy, or from fidgeting. I remember on one occasion Grandma took us to her room and she cut up some canvas and gave Flora, me, and Flora Waller each a piece of canvas with some strands of bright-colored wool, and Grandma taught us how to weave or cross-stitch a top for a pin cushion. I always loved colors and making creative craft things, and I finished quickly. Then Grandma helped me put on a backing and stuff the cushion with clean wool.

Once I remember we were staying at Grandma Stuart's and bedtime came at about nine o'clock or shortly afterwards. As always, Grandma gathered up the family silver (mostly the Tazewell silver and some of the Stuart silver) in a basket and put it in Uncle Page's room, while Flora and I found our way to the guestroom by the gas-lighted halls. In our room the gas burned dimly, and our bed had been neatly turned down by the maid. We started undressing and stopped and flung back the blinds to the two windows on Pembroke Avenue. When Grandma came to kiss us goodnight she quietly pulled in the blinds and turned the shutters to allow a passage of air. After we got into bed we found the room suffocating with the door closed, so we flung the blinds wide open again. We were unable to sleep, but when we heard Grandma tip-toeing in again to see that all was well, we feigned sleep. Again Grandma adjusted very quietly the shutters. Maybe we accepted this, but I think we again let in the lovely night air and resolved to rise at dawn, before Grandma called us, and pull the blinds into their proper position.

In the summer, the Persian rugs in the parlor were packed away and the floor was bare and the light was shut out of that room, and likewise the library or sitting room was darkened, but the dining room had its large bay admitting light with sheer curtains giving privacy. In the living room over the fireplace hung a portrait of General J.E.B. Stuart that Colonel Heros Von Borcke (the

Flora Cooke Stuart in her later years (Courtesy of Sharon Stuart McRee).

young Prussian on Stuart's staff) had had painted by an artist in Germany from a photograph he provided. He had later given this to Aunt Virginia. Grandma had her niece, Cousin Ellen Stuart, copy this portrait exactly, and she had the copy framed and gave it to my father. This cherished copy is now in the possession of my brother. In the library, over the fireplace and near the Stuart portrait, hung the John Brown "Bowie knife," and the sword that Colonel Von Borcke gave to General Stuart was also in the arrangement. There were many bookcases, and a piano that Grandma sometimes played, though she later complained of her fingers becoming stiff.

I can remember one night that Judge Theo Garnett (formerly on Stuart's staff), and Mr. Robert M. Hughes (nephew of Confederate General Joseph E. Johnston) both called.[9] A lively discussion went on about the campaign of Gettysburg. Maps, newspapers, reports, and letters were brought out and spread on the table and read. Different points were emphasized and the following interpretation of events took shape: Grandpa Stuart was following Lee's orders to scout for supplies and find out about the enemy. It was impossible to return the way they had gone because the Federals were alerted and on the lookout with defensive forces along the river. The Federals had forces between Lee and my grandfather, making a circuitous route necessary. Also, the young officers, who were not so active and did not receive as many promotions, were jealous of Grandpa Stuart and encouraged criticism and slander. Longstreet[10] was over Grandfather and he did not support his judgment. Lastly, Longstreet had disobeyed Lee and was transferred to another section. It developed that Grandpa Stuart's message by courier was intercepted and did not reach Lee. Blackford writes that General Lee was ill with dysentery and was forced into the Battle of Gettysburg before he was ready. When Grandpa Stuart did return while the Battle of Gettysburg was raging, he protected the retreating army in a magnificent way.

Back in Newport News and living in the new 29th street home, we were in the middle of the industrial activity taking place in the city. When the shipyard whistle blew for the grimy and dusty men to stop work, they poured in black hordes out of the numerous great gates. Most bolted for the cars while some started walking home. These made black ribbons across the fields. Father had cautioned us to be in our yard when we heard this whistle. We were never allowed to be out after dark unless for some special reason, and then to be accompanied by an adult. One time at dusk a very rough man kept passing our gate as we sat on the steps. When he became aggressively disagreeable we went inside. However, during the day we roamed the fields behind our house. I had never seen such beautiful black dirt. The trees had been cut down–some stumps were there, and puddles developed when it rained. Wild iris and pansy violets bloomed in profusion. We went beyond this black, swampy land to a turnip patch and a sweet-potato patch while skirting the woods.

I sometimes brought back some of this dirt for my garden. I later asked for a spot that I could call my own. My parents gave me a shady spot about four feet wide and six or seven feet long at the back porch and near the servants' water closet. Since it was so shady, I had to find out what would grow in the shade. I raised many varieties of begonias and large, double white and purple violets. Then I needed a fence to make it all the more possessive. I earned money by cutting the lawn grass, and later bought a bundle of laths and built my fence that included a gate and handle. This enterprising garden was really an achievement. In the winter I nursed the geraniums and begonias on a window shelf in my bedroom. I think Mrs. Clements gave me the begonia slips, and Mrs. Collier gave me the violet roots. I also may have sent off and ordered some.

Grandma Phillips had ordered various roses from Peter Henderson and had that catalog. Father ordered trees and set them out wherever he lived, but so often we never stayed long enough to enjoy the fruit. In Richmond, we planted a yellow transparent apple tree along with grape vines and a pear tree. Here he set out an apple tree (wine sap), a pear tree, a plum tree, and some evergreens—blue spruce if I remember. The borders where the roses were planted had to be worked constantly. I often did this for twenty-five cents, while Grandma Phillips sometimes did it for the exercise. I also raised wonderful sweet peas in early spring and had them climb on chicken wire. Mother planted some cucumbers on a sunken barrel, but they later died from dryness. We were proud of our roses—the Jacque Minot, deep red, the Paul Neron, and pink and yellow climbers. We had a red rambler on the porch, and also a paddy vine at one end of the porch.

My interests were not all on the outdoors but were balanced by two other hobbies. I loved pictures and cut out the best illustrations I could find from Father's magazines. I then pinned these on the walls of our room. Father said I could use pins but not tacks, so I literally covered the walls. My taste was excellent, I think. Then, Mrs. Collier taught me to embroider when I visited her for a week in the summertime. She gave me a pattern of strawberries on a small dolly along with the silk. I was fascinated by the colors and I loved flowers passionately along with creating lovely patterns. I made a large forget-me-not centerpiece with maidenhair fern. Since the church was struggling with its debt, I gave it to be sold at a church sale. It was sold for seven and a half dollars and I was so proud. At Christmas we always made all of our gifts, and gave all of our numerous relatives something. I made "Aunt Lizzie" a carnation centerpiece. She treasured it for years and did not let anyone launder it except herself. I also did a large, handsome pansy centerpiece along with a red rose one—and I think that these were kept within the family. There was so much heavy padding and work on these—the leaves took so long. As I was a high-strung, restless child, I now marvel at how I sat and embroidered. It was color–and more color—and that was my world. Mother later taught me how to make white cotton flowers, and I made several bureau scarves and circular doilies in this way.

St. Paul's Church was also part of my world.[11] We did so many things to help raise money to pay off the tremendous debt on the church. Tableaux were to be given by the Junior Auxiliary. We were to say what we would be and bring in the advertisement picture we would enact, and admission tickets cost fifty cents. This was a real occasion. I decided that I would advertise Armstrong embroidery skills. There was pink tarleton over a frame, and no one could move while the lights were on the tableaux. One tableaux was of the Gold Dust Twins, and that made the hit. Flora and I went to Miss Nellie Carr's home to be dressed and made up for the occasion. We had supper there, and the ladies helped dress us. Later on these church affairs became more and more demanding. There were night bazaars, and Flora and I spent many a Saturday making cakes, fudge, coconut balls, or black walnut candy to be sold at those events. We loved to cook and were considered experts. In fact, we got such a reputation that the ladies auctioning off the wares would say, "This is the Stuart girls' cake—$1.50"—and if it had nuts, $2.00. We learned to cook by watching Cousin Mary Blackiston and Great Aunt Maria Marrow, who made cakes for the family and the Hampton Church Guild. People would call up and ask for a cake to be made, and when sold the entire amount was given to the guild. We memorized our recipes, and the one-two-three-four recipe was a favorite, with English walnuts on top. We also made devil's food cake. After Flora went to Columbia University to study domestic science, she insisted on using only pastry flour and sifted it about four times, talking constantly about the grain of the cake. She would no longer make cakes with me!

Meanwhile, Mother had her usual duties. She directed the cook, gave out provisions for the day, weighed and measured everything, and then locked the pantry door, putting the big folding key in the pocket of her petticoat. After breakfast she had the servant bring into the dining room hot water on a waiter. Mother had a soap shaker and a mop. The silver was washed first, and then the glass next. Then the servant finished the dishwashing in the kitchen. We had our barrel of flour for homemade bread, and Mother was forever teaching some cook how to make good bread. There was also plenty of mending, repairing of clothes and making of clothes. Grandma usually helped with this sewing. By this time, Mother was expecting an addition to the family and her routine was lightened. She wore a pretty dark-red housedress with a creamy lace collar. She told us nothing, and we were curious and asked questions of our playmates. We found the baby garments everywhere. Finally, when Elizabeth Letcher Stuart (named after General Stuart's mother) was born on September 5th, 1901, I claimed her as my baby. Flora disagreed and claimed that Elizabeth was her baby. Although the rest of Mother's babies were bald-headed, Elizabeth had blue eyes and some dark hair. I was passionately devoted to her and hardly gave anyone else a chance to look at her. Fortunately, Mother had a white nurse, Miss Garner, who was an English woman. She cared for Elizabeth and also for Mother, who had erysipelas and was very ill.[12]

Father also kept busy during this period. He liked Mr. Collier and usually spent Sundays at the Collier farm on Back River. Flora and I often went with him and it was a real treat. We usually came home loaded with provisions from the farm, including eggs, chickens, oysters, hams, (and in the summer) watermelons and fresh vegetables. The Colliers had thirteen children. There was Howard Jr. (a farmer), Francis, Charles (a pilot who died), Henry (who became a doctor), and Fannie (the eldest daughter) who were all grown. Fannie looked out for all of the little ones, who included Georgia, Martha, Molly Hazen, Will Causey, and others. Although the big boys teased me, I enjoyed these trips out to the country. We often started the trips early Sunday before the sun got hot–at about eight or nine o'clock. The air was clean and fresh and the farms along with way were pretty. I asked hundreds of questions and Father always answered them. Then, as we drove into the long lane, all the Colliers came and greeted us and made a fuss over the "Captain." A big Sunday dinner was served and Father looked over the crops, hunted, or sat under the trees and talked. At nearly dusk we said goodbye and the buggy was loaded. I did not ask questions as we returned because I had used up all of my energy. I just sat there quietly and was so tired and sleepy when I got home. These trips made lasting impressions and constantly kept up my interest. Mrs. Collier always had time to show me a piece of embroidery and a new way to make French knots or something. She also showed me her garden and sometimes even gave me plants.

Father's happiest years seemed to be in Newport News. There was a great freedom of a new place. Father was democratic in that he accepted all men for their ideas. He took an active part in the church, belonged to civic groups, and loved politics.[13] He also enjoyed the splendid horse, "Bill," and his buggy that he had purchased to use in the real estate business. Father normally went on Mondays and Tuesdays to collect rents, largely from colored tenants who worked at the shipyard. He then occasionally took people to see something he wanted to sell. When these sales commissions came in, Father would improve our home property or we would buy something extra—maybe a nice set of books or a new bed with an eider-down quilt.

Conversely, I never felt that I liked Newport News. I did not like the girls I played with—they were not kindred spirits. We played with Annie and Lucille Wilkinson, who lived across the street from us, and they were ungainly, tall, and rude girls. However, they could play a good game of hide-and-seek or hop scotch, or jumping rope. They also liked to go to kissing parties. The Wilkinson girls came from a large family of about nine children, with many grown brothers. There was Will (the oldest), John, Duncan, and several others. Among them was poor little Hoge, who was the youngest and a hopeless cripple with withered legs. We always looked out for him. If we forgot him he made us help him by scolding us. Sometimes, Mrs. Wilkinson made Annie and Lucille stay at the steps and play games he could enjoy if he did not have someone to play marbles with. Although Hoge had braces on both legs up to his hips, he got around and crawled faster than we could walk. He was demanding, spoiled, and highly self-confident. Hoge was also the baby in the family, since Will was over thirty and he was only nine or ten. I have since heard a Newport News radio announcer sign off by saying, "this is Hoge Wilkinson," and I feel that it must be our little Hoge. Annie was quite beautiful, with dark eyes but so jealous. Lucille was softer, gentle, and domesticated—but so tall.

I also met Edith Boswell at school. She was dumpy and wore a white apron, and seemed so old and settled for her thirteen years. One day her brother Cornelius came out of the house to go hunting with another boy, and the boy, thinking his shotgun was unloaded, aimed at poor Cornelius and shot him. We were all so sorry for Edith, and I went to console her. She wore black for two years after that. The Gayles also lived across the street and had three children. Mordecai, the boy, was older than me and was the pride of his father. He was indeed a nice, wholesome boy. Mary was a few months (or maybe a year) younger then Flora, and Alice was younger than Jo. Mother and Father often played cards with the Gayles. Mr. Gayle was a widower with a grown daughter from his first marriage. Mrs. Gayle was a Miss Wilson before she married Mr. Gayle. They were staunch friends of the family as long as we lived in Newport News. When I later went to art school at the University of Virginia, Mordecai Gayle and I sent each other letters every day. We also knew the Clements from Surry County. Although they had some problems, they were nice people who lived on our street about two blocks away. Mrs. Clements was clever with her needle and often helped Mother with her sewing for a small compensation. She had three girls near our ages—Nannie, Louise, and Alphire—along with other children. Cora Spratley, their cousin from the country, also lived with them so that she could attend school. However, they were all so uninteresting and they always bored me!

Eventually, Father decided to give up the real estate business because Mr. Collier was resigning his partnership on account of poor health. He longed for the freedom of his farm life, so Father returned to the world of finance and became a cashier in a prosperous bank. He also sold our 29th Street home and received a grand price for it, but that transaction left us without a home. Where would we go? Another home sufficiently large was not to be found all at once. Fortunately, Grandma Stuart allowed us to live in an apartment over a store that she owned on 26th Street, about half a block from the beautiful James River.

During this period I was allowed to have art lessons. Aunt Lizzie Ivy was my teacher, and I went on Saturday mornings to her apartment for these lessons. Since our temporary apartment lodgings were so small and there was no yard space—we also spent a lot of time visiting Mary Gayle, who had moved to one of the side streets leading to the James River and skirting its park or bluff. Her brother, Mordecai Gayle, liked me considerably. If we sat on the steps to rest he would usually join us and sometimes hold my hand— of course this was done behind the dress fold. I also got my first tastes of babysitting during this time. One night in 1905, Mother and Father went to the Gayles' to play cards and I was left in charge. At the time, Elizabeth was about four years old. She had eaten nuts that day, and shortly after Mother and Father's departure had a terrible spasm, which was only the second one she ever had. I was only about fifteen years old, but I acted at once. I put her—stiff as a board and purple in color—in a tub of hot water and placed a pencil between her teeth. While holding her head, I directed Flora to go to a neighbor and call Mother to get her to come home immediately. When Mother arrived, breathless from walking fast, Elizabeth was pulling out of the spasm. Mother told me that I was "mighty smart" and asked how I knew what to do? I said, "I saw you take care of Elizabeth once."

Aunt Lizzie worked out a scheme to have me go to the previously mentioned University of Virginia Summer School in order to study art from the costumed model—and Father consented. The instructors were Sloan Bredin (the painter)[14] and Graham Cootes (the illustrator).[15] I attended the institute with a fellow art student named Margaret Burbank, Aunt Lizzie, and a colleague of Aunt Lizzie's named Margaret Jervis. We had a large dormitory on the East Ridge that did not cost too much. We ate our dinners at Mrs. Rowell's—a very elegant place. For lunch, Aunt Lizzie brought beaten biscuits with Smithfield ham. This arrangement lasted for six months. The artwork was really over my head, but I learned. I struggled with charcoal to get the perspective of the face. The model posed from about nine o'clock to one o'clock five days a week, and at twenty minute intervals with five minute rest periods in between. All of this was done in an outdoor setting. I enjoyed the rest periods and would linger more than five minutes between poses.

Mr. Sloan Bredin was a good-looking man, with dark and rich coloring. However, he was also very shy and sensitive. He lived in an art colony near New Hope, Pennsylvania and made his living through teaching and making society portraits. Mr. Bredin told me again and again about the features above the eye level coming down like a barrel hoop—on the eye level, straight; below the eye level—curving up. Years later this truth was really etched into my being. While I did some work in charcoal, I loved the freedom of my watercolors and practiced landscape painting in a flowing, spontaneous style. However, I did not feel sure about what was a good composition. The class would also paint in oils or watercolors and bring these sketches to morning class for criticism. At the end of the six weeks course there was a fine exhibition, and Aunt Lizzie had several of her oil paintings on display. I remember one of Mary Selden she did that was a good likeness and had style. That was ultimately the test—for the painting to really look like a person.

During the art camp we also walked to Frye Spring on some afternoons and brought back bottles of the iron water. The red clay ruined my lovely white petticoats. We returned by trolley for five cents per person. Every day, Mordecai Grist wrote me an amorous letter—and every day I wrote to him. I had been taught not to put anything in a letter that could not be shown to anyone—so I wrote with restraint. There were also some plays and concerts at the University and I attended these. A group of young men serenaded us one night about twelve o'clock, and Aunt Lizzie threw a ham bone to them as a reward. I will always think that Aunt Lizzie got Charlie Rowell and his University gang to do it, since I was a little young and undeveloped for college men and dates. When the exhibition came off I received "Honorable Mention" on a watercolor of a landscape. Aunt Lizzie had made me go on the back porch one day and paint the mountains after a storm. They were impressive, and I dashed off a very emotional rendering of those massive mountains with the dark hanging clouds. She liked it and put it in the show. Afterwards, I gave this painting to Grandma Stuart. When I returned home I proudly got out my portfolio with some terrible monkey faces that I drew and showed them to Father. He was teasing, but he said, "Is this all I get for my money?" This nearly killed me—no one else was interested in my art—so I resolved from that day to keep it to myself.

[*Along with Marrow's art, her educational pursuits were taking her in other directions.*] By this time, Flora and I were enrolled in Newport News High School and I was interested in a variety of subjects. At one point, I decided that I wanted to study German, so I found a young German teacher who said that he came from Switzerland. His name was Otto Wagner, and I think he was getting out of military duty by living in America. Although he had some difficulty with English once in a while, he was gentlemanly and bright, and came to our house twice a week. I loved translating, but had a hard time with guttural sounds. I also became interested in geometry, so Miss Gildersleeve from Cornell University helped me with that subject. In addition, Miss Baker taught Flora and me dancing and physical culture. Our lessons certainly kept us busy! After supper we went immediately to our room to study. There, Flora and I wrestled with long and heavy homework assignments. We usually had an English paper to write, along with pages of Latin to translate, and plenty of math problems to work. Then we would have a few pages of delightful German to read, and if it was not too late by then, we glanced at a history lesson along with the horrid chemistry or physics.

During this period, Flora and I were also beginning to date boys. We could have dates on Friday, Saturday, and Sunday provided we did not neglect our lessons. I had dates with Mordecai Gayle, while Flora had an ardent swain named Edward Lash. Several young men from the shipyard's drafting department were also encouraged to call. We usually served olive sandwiches and grape juice with ice and a piece of lemon, and either went skating, played cards, talked, or just sat on the porch. Arnold Buxton was attentive to me, but he seemed to understand that I preferred Mordecai Gayle. Despite my affections for Mordecai, Father would often bring some young man from some transport to have dinner with us.

Following the short six-month stay in Grandma Stuart's second floor apartment, we spent several years living in a lovely riverfront home on West Avenue, only a short walk from the beautiful James River. Father loved the moonlight on the James River, and bought several photographs taken by Harry Mann.[16] There were also amenities that delighted us Stuart children. For instance, there were tennis courts in front of our house, and Flora and I played regularly. During this period, Father also resigned his position from the bank and entered politics with vim. Theodore Roosevelt was my father's friend from the days when he led the Rough Riders at Havana, Cuba, where Father was in charge of the Army Commissary Department.[17] As such, President Roosevelt later appointed Father U.S. Marshal for the Eastern District of Virginia.[18] However, this meant constant travel and unpleasant duties in arresting men, so Roosevelt made Father collector of customs for the Port of Newport News.[19] During the customs service, Father loved the perfect harbor and the many ships that anchored in its protective waters. The government furnished a launch for his duties, and when he checked the lights on ships at night, we were often taken along. During these trips, he explained what a tramp steamer was, a schooner, a battleship, a cruiser, a collier, a freighter, and so on. He also taught us the difference between starboard and port lights.

With Father's political appointment, we lived in style and did some entertaining during these years. Father allowed us to buy any good books we desired. He also allowed us to buy dress materials if we would make the dresses all by ourselves, so I expressed myself creatively by designing stylish dresses. Conversely, Flora took forever to make her dress, and seldom finished it. During these years, we also had big dinner parties, dances, and beach parties, and many friends and relatives attended. One friend of Father's was Captain Grant, who was director of transports. He had a son named Bruce Grant and a daughter named Mary Grant, along with two younger girls. We saw a good deal of the Grants and Bruce fell in love with Flora. Around this time, Flora also accepted a position to teach at a country school in Warwick County, about seven miles away. It seemed that life was stepping up!

Sometime following his appointment, Father was the subject of an article in *Pearson's Magazine* for the honest and efficient handling of his duties in this position.[20] During this time, he went into the creosote problem and by his discoveries saved the United States Government thousands of dollars.[21] The article commended him for his honest, efficient, and vigorous administration as collector of customs, and especially for his vigilance in seeing that the government received a full quota of duty on imported material. In politics,

Father was honest in his belief in the Republican Party, but this stirred up considerable criticism, or "digs," in the local papers.[22] Despite the challenges, he continued his membership in the Sons of Confederate Veterans organization.[23] Consequently, a newspaper once featured an article stating, "J.E.B. Stuart, son of the Confederate general and a member of the Confederate Veterans Association, has taken off his coat and rolled up his sleeves and is working with laborers on the piers."[24] It seemed that Father was showing or training men in handling logs on the piers. Father had been an engineer, and thought that any honest work was all right. His father had been an old line Whig in his political views, and Father did not think that he had switched his family's politics. We children were quite disturbed and knew we would have to face our high school critics, and we rallied to his defense.

NOTES

1. Founded in 1886 by Industrialist Collis P. Huntington (1821–1900), Newport News Shipbuilding and Drydock Company was once the largest privately owned shipyard in the United States. Purchased by Northrop Grumman in 2001, it is now the only shipyard in the country that can build large aircraft carriers, known as "supercarriers".

2. The Chesapeake & Ohio Railway was formed in 1869, connecting Richmond, Virginia to the Ohio River by 1873. It ended passenger service in 1971 and was later merged into CSX Transportation in the 1980s.

3. The Chamberlain Hotel was in recent years renovated into a high-end luxury retirement community for people over the age of 55.

4. During World War I, Newport News was a major embarkation point for soldiers and supplies. One of five camps in the area, over 115,000 soldiers processed through Camp Stuart alone to serve in Europe. A historic marker at 16th Street and Roanoke Avenue now commemorates the original location of Camp Stuart.

5. The Catlett and Sinclair families have resided in Gloucester County, Virginia for generations. Members from both families served in the American Revolution, the War of 1812, and the Civil War.

6. The desk is now owned by MSS's grandson, Drewry McRee Smith III.

7. Robert Page Waller (1853–1923) belonged to a family of distinguished ancestry rooted in Virginia since the 17th century. His maternal great-grandfather, Henry Tazewell (1753–1799), was a Revolutionary War veteran who served as a U.S. senator from 1794 to 1799. His maternal grandfather, Littleton Waller Tazewell (1774–1860), served as a U.S. congressman (1800–1801), U.S. senator (1824-1832), and as Virginia's 26th governor (1834–1836). Robert Page Waller's younger brother, Littleton W.T. Waller (1856–1926), served as a major general in the U.S. Marine Corps.

8. Virginia Polytechnic Institute and State University (V.P.I.) is now widely known as Virginia Tech.

9. Theodore S. Garnett (1844–1915) served as a lieutenant and aide-de-camp to Maj. Gen. J.E.B. Stuart during the Civil War. A grandnephew of Gen. Joseph E. John-

ston, Robert M. Hughes (1855–1940) was a prominent Virginia lawyer who helped establish what would later become Old Dominion University in Norfolk, Virginia.

10. Lt. Gen. James Longstreet, CSA (1821–1904) of South Carolina.

11. St. Paul's Episcopal Church is located on 34th Street in Newport News, Virginia.

12. Erysipelas is a type of superficial bacterial skin infection.

13. During this period, JEBS II served first as junior vice-national commander (1907) and then senior vice-commander (1910) of the Army and Navy Union. Founded in 1886, it is considered the nation's oldest veteran's organization.

14. Rae Sloan Bredin (1880–1933) was a prominent portraitist and landscape painter. A member of the New Hope Group of Landscape Painters, he was best known for his murals of the four seasons and the Delaware Water Gap, now exhibited at the New Jersey State House Annex.

15. Frank Graham Cootes (1879–1960) was a prominent portraitist and illustrator. He served as an illustrator for the *Saturday Evening Post* and was also an official U.S. president portrait painter (best known for his portrait of President Woodrow Wilson).

16. Harry C. Mann (1866–1926) was an award-winning commercial photographer based in Norfolk, Virginia who specialized in landscape and portrait photography.

17. The true extent of the friendship between Theodore Roosevelt and JEBS II is currently unknown. Stuart family tradition maintains that they were acquaintances who met during the Spanish-American War.

18. JEBS II originally applied for the position of U.S. Marshal for the Eastern District of Virginia in 1901, with recommendations from Maj. Gen. Fitzhugh Lee, Col. John S. Mosby, and John S. Wise. President Roosevelt nominated him for the position in December 1904. Beyond assisting a friend, another motive behind this appointment was to demonstrate President Roosevelt's willingness (in the spirit of reconciliation) to grant federal government positions to prominent Confederate leaders or those associated with them.

19. JEBS II served as collector of customs in Newport News from late 1905 through late 1910. Prior to that, JEBS II served briefly as U.S. Marshal in early 1905.

20. See A.L. Benson, "Instinct Above Law: The story of the rebates of creosote duties by the Treasury Department because—'it meant a great deal to the railroads,'" *Pearson's Magazine* (1911), Vol. 25.

21. The "creosote problem" to which MSS refers was a circa 1901 controversy where railroads were not paying the transport taxes on creosote as required by law.

22. In September 1905, there was a resolution introduced in the Lexington, Virginia Sons of Confederate Veterans Camp denouncing JEBS II. The proposed resolution declared JEBS II to be a disgrace to his father's memory as well as an individual unfit to garner the respect of SCV members. After considerable discussion, the proposal was tabled and ultimately never passed. This episode was later the subject of a short announcement in the September 27th, 1905 issue of *The Lexington Gazette*.

23. JEBS II was a founder and longtime member of the Sons of Confederate Veterans. In 1896, he was selected to be the SCV's first commanding general at its inaugural convention in Richmond, Virginia.

24. This source has not been clearly identified at the time of this writing.

Chapter Five

The Struggle for an Education

In high school we had four years of intense studies—four years of Latin, four years of mathematics (algebra, geometry, and some trigonometry), four years of history and civics, four years of English and literature, two years of physics and chemistry, and two years study of the German language. The last was a choice instead of French, as Father thought Germany would become a great nation as so many German ships came into port. That made five or six classes each day with study bell coming at the end of the long day. The preparation for these classes at home was terrific! Creative composition had to be written, and that was done each night. Long passages in Scott's "Lady of the Lake" had to be understood and often memorized, or pages of numerous English and American writers had to be read, such as Hawthorne's "House of Seven Gables." Then the Latin teacher, Miss Edwards, who became Mrs. Mardsen, gave us long passages in Caesar, Cicero, or Virgil's "Aeneid" to untangle and learn the vocabulary, because the next day she turned it all around and made us go to the blackboard and write it a new way.

I always studied my mathematics first. We had a young instructor, Mr. Dutrow, who had just graduated from college. He was very short and neat in his dress. He gave us each day an original to work out (if we so desired) and our regular problems to be studied so we could go to the blackboard without the book and prove them and then explain to the class. This class was the joy of my life! I was so interested that I begged Father to let me do extra work with a private tutor. He found Miss Laura Gildersleeve, who had a Ph.D. from Cornell University, and she afterwards taught at that institution. She was a marvelous teacher and made me feel that doing originals was like eating cake. Philip Murray, a bright pupil in our class, and I were about the only ones who could tackle those originals that Mr. Dutrow put up. Mr. Dutrow later wrote a reference letter for me a few years after my graduation. He said, "Mary Marrow Stuart is one of the most brilliant students who has ever gone through our high school–and I predict a bright future for her."

At night after attending to math, I tackled the creative writing problem, and then the horrid Latin—not that I disliked it, but because I was dreadfully afraid of the Latin teacher. She could awe me into not knowing anything. Then, if there was time, I could hurriedly read over my history or civics, whichever we were having for the day. This was not completely learned, and Miss Mary Jones of Newport News, who was a wizard with her history, could make me stammer, but when she finished, the important events stood out against minor happenings. Now what happened to physics (or, if it was in the last year, chemistry)-well—maybe it was caught on the fly somewhere the next day. Or if the class had not studied this subject, someone in the class trapped the poor young teacher—the blushing Mr. Howard—into explaining for the whole period, or we would bring some sparklers to school and get him to tell us how they were made. I hope Mr. Howard never knew how we plotted and diverted him. How can any teacher refuse to explain something to a student who wants to know? Or to a student who does not quite understand? It just seemed to me that we could not quite hold the line set for us and we dared not fail or flop, so we skirmished. I loved the English literature teacher, Miss Lydia Coghill from Petersburg. Although she dressed in black and was dumpy limping on her cane, she was amiable and jolly, and had the real appreciation of literature in her. Somehow she could keep everyone in her class on tiptoe with interest. We were all very breathless with the romance of Ellen Douglas and Roderick Dhu when she taught "Lady of the Lake." Someone always offered to carry her books just to talk to such a magnetic, happy soul.

One day near the finals of my junior year my instructors told me that I had to debate in public with three seniors, to which I replied, "I can not... I just can not." The instructors then said, "but no one graduates until he or she does some debating in public." I thought, "I just cannot do it!" They were firm. "We think you can and we cannot take 'no' for an answer"—and right there Miss Cogbill gave her merry chuckle. I went home and told my parents. They said they thought it was a great honor for a junior to be selected with three seniors. I prayed, "O Lord, please help me through my duties and tasks." I was given the unpopular affirmative side of the question—Resolved: "That the License of the Press shall be limited." I was ill unto death over it all—I spent all my nights suffering—I could picture myself going to pieces on the stage before the crowded house.

Finally, I said to myself, "you are a coward—come now and face it—nobody wants you to be a timid mouse. If you do the very best you can do—well, then no one can blame you!" So I began to write out my thoughts, and Father helped me by giving me several excellent points, which I had to shape into debate form. I went to the school library, whenever I could, to do research. I remember that one of my best points was on the distorted art shown in the comics—and to this day I will not bring myself to look at the comics. I gave up my playtime in the afternoons and literally slaved over that paper. Then I practiced reading it before Flora; then before Father; and finally before Miss Cogbill. She beamed.

On the festive night I found the newspaper had sent three judges. I was so afraid I would not be heard that I almost yelled, and my delivery was jerky. A girl from the North, Gertrude Loomis, was my opponent, and Guy Via, the editor of the high school journal, was my other opponent. Lily Harrison was my partner and she and I ultimately lost the debate. Miss Mary Jones met me as I was leaving the hall in a crestfallen blur. She said outright, "You should have had the medal. Your paper had more content in it than any of the others." Although disappointed, what I got out of the struggle was a new confidence in myself–to tackle the impossible when you have to do it.

Flora and I finished high school in February 1908. I was nineteen years old, and Flora was eighteen. I was relieved that the ordeal was over. Once I had gone to Father and asked if I could drop Latin and get a partial diploma, as so many girls in the class were doing. Father acted as if he was shocked. He said, "I want my girls to get a full diploma—not any half-way business!" That settled it. Overall, these years had pleasures, tenderness, and a happy, protected home life with occasional sorrow. A sensitive and wistful girl, I had found that trying to live and learn and adjust myself to an adult world felt almost tragic at times.

[*However, back in Marrow's days as a young high school graduate, she was pondering her next great adventure.*] Having witnessed my seriousness as a student, my parents turned their attention to how best to meet my hopes as an artist. How could Father and Mother manage an art education for me? About this time, Cousin Annie Ramsey (daughter of General Charles Ruff of Philadelphia, Pennsylvania),[1] paid a visit to her second cousin, my Grandmother Stuart, at Uncle Page's home on Warren Crescent in Norfolk. She had planned to see the Jamestown Exposition Tercentennial.[2] We were invited to Grandma Stuart's to meet Cousin Annie, and she was very nice and jolly. I asked her about art schools in Philadelphia, and off-hand she said there were four art schools there—namely: the Philadelphia Academy of Fine Arts, The Pennsylvania Museum and School of Industrial Arts, Drexel's Art Institute, and the Moore's Art School. She added that I should come and stay with her and study art. I could not forget that invitation and kept talking about it. Father said he wanted me to have a very practical course in art—"one that would always allow me to earn my living." He did not want me to be like Cousin Ellen Stuart of Wytheville, Virginia, who studied eight years in Paris

Marrow's mother, Josephine "Jo" Phillips Stuart, circa 1908 (Courtesy of Sharon Stuart McRee).

and Brittany and spent a fortune, and then could only get a meager position as an art teacher in America. She taught art in various studios in various girls' boarding schools. She really was an excellent portrait painter and water colorist, and she had done original compositions while on the Brittany Coast, with groups of people in them, that were later exhibited in the Salon, Paris. She had also painted some portraits of the Taylors that hung in old Williamsburg. Of course, America had not accepted painting in its formative years because the practical problems of life and living were so demanding.

Cousin Annie Ramsey and Father wrote many letters back and forth about art schools. At one point in the interchange I thought I could not go because Father would not consider "turning me loose in a big city." Also, despite her invitation, Cousin Annie could not see how she could fit me into her small apartment. However, I never let go the idea that I would study art in Philadelphia. Finally, Cousin Annie took a larger apartment on South Washington Square, with her daughter Ethel and son Fred. He would rent a room in the next house and would let me have his place in the apartment. I would pay only the extra cost of his room. He came over for his meals, and this proved a fine arrangement. At last, after much study of art catalogs, a decision was made on The Industrial Art School at Broad and Pine Streets.[3] I packed a small steamer trunk and carried my huge black cardboard portfolio that I had used at the University of Virginia Summer School. At the big Pennsylvania Railroad Station (Broad Street Station), I hired a hansom cab (a two-wheeled vehicle) and told the driver that I wanted to go to South Washington Square. I was really afraid I would get lost or that I would be left at the wrong place, but it all worked out beautifully. I arrived and received warm greetings.

Cousin Annie had a lovely apartment on the second floor–a large, bright living room and dining room combined—two large bedrooms, one for Cousin Annie and me with two beds and a wardrobe and one bureau. The far bedroom was for Ethel, her daughter. A little hall, a wee dark inside bathroom, and a wee dark inside kitchen were tucked into the plan. There was a very nervous maid, Minnie, and Cousin Annie worked to teach her. She finally could cook and serve with ability and she made excellent bread. Cousin Annie had learned to like the French cooking and the French style of several courses in serving meals. There was nearly always a soup course, meat and vegetable course, a salad course, a dessert course, and lastly coffee and cheese with crackers. These meals were real works of art! I learned to like olive oil on my spinach and on my salads. Sometimes there were sweetbread patties, beefsteak with mushrooms, or lamb with caper sauce or chicken fricassee. Pennsylvania was noted for its dairy farms and Philadelphia had elegant and rich ice creams that I enjoyed. Burnt almond, walnut, pistachio, peach, and caramel were favorites.

Cousin Annie Ramsey was the daughter of General Charles Ruff, and she at an early age had married an artist and lived for years in France, chiefly on the coast of Brittany. Her two children were born in France. However, living on an income from painting was precarious, and General Ruff sent checks and sent checks, and finally persuaded Cousin Annie to return to America and bring her two children, let him arrange for a divorce, and permit him to provide a settlement upon which she could live. So she parted from the artist husband forever. Cousin Annie later established the first juvenile court in Philadelphia under Judge Lindsey of Denver, Colorado.[4] She was an important person in starting a Presbyterian Deaconess Home on Spruce Street. She also belonged to several important women's organizations and was extremely interested in all the great suffrage leaders, whom she knew personally. They included Mrs. Carrie Chapman Catt, Mrs. O.H.P. Belmont, and Mrs. Joseph Widener.[5] For the sake of the cause, Mrs. Parkistan was already in prison in England.[6] I considered Cousin Annie a great intellectual and a very cultural person. She knew music and opera and spoke French and Italian fluently. She was constantly having some lessons to brush up on her French. She knew artists and their paintings, and was for the new human movements. She was a tremendous influence on my life. She said to me one day, "Many Southern women are light and frivolous and they do not have any depth. Try to understand the important things—make yourself into an intelligent person." This was serious advice and I knew what she expected of me, and I would do my best.

Cousin Ethel Ramsey had been educated in French convents and was about thirty-five years old. She worked at the William Penn Building in the Bureau of Social Charities, and was writing a book on Philadelphia's charities that took six years to compile. She finally had it printed, but I doubt if it is ever read. She and her boss, Mr. Marsh, had to shut their eyes to the political corruption in this City of Brotherly Love. So all of this book writing meant Cousin Ethel always slipped into a dressing robe and retired to her room immediately after dinner. She had a capable stenographer there three or four evenings each week just to take dictation or to do typing until about eleven o'clock. Her brother, Cousin Fred was curator of the Academy of Fine Arts, and I heard many stories about their management problems there.

Meanwhile, my art course was my immediate business. Father required that I put down every penny I spent and account to him for all of my purchases. He did allow me to, write, "sundries" for a few cents for which I did not need to account. I generally spent this money on art supplies and chamois—Bristol board and watercolors were expensive. Grandma Stuart sent me a check each month that I used to buy a suit, a hat, a pair of shoes, take a trip, buy lunches, or pay the room rent of $20 per month for Fred's room. I did not have a great deal compared to some of the girls at the art school—but I was extremely happy and satisfied. Once Father did not send any check and I was counting on it coming. I think I had to borrow from Cousin Annie. Then I sent a telegram C.O.D., saying that I was broke and to please rush a check. Father sent a check, but also scolded me, telling me not to do that again. I felt quite upset that I had worried my poor Father, who was now busy working as collector of customs in Newport News.

On Tuesdays we had mechanical drawing and a very acid little man, Mr. Dougherty, taught this class. He gave us machinery to draw to scale, a staircase to translate into three scales, many problems in projection and shadows, many in perspective, and a sheet on designs. It all nearly drove me crazy—twenty sheets of this—but wonderful discipline. *I learned that a pinpoint made a difference.* Cousin Annie said I had a nightmare one night and kept talking in my sleep and seemed so worried, saying, "I could not find it." She said I then arose upright in bed and said, "I have found it!" "What?" she asked. "Oh, the vanishing point!" It was quite clear to me. I had worked it out in my sleep.

The day started off with a class in charcoal or pencil drawing under the famous illustrator, Mr. Albert Barker.[7] He was an excellent teacher. Once he took a corner off my drawing, which meant that I had to start again. We drew wheels, chairs, plinths, cubes, etc. He required sharp pencils, an "H" eraser (that he hoped we would not use), and neat looking work. In this class I got a dose of perspective from the practical point of view. We learned to do many types of letters, including Gothic uncials, Roman letters, and Old English letters. These were inked in with a sharpened stick and waterproof ink. He also taught me to measure or judge space by comparative angles. If one did not reach his class at nine or before, the doors were locked and not opened until nine-thirty. Consequently, the student had to go to the principal (Mr. Fred Stratton), and tell him why he or she was late. He then wrote your excuse and it was later given to Mr. Barker. Minnie, the maid, just would not come early on those cold mornings, so I resorted to going without breakfast in order to arrive in time. Then, at ten o'clock I would slip from class and go to a little French pastry shop behind the school and get a cup of hot chocolate and a bun or cream-puff. It pleased Minnie that she did not have to get my breakfast, and of course the cost came from my small spending allowance. But I was a guest and could not demand or interfere with the house schedule. At school, I had long talks with Mr. Barker and told him that I wanted to be famous. I wanted to do something worthwhile and not just die with a tombstone over me. He looked at me and said, "Have you read Marcus Aurelius?"[8] I said, "No." "Well, you should read that and then you will not want to be famous—and then when you reach my age, you will not even bother about such a thing as wanting to be famous." That did not discourage my burning ambition.

In the afternoons we drew from casts or from the living model (after the first year if we did good work). There were classes in watercolor rendering under Miss McFarlane, in which we sketched drapery folds and imposed watercolors over it. Clay modeling under Miss Bradley, classes in historic ornament under Miss Elizabeth Dow, who sent us to the Museum at Fairmont Park to make a concour on Egyptian Art. We selected objects we thought were important and planned the sheet, drew objects, lettered the sheet, and colored it—all accomplished in that morning-and reported back to school for the afternoon program. Very exciting! I selected a mummy and its enclosing case as my center of interest and added other minor objects. I scratched the Bristol board with a penknife and put a wash on and scraped it again and put on another wash. When I finished I really had an ancient looking mummy. I earned an "A" and was asked to contribute this sheet to the school for exhibition purposes.

There was one class I detested under a Mr. Andrade. We did designs of wrought iron, wallpaper, oilcloths, and furniture. Mr. Andrade was so sarcastic, and he tried to flirt with the girls. He was not popular. He held up my certificate because of one assignment. After I came home, sick with overwork, I had to do that design all over again. I worked over and over it, and finally shipped it and received a "C"—the first one on my record–and then received my certificate. Also, I received a Temple Scholarship for merit of work. Father had a Newport News newspaperman, Mr. Horace Epes, write up the scholarship award to me. I had gone to a Northern school and taken two years of work in one year. Father was now quite proud of me and he resolved to send me back for another year.

Meanwhile, my sister Flora had accepted a teaching position at Morrison, Virginia.[9] She boarded with the Archie Ham family. On weekends she had a devoted admirer, Bruce Grant, who was the son of Captain Grant. He drove to Morrison on Fridays and brought Flora home, and also took her back on Sunday when she did not go by train. Archie Ham seemed to be in love with Flora. But someone said that Archie was always in love with the teacher of that little red schoolhouse. He finally got one teacher to have him—Miss Isabel Richardson. For me back in Pennsylvania, "all work and no play" sometimes made me a dull girl. But I did have many lovely weekends visiting my Quaker friends—the famous Hovenden family at Plymouth Meeting.[10] Mrs. Hovenden had been Miss Helen Corson, and as an artist had studied abroad and in Paris. In art circles she met Mr. Thomas Hovenden, of warm Irish background, and they married. He painted the famous work, *The Breaking of Home Ties*—showing a very young man going forth to war and saying goodbye to his mother and the home. Tragically, Mr. Hovenden was killed saving a small child from a Pennsylvania Railroad train bearing down on her at Spring Hill.

The Hovendens were strict abolitionists, and during the War Between the States hid some of the escaping slaves from the South. It all seemed strange that I, a granddaughter of a Southern rebel leader, was thrown into their midst and loved them so. I never mentioned the fact that I had heard the "slave hiding" story secretly from Cousin Annie Ramsey. The daughter of this marriage, Martha Hovenden, was a well-known sculptress.[11] Their son, Thomas, was a capable and outstanding engineer who had graduated from the University of Pennsylvania and accepted a position as manager of the Lindsey Construction Company of Philadelphia.[12] He was then twenty-six years old and I was nineteen.

These weekends with the Hovendens were the joy of my life. There were nearly always distinguished guests invited to visit at the same time I was there. One was Miss Paula Himmelsbach, an artist who designed exquisite stained-glass windows in Philadelphia.[13] She was married to a Greek who somehow had remained in Greece. Two young brothers named Smith, both professors at Columbia University, came on one or two weekends when I was there. These two men were very sophisticated. They had gone in a canoe on many streams in Canada with Thomas. Also a visitor at the Hovendens' was Livingston Carson, who had taught at some Northern university. He had just published a book of his poems and had received his honorary doctorate from the University of Pennsylvania. There was a marvelous and sacred studio in the Hovenden home just peppered with Mr. Hovenden's oil compositions and sketches for these paintings. Outside over the barn and horse stalls was a working studio where I often posed for Martha. Once I remember posing in a Nile-green satin low-neck dress. She rendered me in colored wax in a seated, full-length pose—very graceful. This was sent to several exhibitions, including New York's Academy of Design and some exhibitions in Philadelphia. I also posed in Martha's Philadelphia studio. Martha was so sincere, honest, selfless, and sensitive. She seemed happy when I posed for her, and took me home with her.

There was a fine old Irish cook named Maggie, who made tasty cottage cheese and all kinds of jellies. Often supper consisted of elegant bread, cheese, hot chocolate or iced tea, and jelly. But it was served with style in a beautiful dining room with antiques. Upstairs the tester beds were so distinguished and tall that a small stepladder was needed to climb into bed. Above would be the snowy white crocheted canopy. There were four bedrooms upstairs and a bathroom. Thomas had his quarters on the third floor, where everything looked masculine. The Hovenden home was at the intersection of several roads, and in horse-and-buggy days there was not so much dust. But when the "devil wagons"—as Thomas called the first automobiles—appeared, there came from them an endless vaporous dust–and the road was oiled, making a dreadful smell. Diagonally across the road was the Plymouth Meeting House and graveyard. I attended here once and the spirit moved on one. We came home after sitting for hours, thinking. At first the Hovendens kept horses for a surrey and we had many enchanting drives over the lovely Pennsylvania terrain—over toll bridges—to Valley Forge and to the Memorial Church in honor of George Washington, and where the original thirteen states were honored by each having a separate chapel. We drove to the pottery factory at Enfield. On one such trip, a fine horse slipped on a wet, sleety hill in Conshohocken and was hung in a sling for six months rather than being shot. After that Mrs. Hovenden lost her interest in driving and let Martha drive. So Martha bought a car and there were longer drives. Pennsylvania is so beautiful!

Thomas loved me and I was close to his family. Over time, I had opportunities to return some of the Hovenden favors. First, by posing, because attractive models were hard to find. And then one day Cousin Annie came home and said she had taken a box at the Yeats Play, *The Land of Heart's Desire*.[14] She was helping some cause, of course—and I was to invite my friends and she would chaperone the party. So I asked Martha and Thomas–and I invited my devoted art school friend Sophie Hudgkins, from Westmoreland County, Virginia. She was a daughter of an Episcopal minister and a real lady. She and I were the only Southern girls at that Industrial Art School. Sophie had little in looks, but was so charming. I also asked Dorothy York, who lived with her mother in an apartment behind ours near the landing steps. Her mother was the art editor of the *Ladies Home Journal*. Dorothy had coal-black hair and was poised and beautiful. I think Ralph Boyer, an artist friend of Fred Ramsey, was invited along with Fred—so each young lady could have a partner. The young men were so attentive and looked handsome. Martha talked with Ralph Boyer about art. I chatted with Thomas. Fred and Dorothy seemed interested in each other, and Sophie had some young man from the textile side of the Industrial Art School. I think Thomas presented me with a large box of chocolates, so they were passed around during intermission. Afterward, we strolled through the galleries and talked in our group, or went promenading with a partner. It all turned out a success. The promoters of the play made money. I won some popularity, and Cousin Annie was so good to allow me to call it my party.

On another occasion Fred asked me to a masquerade ball at the Philadelphia Academy of Fine Arts. Fred said I must go as Botticelli's "Prima Vera" (Springtime).[15] Well, Cousin Annie got a lovely print of the *Dance of Springtime* with the Hours gathered around her. She copied the main costume. She bought with my money sheer lavender-colored organdy goods and engaged a dressmaker, and she and Fred worked over my costume. Then a string of Smilax[16] was draped around my neck and a flowing lavender ribbon accented my high waistline, and some ribbon bound the sleeves in puffs. The dress had a low, rounded neckline. As a surprise, I wore my golden tresses braided to below my waist. Fred went distracted over my appearance and over the success of my costume, which he had managed. We went in a cab, and when I arrived people exclaimed—"Oh, look at Spring!"

I later found out Fred had been so wild over Botticelli that he had wanted me dressed that way, and I really think he convinced me that everyone would appear in a Botticelli costume, but some of the costumes were messy indeed; the usual clowns, gypsies, Spanish dancers, and a sheik. I knew few people and was completely dependent on Fred and Ralph Boyer for dances. The couples kept to themselves—there did not seem to be anyone to mix the crowd. Fred was a slave to me, and I felt that was not right–so I disappeared into the dressing room. Then Fred looked for me and seemed to be distracted that he could not find me. I looked at the dancers and discovered four Negro couples on the floor. "Oh," I said, "look at those Negroes dancing—let's go home." Fred talked with me. He said, "you know they are students of the school— they are respectable and are acting correctly—and seem to be dancing just with themselves. Don't be silly." There was one Negro girl student at the Industrial Art School, but she did not try to mingle with us. So I stayed and danced—and thought many things in my Southern soul. I had never before been to a party where there were Negroes! I decided that I must be careful and not let Father know these Northern customs. He would make me come home. So I said, "in Rome do as the Romans do."

Meanwhile, I continued my struggles with perspective and Fred helped me—going over my problems with me. Then he would say I needed to take a walk and get a breath of fresh air. So we tramped for several blocks—watching the beautiful effects of light on certain sections of Old Philadelphia. Philadelphia by moonlight is bewitching, and the waterfront is magical. At times, Cousin Annie Ruff would invite Cousin Annie Ramsey (her daughter), Ethel and Fred (her grandchildren), and me to her home on 42nd and Walnut Streets for a special Saturday dinner. There was a white, Irish maid (or a German maid) and a white cook in the kitchen. The meals were quite finished, but much heavier and more English in character than at Cousin Annie Ramsey's. Soup first—then roast beef with Cousin Mary carving—and always mashed white potatoes with another succulent vegetable. Along with these dishes were maybe salad with cheese and crackers—and ice cream and cake for dessert.

Sometimes Cousin John Ruff and his wife (Mamie) and son (Charles) would come in to talk with us and maybe have cheese and coffee with us. Cousin Annie Ruff wore her little white organdy cap and smiled with charm and gentleness. She was so like my dear Grandma Stuart, and rightly so, as they were first cousins. Their ancestry went back to the Hertzogs.

I often found myself studying how this predominant German strain was asserting itself. John Ruff Jr. was for years the Sunday editor of *The Philadelphia Ledger*. He was so learned and heavyweight in his thoughts, and I never felt that I could reach his level. I am sure he could hardly talk to me, but Cousin Mamie from Kentucky was a perfect dear, and she and I could chat by the hour. The son, age twelve, was well behaved and polite. At Christmas the Ruff ladies sent me a delicate little gold necklace with a turquoise and pearl and gold pendant attached. I have not mentioned frail little Cousin Margaret, who had gone over to the High Episcopal Church. She often went without her meals during fast periods. So to repeat, Cousin Mary, Cousin John, Cousin Annie, and Cousin Margaret were all the descendants of General Charles Ruff and his wife, Annie.

Dorothy York and her mother invited me to their apartment for tea, and simple refreshments were passed. There I met a fascinating girl, Dorothy Parker, and her escort. Afterwards I went to see Dorothy Parker, who wrote magical poems. Her mother and father were separated—I think—and Dorothy and her mother lived in a huge home on a nearby residential street. There were also visits to the Brewers at Vineland, New Jersey, especially at Easter, Christmas, and Thanksgiving, because I did not go home for those holidays.

Now to go back to the Brewers of Vineland, New Jersey. When my courageous Grandpa Stuart received his mortal wound at Yellow Tavern, Virginia, he was carried to Dr. Charles Brewer's home on Grace Street in Richmond. Dr. Brewer, who had married Grandma Stuart's sister (Maria), attended the general in his last hours. They had been stationed in Richmond during the Civil War. Now, Dr. Brewer was the physician for the Vineland Feeble-Minded Home.[17] He lived in his home on Grape Avenue with his wife, my Great Aunt Maria, and a daughter (Cousin Maria) and a son (Charles Brewer). Cousin Maria worked in the office of the Feeble-Minded Home. Charles was a young lawyer and Yale graduate who was just starting in the legal business. Dr. Brewer died shortly after I arrived at art school in 1908, so I never saw him. Cousin Annie said I had to write a note of sympathy and send flowers–which I did.

At another home was Cousin Wirt Brewer, who had married Henry S. Alvord–a small, short man, but a keen and outstanding lawyer in Southern New Jersey. He was wealthy but close with his money. This was his second marriage. Ruby, his daughter by the first marriage, was about eighteen years old and lived with Cousin Wirt. There were three small children by Cousin Wirt–Dot (or Dorothy) who was age ten, Brewer (the son) who was age five, and Rosalie the baby. Cousin Wirt was very dear to me. She had passed the New Jersey Bar and often helped her husband with his legal research. She was rather haphazard in her housekeeping and whimsical in disposition. I made a big fuss over Cousin Wirt's children and tried to help. Another daughter of Dr. Brewer, Cousin Rachael ("Ray"), lived with her husband, Dr. Jack Halsey, and they had no children. He was so interested in his various Italian country patients. Vineyard was scattered. It had been settled largely by the Italians, as it was advertised in Italy. The Halseys had a large Irish cook named Maggie, who lived on the place and helped especially in answering the doctor's phone calls.

Cousin Jack would often take me with him when he was driving his rounds. At first, there was the horse and buggy (in snowy weather, the horse and sleigh), and later he had two automobiles. I happened to be in Vineland when a terrible blizzard came during Christmas in 1908. Vineland was cut off from all communication with the world for twenty-four hours. The whole world around us looked magical. Telephone wires were weighted down. I went with Cousin Jack to see some of his Italian sick. I never went inside, but they came to the door and offered me wine. I did not accept any because I was so afraid they might poison me. They stood at the doors and stared at me. It was so cold—my feet were numb under the heavy lap robes. Afterwards, I had dreadful chilblains.[18] We also went to dances in spite of the snow. The streets were full of sleighs and the silvery bells echoed through the stillness. I was enchanted–such a fairyland of beauty and melodious sounds. There were three dances in succession. I had pretty party dresses that an expert dressmaker in Newport News had made. With my Nile-green satin dress, I wore pale green lisle hose, as there was not any silk or nylon hose of which I knew. On the dance floor Charles Brewer said, "this is the Schottische—do you dance it?" I said, "no, I have never heard of it." Well, he took me over to the side and taught me in a few seconds and I just had to learn quickly to dance it with him. I was rather awkward in doing it, I am sure.

I stayed on my *first* visit to Vineland at Aunt Maria's home. The whole clan came for that Christmas dinner of turkey with its trimmings and special verses and favors. I helped Charles put up the Christmas decorations of holly and the like. While I was on the stepladder, someone stole my slippers to see the size (my feet were small), which was 2 ½. That night when I returned with Charles from a dance, I said "Good Night" and returned to my room. I could not undo my dress from the back—it was so complicated. I could not wake up Aunt Maria or Cousin Maria, and I would never ask Charles Brewer to unfasten my dress. Finally, I did get it off after two hours of work. The next morning, someone said, "you burned your light late—I saw your light burning at two o'clock." I told the truth about my dress and its fastening problem. They scolded me for not calling for help—all the cousins loved me, and I felt the importance of being on my own. Another time, I remember staying at Cousin Ray's at Thanksgiving and they allowed me to sleep in a gem of a carved Rosewood bed made in Italy. An old Italian woman had given it to Cousin Jack. He had brought her numerous children into the world and treated them faithfully. They could not pay the bills, and as they had about a dozen children they could not divide the bed, which was their one treasured possession from the Old World. So out of admiration for Cousin Jack, and remembering his trips in all kinds of weather, they bestowed this masterpiece of cabinet making on "Dr. Jack."

There was a Christmas spent at Cousin Wirt's home with the cheerful open fire and the children and toys all around. Also, a lovely Easter was enjoyed there with my sister Flora. I wore a wisteria colored suit and hat to match, and had a bunch of violets to wear. They wilted before Easter, and Cousin Wirt bought a huge bunch of Trailing Arbutus and arranged it for me to wear. Before I had this wisteria suit, I had a rather raw green suit that I had bought myself at Bloomingdale's in Philadelphia—and a very bright green hat with ostrich plumes. Cousin Jack teased me about being so Irish and green, and he called the Italians to the door to look at me. I was young and healthy—I was living my happy days. After church and dinner we went in two cars to Atlantic City. Among those included were Aunt Maria, Cousin Wirt, Cousin Ray, Cousin Charles, Cousin Jack, Flora, and Ruby and Russell Browne. Maybe Philip St. George Prince, about sixteen years old, and I sat on pullout stools. He was the son of Mr. and Mrs. Henry Prince. Mrs. Prince was Flora Brewer, the second oldest daughter of Dr. and Mrs. Brewer. The oldest son of the Princes, John, was graduated from Cornell and was a fine athletic type. He danced with me at some of the Vineland hops. He was wholesome, and was quite a Northern type of man. One winter he contracted a terrible cold that went into a virus infection in his head and ears, and God took him away in his fine young manhood. So all affection was showered on Philip St. George, named after his great-grandfather, General Philip St. George Cooke. He and I bear the same kinship to our noted forebear.

Back in Philadelphia, Cousin Annie thought that I should attend at least one grand opera performance, so she bought two tickets to Gounod's *Faust* and gave them to Fred and me.[19] I was so excited, but I also wondered if I would really like the terrible tragedy in music. I did, and have never gotten over my love of opera. Fred shed a few tears when "Marguerite" was under the spell of "Faust" and "Mephistopheles," and again when her brother "Valentine" returned from the wars to champion her cause and it ended in his tragic death. I was quite overcome but managed to control myself. Fred said he thought it was "honorable to show one's emotions," and we had a long discussion. One evening Fred went to see *Tannhauser*, and the next day he kept whistling, "Oh thou sublime sweet Evening star."[20] On another occasion I went to see Puccini's *Tosca* with Caruso and Geraldine Farrar acting and singing.[21] Cousin Annie had been invited to use Mrs. Widener's box at Hammerstein's Horse Shoe Opera House, and there was a European count who was also invited to share the box with her. She immediately invited me to go with her and some friend! When Tosca threw herself over the castle parapet in the final act, I was so overcome I could not move or talk. I am afraid I did not even notice the count! I was in a daze.

Meanwhile, Cousin Annie said that she wanted me to meet some of the girls from the old Philadelphia families. I was quite shy and did not encourage this idea. So she introduced me to Polly Hughes, daughter of Dr. Hughes. Polly was taking some art classes at the Industrial School. To me the most remarkable thing about Polly was that she had red-gold hair like mine, but she could wear old-rose colors and even a neutral pink. She was bright and gay. At one point, we agreed to go Dutch treat to see a Saturday matinee of Fritzi Scheff—and I think we went on another occasion to see Billie Burke in some light play or comedy.[22] I called at Polly's house. I do not remember whether she came to see me, but she was a dear child—very friendly and attractive—and we had a happy friendship. On a more serious note, Fred, who was a Socialist, would spend hours trying to get me to see the light. Once he said, "if I taught school for five years, I would have done my socialist duty— or if a man did some dirty work like sweeping the streets or digging ditches for two years, he would have done his socialist duty." He began calling me "Mike," and I hated that. He said I was just the opposite of "Bluff Old Mike" or "Noisy Mike." It was his silly little joke and I had to take it. Fred went to some meetings and brought several workers to our home—one outstanding person was Miss Frances Perkins.[23] He put questions to her, and she really knew how to answer about labor, workers, etc. She was a brilliant and nice-looking person, and I wondered why she would bother to spend her life for the cause of Socialism. Fred kept trying to convert me. I would never accept it all, but I did see some good in the theory.

In June 1909, I went home sick, confused, and worn out with the terrible struggle. I was trying to keep at the top of my art class, trying to fit into a new environment, watch my manners and thoughts, and listen at every un-occupied minute to Fred's arguments for Socialism. When I reached home Mother called the doctor. My temperature was 103 degrees and stayed that way—and I was dizzy and suffering from nausea. I had a bad case of appen-dicitis due to rushing to school each morning and neglecting my health—so Dr. Burton said. Later he said that I had peritonitis. I went to the hospital and had an operation. Father would not let me even walk up and down the stairs. He carried me all that summer. I recovered, and as strange as it may seem, Father consented to my returning to art school. However, Cousin Annie felt that I was "too much responsibility." Maybe Fred was too interested in me, as he was thirty-three and very foreign in his ways. I did not care for any of the men artists I saw or met in Philadelphia. So the second year in Philadelphia I stayed at a Presbyterian Deaconess Home, on Spruce Street, which was struggling to organize.

I roomed on the fourth floor in the Deaconess Home with Viola Sourbier from Harrisburg, Pennsylvania. Our room cost eight dollars a week, which we divided. We had running water and a stationary washbasin. Viola was Pennsylvania Dutch in every sense of the word. She would say, "let's ready up," or "does my skirt stick out?" meaning does my petticoat show. And she would ask, "what does the clock say?" and say "oncet" and "already yet." She liked to get up at sunrise, and I liked to stay in bed until 8:30 or nine o'clock on Saturdays, especially. The doctor had told me that I must rest often. Viola was dreadfully moody, and I had a terrible time trying to get around her moods and sensitive feelings, and I had to watch every word I uttered around her. We had nothing in common. She loved me, but could not understand my liberality. At one point, our school gave a dance and I invited

Charles Brewer to be my escort. He sent me a lovely bouquet of Lilies of the Valley that I wore tied to my left arm. I wore a lovely plain creamy crepe-de-chine dress trimmed with white satin. Cousin Ethel had given me one of her dresses, which I had carefully washed and ripped up. I then had a Newport News dressmaker design it into an entirely different style. The satin crossed in bands over my chest, and there was a crushed-satin girdle, and bands of satin trimmed the sleeves. A string of pearls gave style at the neck. Beforehand we took our dance cards and exchanged dances with our friends. This was another Northern custom. A girl could go to a dance and feel safe—no wallflowers and no bashful swains. Elmer Gottlieb took Viola. He was from her town and his brother had married Viola's sister. He was studying medicine at Jefferson Hospital. Well, I had a good time. He kissed me goodnight inside the Deaconess Hall, and I wondered if Miss Pine was peeping. He left to spend the night at a hotel. It must have cost him a good deal—flowers, cab two ways, railroad fare from Vineland, and hotel bill. Charles Brewer said I looked beautiful—and that made me happy.

When I moved to Philadelphia, Grandma Stuart wrote a letter to Dr. Grammar, rector of Old Saint Stephen's Episcopal Church. He had been Grandma's minister serving previously at Christ Church in Norfolk. He called and I went to church rather regularly. His daughter wrote a note to me and asked that I call on her one day at home, which I did. She served tea beautifully, and we carried on a conversation that got nowhere. I wrote her a note of appreciation—and as she was much older than I was, we just dropped matters. On another occasion, Cousin Annie invited an actor, Mr. Thompson, and his wife to Sunday breakfast at ten o'clock. They had acted under Sothern and Marlowe in Shakespeare plays.[24] They were delightful, charming, and cultured—and I learned then that theatre people are all right. They of course talked about theatre, and I listened. During this period, a favorite afternoon pleasure was stopping at Salter's and getting a watercress sandwich minced with olive oil and a cup of tea for fifteen cents. The meal was out of this world and relaxing. Sometimes I had enough to buy a saucer of burnt-almond ice cream for another fifteen cents. All could cost thirty or forty cents. We never treated—instead we went Dutch treat. Florence Locke, a native Philadelphian, and Alma Grumann, a little German girl from Indianapolis, were kindred spirits and often chatted with me as we reviewed a day at art school.

I signed up for illustration the next term, as I wanted the drawing and original composition and not any more general course or drill in teaching methods. I had dear Mr. Fabre to teach me artistic anatomy and drawing in life class, and Mr. Diegendisch kept me busy with cast drawing. Mr. Fabre painted miniatures to augment his income. He also taught bone structure and anatomy to a class studying to be doctors at the University of Pennsylvania.

These two men were entirely different. Mr. Fabre was thorough in his teaching and French in disposition and manner—a gentleman. Mr. Diegendisch was a rougher, bolder type—and rather German, but he was human. Both men showed patience and a love of their subject. I lived for a word of encouragement. One day, Mr. Fabre was studying my face as he took up the charcoal to mark my proportions down. He said, I "always saw too large." I said, "I liked it." He smiled and marked down my whole drawing. This always happened. Criticisms were severe. Then he looked into my face—and remarked, "my, what color!"—and I blushed furiously. He had been working on a miniature, and he was terribly conscious of the coloring of the skin—and he was making a miniature portrait of a lady. In life class I always seemed to get a bad angle for the figure posing. This class was extremely hard–a living line instead of a static line—and then Mr. Diegendisch would take out his spectacle case and say, "is it as black as this?"—"No! No! No!"

On Sundays, I took long walks with Fred Ramsay along the beautiful Wissachickon. We took lunch that he made, as there was no Minnie on Sundays at Cousin Annie's. There would be about four sandwiches and some fruit and cake. We would take a trolley to get there and get out and stroll along the stream. We talked about the water-willows that William Penn had dutifully planted so the early people could make baskets, and Fred said that he "liked yellow-haired girls." I looked up and thought he looked romantic, so I turned the subject very quickly along very serious lines. But I am sure it helped our eyes to rest them on the subtle changes of light and color along the winding stream. I would always be physically tired after the tramp—and sometimes I went to Cousin Annie's for supper with walnut ice cream. Meanwhile, Ethel had bought a cottage in the Artists' Colony at New Hope. She was a neighbor of Mr. Lathrop, the painter.[25] He lived about a mile away and had ten children, I think. We went to see them once. Ethel's place was situated on a narrow strip between the Lehigh Canal and the Delaware River. The front was one story high and opened on the Tow Path, and the back end of the cottage was two stories tall and sloped gradually to the river. I spent many weekends with Ethel. Fred would come sometimes and make me walk for miles. On one of these tramps I thought I would not be able to get back. I sat down on a large rock and cried. Fred came back and jogged me on.

At her home, I helped Ethel all I could. I set the tray and carried the pot roast and biscuits or tea—all on a large tray. Ethel said it must be efficient–nothing left off. I thought and thought over it—and I am sure that stepping back for a forgotten object would not be as bad as using all this gray matter in thinking. Often, we could hear the mule driver cursing and driving his poor mules—even in the dead of night. Some mules had bells—and the barge would follow at a distance with ropes and ropes. Ethel was told to buy a pistol and learn to shoot. She did—and often she would practice when the barges and mules were pulling. During this time, Ethel was interested in Don Davenport. I think the Hovendens introduced Don to Ethel on a weekend party at their home. He wanted to settle at New Hope and farm. He had raised onions on a farm in Canada, and then raised onions in Texas. He had also studied textile design at the Industrial Art School and had tried designing, but found it too confining. Ethel invited him to our parties. At the end of the year I left there was a happy marriage–and the Davenports lived in the little cottage and did weaving. They employed several girls and had several looms, and Ethel made the designs. Don managed the business end.

Life after school in the Deaconess Home was important. By this time I was allowed to serve tea in my room, and I bought nice cakes at the French shop. I served the tea with lemon and cloves. I think I had a Sterno Burner, and various girls came to see us. Viola and I often had tea by ourselves. At dinnertime, at night, I was seldom hungry because of the tea refreshments, but I missed Cousin Annie's lively meals. Miss Pine was the housekeeper and she served Pennsylvania Dutch food—scrapple, grits, potatoes with parsley, and sometimes a meat loaf. My lunch and breakfast were light. The morning prayers took so much time. The new girls, Miss Craig, Miss Longstreet, etc., were so fumbly with praying out loud and composing the prayer as they went. Deaconess Stone was the spiritual head of the home—a fine Christian—and her prayers were uplifting. She had a crippled back and wore a support. Mrs. Elaine Williams was a devoted friend who loved the Deaconess. She helped the Deaconess dress and also kept her company. Mrs. Williams had lost her husband and it had crushed her. She had a lovely daughter named Elaine, who was shipped off to school so she would not be spoiled. It also gave Mrs. Williams more time to help Deaconess Stone.

I loved the Deaconess and I think she and Mrs. Williams admired me. I kept so busy with art school and was seldom around. It was decided that the Deaconess Training School was doing so well that there would be an open house. We all cleaned and cleaned our rooms, and I did not feel well. When the guests came, Viola went away but I was left. We all had bells that rang in our rooms so Miss Pine would not have to go to each floor to find us. I heard my four bells calling me but I did not answer. Finally, I crawled under the bed. Miss Pine then came looking for me and I heard her say, "No, Miss Stuart is not here!" Finally, Deaconess Stone came and looked under the bed. I felt abashed but told her that I was sick and did not want to see anyone. I was just getting out of the way—but my room was certainly open for inspection. "Well," she said, "your cousin Fred Ramsey has just called and left his card. He was worried about you!"

A little later, Ethel decided to give another party at New Hope. She asked Thomas Hovenden, Martha, Don Davenport, and me for a Saturday in springtime. She planned we would walk or wade in the Delaware River. The rocks were cold and slippery, and I was acting coy. Thomas said he would carry me over it all—and as he had paddled a canoe in Canada I felt that I could trust him. But I then asked myself why I should be carried and no one else. I came to my senses, and struggled on. We had an interesting lunch served on the lawn—then Ethel suggested that I read to Thomas while he rested in a hammock down by the river where we went wading. I did, and my voice was so soothing that he went to sleep. I left him in slumberland. Martha said it was cruel and there was some teasing. Then, Thomas woke up and never ceased apologizing. He did work hard—rising in the early morning hours to go to work in Philadelphia.

Around this time, I heard much talk about the Philadelphia Centennial and a historical pageant. All of us bought grandstand tickets. Martha and Mrs. Hovenden were also coming to see it and would join us. Everyone was talking about the noted artist, Violet Oakley, who had designed the various floats.[26] Fred knew her well and had called on her and also had dinner with her. She was invited by Cousin Annie to one of those marvelous dinners. Violet Oakley was so attractive—dark, slender, ethereal looking. I liked her at once. She lived with her noted artist cousins, Elizabeth Shippen Greene and Jessie Willcox Smith.[27] They called their place "Cogs" (for Cousins Oakley, Greene, and Smith). I did not see the place, but heard it was artistic and beautiful throughout. There were also apparently roses, hollyhocks, and delphiniums growing in the garden and around their entrance gate or door. These three women had enviable reputations for turning out high-grade illustrations for books and magazines of quality. They seemed to be busy all of the time. I believe that they had studied at the Academy. I kept asking questions about them. In her later years, Jessie Willcox Smith featured children's stories and I always saved her illustrations. Anyway, a beautiful day came and the beautiful Philadelphia Pageant passed slowly down Broad Street. Its beauty and choice remains in my memory. Years later, I planned a pageant for Norfolk (for its tercentennial), and I could recall the marvels of Violet Oakley's designing in her historical production.

My scholarship was good for one more year of study, but Father asked me, "don't you want Flora to have a year at some school?" I could not be selfish, and I said, "yes." I went back to our West Avenue home and settled down to the pace of Newport News. Father allowed us to have some lunch parties and give a dance, or have some card parties, and we asked young men. We also went to Old Point for the hops, if we were invited and had a chaperone. Bruce Grant, son of Captain Grant (in charge of transports running to Cuba), was very attentive to Flora. Everyone thought that this was a serious romance. But Flora decided to visit her Stuart Hall chum, Harriet James, that summer. In fall 1910, Flora went to Columbia University to study domestic science.

Around this time, Father lost his political position as collector of customs. His job vanished when the Democrats elected Woodrow Wilson as president.[28] Nothing turned up in Newport News of the kind and nature of a position that fitted Father's capacities, so he left the family to seek employment in New York. He first went with the Adams Express Company and made enough to take care of himself. Jo had only her high school diploma, but she took a teaching position in Newport News and supported the family on her meager salary. She was teaching third grade and made forty dollars a month. In this house we still owned, there was Mother, Jo, J.E.B. III, and Elizabeth—no cook. Mother could not join Father in New York because his salary was not large enough to take care of four people—or five people if Jo went. However, the West Avenue home in Newport News was large and hard to keep. Therefore, it was later sold. At that point, Mother decided to move to Norfolk and live in a home Father partly owned on West York Street, near Botetourt Street. This former Episcopal rectory had a debt on it, and paying the interest was an undertaking. Mother decided that she would take roomers

Marrow's sister, Josephine "Jo" Stuart, circa 1911 (Courtesy of Olivia Stuart McFadden).

and employ one servant to get the family into new surroundings and keep it on a solvent basis.

During the summer of 1910 I took a heavy normal course at Newport News. I studied painting methods under Miss Salisbury of Dayton, Ohio, school management under Mr. Davis of the University of Virginia, and craftwork (such as basketry, chair caning, and some clay modeling) under Miss Lulu Jones of Newport News. I also started looking for a position. Grandma Stuart was helping me in Norfolk. She knew a trained nurse, Miss Evelyn Santos, who had nursed in the Page Waller home, and she had a sister, Miss Lelia Santos, who was a supervisor of art in the Norfolk Public Schools. Miss Lelia had organized the artwork of thirteen schools. At first the pupils were required to buy a Veri black pencil for five cents and a package of drawing paper. Her art ideas advanced into the system, and she was allowed to add to the required supplies on the book-list a watercolor box, a box of hard-pressed crayons, and a small water pan.

Miss Santos had been allowed one assistant, who married, and she now asked for another. I looked like a prospect. I quickly took my portfolio to her home and showed her my work. She thought my training was excellent—she liked my careful work, and my personality and appearance. Accordingly, she requested another art teacher to assist her, and recommend me. I had a very fine letter from Mr. Fred Stratton and one from Mr. Albert Barker of the Industrial Art School (then called the Pennsylvania Museum and School of Industrial Art). Another young lady wanted the position and had fifty letters saying how good she was, and Mr. R.A. Dobie (then superintendent of Norfolk Public Schools) and Mr. Spence (supervisor of instruction), wanted to see her selected. However, Miss Santos said that she wanted me. She had seen my work and thought it was excellent. Therefore, in 1910 I was selected to the position of assistant art supervisor for thirteen schools at the salary of $55 per month for ten months ($550 per year). I was proud of the honor and worked in all sincerity and with exhausting energy. Mr. Dobie later said to me, "young lady, you should be proud of being selected—you are lucky—you had *only two letters* of recommendation and another applicant had *fifty letters*."

Next, Father sent me with Mrs. Bernard Semmes across the river on a steamboat to Norfolk to look for a proper boarding place. We spent a weary Saturday going from one elegant home to another. One person would send us on to another but we found nothing. The nice places wanted men as they were less trouble. Finally, Grandma Stuart asked Mrs. Willie Waller to say she would take me. She did, and I paid thirty dollars for a little bedroom on the third floor without heat. Dusty, trashy books were on the shelves in that room, and a narrow oak bed, an oak bureau, and one chair—that was all. Two other rooms on that floor had about four men occupying them, and we had to share a bathroom on the second floor with many other roomers on that floor. However, Grandma Stuart was so happy to have me in Norfolk and starting a career, so she gave me a check for fifteen dollars each month and sometimes she made it twenty dollars. Bless her soul for all her intimate goodness and love for me, her J.E.B.'s eldest child. I managed to pay my board, buy my clothes, pay for my laundry, pay for daily cab fare to schools, buy my lunches, and sometimes take a trip by steamboat to my parents' home in Newport News.

There was an exciting life at Mrs. Waller's. I had many dates to go to dances, to go to card parties, to go to Keith's Vaudeville on Saturday nights, to play tennis at the country club, and just to stroll. Billy Ayers, Ashby Estes, Mr. Barnes, William McMurran, Luther Matthews, Nivison Waller, and Drewry Smith were all nice to me, but there was no place to entertain a date at night. Before the year was finished I found Mrs. Waller's so noisy and distracting—and the meals served were not nourishing or wholesome—so I went to the Steeds. Mr. Robert Steed was the longtime Norfolk city clerk who was an authority on the city's history. His daughter, Carra Steed, was also in schoolwork and they were kind people. The tomato salads in the spring were so restoring, and I had a quiet, clean room on the third floor. Drewry Smith was interested in me and called quite often, and there was a peaceful and attractive sitting room at my disposal.

After six years of intensive art teaching in Norfolk I made seventy dollars per month for ten months. Art teachers were allowed ten dollars more per month than grade teachers, to cover transportation to different schools each day. One year, I gave my brother J.E.B. III twenty-five dollars per month to help him at the University of Virginia. Flora donated ten dollars, and he could count on our steady help. However, J.E.B. III also helped himself in every way. He made maps, did some tutoring on the side, and corrected a bunch of papers for the professors—and thus worked his way through the University that year. Afterwards, Mother moved to the University of Virginia and gave J.E.B. III his board. After he received his electrical engineering degree from the University in 1919, Father was able to give him a year at the Massachusetts Institute of Technology, where he received a master's degree.

I left the Steeds and came to board with Mother. Jo secured a position as a steady school substitute at twenty-five dollars per month basic pay, and if she taught for any absent teacher that meant more. This relieved her of drudgery, as she stayed in the Charlotte Street School with the gentlemanly Mr. Leland Boush as principal. Jo took a night course in typing and helped Mr. Boush with his reports and letters, rang the bells, answered the telephone, and sometimes relieved a sick teacher. There were about ten or eleven classes of boys at this school. One day, Jo had a funny experience. A boy fixed up an alarm clock in the book closet and asked to be excused. In a few minutes after he left the room, the clock went off loudly. It made everybody laugh and Jo laughed, too. After some moments the clock was found. When the boy returned nothing happened—and that was disappointing! Meanwhile, Flora finished her year at Columbia University and went to teach in Norfolk. I continued as assistant art supervisor in the Norfolk Public Schools, and made a decent salary. I saved a little after paying Mother board, and I went on trips in the summer.

One summer around 1915, I went to West Chester, Pennsylvania to be with Cousin Annie Ramsey, where she was boarding at a wonderful place. This was near the Hovendens, and I was invited for a visit with them. I had made some pretty clothes in Norfolk by sewing at night and after school in the afternoon. Thomas was very attentive to me during my visit. While at the Hovendens' I received an invitation from Cousin Wirt at Vineland, New Jersey. I asked Cousin Wirt if I could bring Thomas and she immediately agreed. So, Thomas and I started forth one Sunday and he seemed eager. We went to Camden and took the electric train from there. The dinner was dreadfully disappointing. There was rice, milk, and New Jersey cantaloupes–no meat as I remember it. The children dragged toys and sweaters around, and Cousin Henry was so prim. I met Cousin Wirt in the hall or kitchen and asked, "What do you think of Thomas?" She laughingly said, "Marrow, if you marry Thomas all of your children will be redheaded!" Therefore, from then on I decided to not be too nice or encourage Thomas. I often had to remind myself of this—I must not have any redheaded children–that would be a crime!

Cousin Wirt suggested that we go to a certain park on the electric train and rent a canoe and go on the lake. The children were so troublesome and the grown-ups were so stiff—so off we went. I had on a lavender lawn dress with a sun parasol to blend. Thomas tried to tell me romantic things on the lake and while we were returning on the electric train, but I was too upset. Around and around we went. Finally, Thomas said, "I will write you something I want to tell you." I loved Thomas and he loved me—but a hidden force always separated us. Then, he went to New Orleans for the Lindsey Company of Philadelphia to inspect a huge factory chimney. On the way back he stopped to see me in Norfolk, and fate acted up again. Mother was so formal and would not be anything but cold. Thomas and I walked to a little boat pier and were happy to talk to each other. This was the last time I saw him. Thomas caught typhoid fever and was delirious. I sent American Beauty roses, but he was never able to see them. Martha wrote and told me how ill he was. I sent more American Beauty roses—and Thomas was placed in the little Quaker churchyard to forever rest in peace. I took out his gifts, his pictures, and his letters—and cried through the night hours. So brilliant—so promising—so placid—so handsome! "Whom the Gods love, die young."[29]

The years that followed seemed hectic. Mother had two or three teachers boarding with us. We had dates with young men at night, and Flora in particular went to some big dances. The officers on the *USS Yankton* also gave us some parties.[30] On Sundays, the family went to Old St. Paul's Church, where Mother rented a pew. Meanwhile, J.E.B. III worked like a slave at a grocery store on Saturdays for one dollar from 7am to 9pm, with a short interval for lunch. He had to sleep late the next day to recover. On Sundays, faithful and loyal old Emma left after serving dinner, and on Sunday nights Mother allowed us girls and our male friends to make supper. I remember Raymond Corcoran (a paymaster in the Navy) could fix grapefruit and could "buttle," and he took infinite pains with fixing a half of the grapefruit for each guest. Someone knew how to make Welsh rarebit and we had that quite often, or ground steak, or scrambled eggs—then tea or coffee and toast with Virginia preserves. At these suppers were Drewry Smith, Lt. Raymond Corcoran (from the *USS Yankton*), Randall McGavock (originally from Max Meadows, Virginia), Lt. Victor McCabe, Lt. Francis LeBourgeois, and Lt. Jack Beardall (who was from the Navy supply ship, *USS Culgoa*). Years later, Lieutenant Beardall became an admiral. He was a naval attaché for President Franklin D. Roosevelt, and was included in the 1945 photograph showing the signing of the peace treaty with Japan aboard the *USS Missouri*.[31]

When vacation time came, Mother always urged us to separate from the family and get new viewpoints, to make new friends, and go on trips to escape the summer heat. I went to Woodstock, New York one summer (1912) to study landscape painting under Mr. John Carlson. I also went to Columbia University for a six-month summer session in 1914. I took a very heavy course in art subjects, which included: design and composition, clay modeling, costume design, and classroom art (elementary and secondary). For several summers I visited the Hovendens. Then one summer I taught art at the University of North Carolina at Chapel Hill's summer session.

Before living in Norfolk, Flora had taught for one year at a rural school at Morrison, Virginia, and for another year in Newport News. Flora also spent many of her summers with friends. In the winter of 1910 she had studied domestic science at Columbia University while I was at Mrs. Willie Waller's starting my career. Flora left the University and went to work at a summer resort place near Albany, New York, called Altamont. In the summer of 1910 she visited the John James family at Danville, and served as sponsor for a Confederate reunion while she was there. Harriet James and Flora were devoted friends at Stuart Hall, and this friendship lasted throughout life. Harriet had four brothers who visited their home when they could, but their service in the Army and Navy restricted such visits. In summer 1910 there were three brothers at home–Russell, Jules, and Bartlett James. Army Captain Russell James later provided a comfortable home for Mrs. James and Harriet James in the summer of 1913 at Fort Slocum, New York. Flora also visited them during that summer. Jules James was the only son serving in the Navy. He had graduated from Annapolis in 1908 and was in time promoted to admiral.[32] Jules also married the daughter of Henry L. Stimson, who was secretary of war in President Franklin D. Roosevelt's cabinet.

In the late summer and fall of 1911, Flora worked in a tearoom in Norfolk under the sponsorship of the Y.W.C.A. She made some interesting friends and her cakes were marvels of cooking. However, Flora left in February and entered upon the duties of a teaching position in the Norfolk schools for two years. Then, she asked for a release from her contract (which was granted) and ended up teaching at the Miller School in Crozet, Virginia. Jo was also busy during this time, and on one occasion went to Abingdon to visit Cousin Katherine Stuart, who was the daughter of Cousin John Stuart and the niece of Cousin Dale Stuart and Cousin Henry Carter Stuart, who would later serve as Virginia's governor.[33] Jo and Katherine later went to a house party at "Elk Garden," Governor Stuart's spacious estate—and Cousin Margaret (the Governor's wife), was the hostess. Among the guests was William A. Stuart (brother of Katherine and Henry Carter Stuart) and two of William's friends. At this time, Cousin Henry was very busy with his political campaign running for Congress and only came home occasionally. The young daughter, Mary Stuart, was there with a French governess.

In 1915, Jo went to the World's Fair in San Francisco and she visited Frazier Bailey's mother. She also spent two summers at the University of Virginia studying English, history, and literature. Meanwhile, Mother and Elizabeth spent their summers (1911, 1912, and 1913) with Father in a furnished apartment in New York. During the summers of 1914 and 1915, Mother was a hostess at a Y.W.C.A. cottage at Willoughby Beach, and Elizabeth was with her. J.E.B. III worked on Cousin Hardin Hairston's farm in the summer of 1915—and during another year he worked at Blue's lovely estate near Charlottesville. He was then at Plattsburg taking military training during the summer of 1918.[34] At the end of the training period he was commissioned an officer in the Army for only twenty-four hours because there was a mistake— his eyes did not measure up to the tests and the commission was withdrawn.[35] Overall, these years saw us crowded into a city home and without our Father, who had always been a strong, dominant influence. All of us were ambitious, and yet like fledglings were trying our wings and trying to find our talents and trying to place ourselves in individual situations to our liking. In June 1916

Marrow's brother, J.E.B. Stuart III, during his U.S. Army training in 1918 (Courtesy of Olivia Stuart McFadden).

I married, and my thoughts began to wander from a sole focus on education and career toward eventually starting a family. In the space of one year, there were three weddings in the family. Flora was married on August 22, 1918, Jo on April 26, 1919, and Elizabeth on June 16, 1919.

NOTES

1. Charles F. Ruff (1818–1885) was an 1838 West Point graduate and career U.S. Army officer who was brevetted a brigadier general toward the end of the Civil War. He spent much of the war stationed in Philadelphia, Pennsylvania, where he served in a variety of administrative positions.

2. This event took place in 1907.

3. MSS is likely referring to what was once called the Pennsylvania Museum School of Industrial Art, which was founded in 1876. It was later renamed a couple of times before merging with two other colleges in 1985 to form the University of the Arts.

4. Judge Benjamin Barr Lindsey (1869–1943) was one of the pioneers in the creation of the American juvenile court system. He was also a leader in the movement to abolish child labor.

5. Carrie Chapman Catt (1859–1947) was founder of the League of Women Voters and the International Alliance of Women. Alva Erskine Belmont (1853–1933), wife of U.S. Rep. Oliver Hazard Perry Belmont (D-NY), helped establish the National Women's Party and organized the first picketing to ever take place at the White House in 1917. She had previously been married to William Kissam Vanderbilt, a grandson of Cornelius Vanderbilt. Eleanor "Ella" Pancoast Widener (1874–1929) was married to Joseph Widener, a wealthy art collector and horse breeder.

6. This woman's identity is currently unknown.

7. Albert W. Barker (1874–1947) was a prominent American artist who served as an instructor at the School of Industrial Art between 1903 and 1913. As an illustrator, he was best known for his work in charcoal drawing.

8. Marcus Aurelius (121–180) was a Roman emperor from 161 until his death in 180. He is widely known for his famous literary work, *Meditations*.

9. Once a small, unincorporated community in Warwick County, Virginia, Morrison was consolidated into the City of Newport News in 1958.

10. The patriarch of this family, Thomas Hovenden (1840-1895), was a famous Irish-American artist and teacher. He is best known for his paintings *The Last Moments of John Brown* (1884) and *Breaking Home Ties* (1890).

11. Martha M. Hovenden (b. 1884) was an American sculptor and medallist. Her best-known sculptures are two limestone relief panels for the Washington Memorial Chapel in Valley Forge. They are entitled *The Declaration of Independence* (1926) and *Constitution* (1936).

12. His full name was Thomas Hovenden Jr. (1882–1915).

13. German born Paula Himmelsbach Balano (1877–1967) was a painter and stained glass artist who created the windows for Christ Church and other Delaware Valley institutions in Pennsylvania. She was the first woman to develop and fabricate her own designs in her own studio and under her own name.

14. MSS is referring to the famous Irish poet and dramatist, William Butler Yeats (1865–1939).

15. MSS is referring to the famous Italian painter, Sandro Botticelli (1445–1510).

16. Smilax is a type of plant.

17. This facility is now known as the Vineland Training School.

18. Often confused with frostbite, chilblains are acral ulcers that occur when an individual is exposed to cold and humidity.

19. MSS is referring to the French composer Charles-Francois Gounod (1818–1893).

20. *Tannhauser* was an opera written by Richard Wagner (1813–1883).

21. MSS is referring to the Italian composer Giacomo Puccini (1858–1924). Enrico Caruso (1873–1921) was a famous Italian tenor who was a pioneer in the field of recorded music. Some have also called him the greatest male operatic singer in history. Geraldine Farrar (1882–1967) was a famous American soprano opera singer and film actress.

22. Fritzi Scheff (1879–1954) was an Austrian-born actress and vocalist. Mary William Ethelbert Appleton "Billie" Burke (1884-1970) was a prominent American actress. She is best remembered for her role as "Glinda the Good Witch of the North" in the 1939 film, *The Wizard of Oz*.

23. Frances Perkins (1880–1965) went on to serve as U.S. secretary of labor under President Franklin D. Roosevelt from 1933 to 1945. She was the first woman to hold a cabinet position in the United States and was also the first woman to enter into the presidential line of succession.

24. Edward Hugh Sothern (1859–1933) was a prominent American actor who specialized in Shakespearean roles. His father was the famous English actor, Edward Askew Sothern (1826–1881). Julia Marlowe (1865–1950) was a noted English-born Shakespearean actress. Sothern and Marlowe had a successful partnership and were widely regarded as the premier Shakespearean actors of their day.

25. William Langson Lathrop (1859–1938) was an American impressionist landscape painter and founder of the art colony at New Hope, Pennsylvania.

26. Violet Oakley (1874–1961) was an American artist widely known for her work in murals and stained glass. She is best remembered for painting a series of 43 murals in the Pennsylvania State Capital Building during the early 1900s.

27. Elizabeth Shippen Green (1871–1954) was a prominent American illustrator who specialized in children's books. She also spent many years working for *Harper's Magazine*. Jessie Willcox Smith (1863–1935) was another famous American illustrator well known for her work in children's books and in magazines such as *Ladies Home Journal*.

28. As noted in Chapter Four, it is likely that JEBS II actually lost the collector of customs position during the Taft Administration in late 1910. Woodrow Wilson was not elected president until 1912.

29. This quote comes out of Greek mythology and is attributed to the Greek mythological hero "Trophonius."

30. Commissioned in 1898, the *USS Yankton* was a gunboat that saw service in both the Spanish-American War and World War I. It was decommissioned in 1920.

31. A 1908 U.S. Naval Academy graduate and Florida native, John R. Beardall (1887–1967) reached the rank of rear admiral over the course of his thirty-six year naval career. He also served as superintendent of the U.S. Naval Academy between 1942 and 1945.

32. During World War II, Rear Admiral Jules James (1885–1957) commanded the U.S. Navy operating base in Bermuda and later commanded the Sixth U.S. Naval District, headquartered in Charleston, South Carolina. He was related to Rorer A. James Jr. (1897–1937), who later married MSS's youngest sister, Elizabeth Letcher Stuart (1901–1982).

33. Henry Carter Stuart (1855-1933) was Virginia's 47th governor, serving from 1914 to 1918.

34. MSS is referring to Plattsburgh Barracks in northern New York State. It was a forerunner of the recently closed Plattsburgh Air Force Base.

35. On January 13, 1915, Flora Cooke Stuart wrote a letter to President Woodrow Wilson requesting his help in securing an appointment to West Point for her grandson, JEBS III. In his response a couple of days later, Wilson explained that the president could no longer confer direct appointments to the Academy. While supportive of JEBS III's ambitions, Wilson also expressed concern that the issue of nearsightedness could undermine his efforts to join the U.S. Army.

Chapter Six

A Focus on Family

As related previously I had met a very impressionable young man at Mrs. William Waller's boarding house in 1910, when I first started teaching as assistant art supervisor in the Norfolk Public Schools. He was brought from St. Louis, Missouri, to Norfolk by Mr. Clifford Millard to serve as his secretary and to do his special type of work. Mr. Millard had been elected president of the John L. Roper Lumber Company at a very handsome salary. This young man, named Drewry McRee Smith, came from a very distinguished line of ancestors in North Carolina. He was the great-great grandson of Justice James Iredell of the first Supreme Court of the United States.[1] Further, he was the great-grandson of James Iredell Jr., who served as governor of North Carolina and also as a U.S. senator.[2] Drewry's mother, born Penelope McRee, was a daughter of Griffith John McRee, of Wilmington, North Carolina, who was a writer and lawyer.[3] Penelope was also a granddaughter of Dr. James Fergus McRee, who was a noted North Carolina physician and botanist in his day.[4] One ancestor, through the McRees, was William Henry Hill,[5] who married Eliza Ashe,[6] and was considered one of the wealthiest men in North Carolina. Asheville, North Carolina derived its name from the Ashe family.[7] Drewry's father, North Carolina native John Dawson Smith, had received his early education at Colonel Kenan's academy for boys in North Carolina, followed by two years at the University of Virginia. He then continued for four years in Germany, first at the University of Berlin and then at Heidelburg, where he graduated in jurisprudence with an *insigne cum laude*. This sheepskin is one of Drewry's treasured possessions. Drewry absorbed something of the European culture and German language in his boyhood days from his father.

This Drewry McRee Smith was young and brilliant—he made a good salary for the day (the second decade of the 1900s), and he was ambitious. While working hard each day, he undertook the study of law at night. I was working faithfully teaching art at the Norfolk schools, and there were a few dates, but mostly on Saturdays and Sundays. Our favorite pastimes were trolley trips to Cape Henry on Saturdays. Drewry had passes on the Norfolk Southern Railroad's electric line to Cape Henry and Virginia Beach. Cape Henry was then a wild beauty with its big open spaces, freedom, and charm. It offered a world of interest in its beach walks on the hard sand, in its infinite variety of shells washed ashore, its ocean beauty with changing patterns of light, its shifting sand dunes, and the old light house and passing ships. We always ended with a ravenous appetite at O'Keefe's Restaurant to eat sizzling roasted oysters and shells, panned in butter and served with crackers and coffee. These Sunday trips took all the kinks out of a person and restored, invigorated, and inspired one. In mild weather, the long car ride to the beach and back was restful. The mighty pounding force and vastness of the Atlantic Ocean was a powerful stimulant to thought, and good company led to appreciation of everything.

In June 1914 Drewry successfully passed the Bar Examination at Roanoke, Virginia. He also went to St. Louis to see his people. It was a hot summer, and the Grand Duke of Austria was assassinated during that time, which led to the World War of 1914-1918. As has been previously related, I taught art at the University of North Carolina during the summer of 1915. Drewry surprised me with a visit as he returned from another visit to his people in St. Louis. Chapel Hill was suffocating and hot, and in the afternoons I was forced to undress and rest in my room. As the sun and its heat passed I would take a shower and dress. Then, after supper we walked to the big rock pile and found a rock and cast it on the pile. This rock pile was a monument to Zebulon Vance.[8] Drewry and I became engaged, and on June 14, 1916, we were married at Old St. Paul's Episcopal Church in Norfolk, Virginia. The birds were chirping and singing in the ivy that covered whole sections of the old church. The music was superb—also very useful, as Mr. Covington had said he could not be there at ten o'clock, the hour selected. He had to offer the prayer at a school commencement at that hour, so we compromised on a time fifteen minutes before ten. However, circumstances played havoc with my earnest intentions. We (Mother, Jo, Elizabeth, and I) were living in a small apartment. Ella Jordan was there during the week, but went home to Smithfield for Saturdays and Sundays. Father came from New York to give me away at the wedding ceremony. He stayed with Cousin Maria Cooke on West Freemason Street, as it was impossible to tuck another person into our crowded home.

On the morning of my wedding day I had a hairdresser come to the home and she gave me a facial. I heard my sister Jo say, "You are the bride and can wait to get into the bathroom. We are using the facilities first." So I waited to

complete my dressing and Father came to go in my auto taxi. Mother, Jo, and
Elizabeth had already gone to the church. My brother, J.E.B. III, was in the
midst of examinations at the University of Virginia and could not attend the
wedding. As I took my seat in the waiting taxi, I handed Father a pair of German steel scissors I had bought especially to cut or rip the ring finger of my
glove. He put the scissors in his pocket, and later wrote Mother, indicating he
had the scissors and did not know from where they had come. He sent them
to Mother at Charlottesville, and years later I claimed them. In the excitement
or worry over being late, I never thought of ripping the glove until I was at
the altar and the minister said in a whisper, "your ring finger." I then hastily
snatched off the glove.

As we prepared for the ceremony, Drewry was on the wrong side and my
petticoat was showing slightly. Of course, I had not had anyone to check my
appearance as they all left me alone in the apartment. I had even locked the
apartment before making my way to the carriage where Father was waiting.
Unavoidably fifteen minutes late for my own wedding, Uncle Edwin turned
to Mother and remarked, "Where is Marrow? Wedding at ten—well, Marrow
got her way as you might well know she would!" At ten o'clock, the music
drifted into the haunting strains of *Lohengrin*[9] and filled the hushed silence

*J.E.B. Stuart II, circa 1917 (Courtesy
of Col. J.E.B. Stuart IV).*

as Mr. Walter Edward Howe pumped the pedals and played the organ exquisitely. He had filled in while waiting for me to arrive with airs that Drewry had selected–Schubert, etc. The dignified and triumphant "Wedding March" by Mendelssohn[10] finished the ceremony. As I left the altar after making the solemn pledge "for better or worse—until death do us part," I looked at Mother in the front pew on the left side. Her face was sad and showed tears. I smiled my bravest, instead of looking demure, and a very frank-spoken cousin said I was grinning and looked too pleased over getting married. Meanwhile, the little birds chirped in the ivy mantle on the old church and the sun was beaming in splendor.

Mr. Covington could not bless us or wish us happiness, as he had to drop his robes and surplice in the entrance alcove and dash to the commencement. I longed for his blessing. Elizabeth was there in the doorway, and while she kissed me she poured rice down my back. A week later it was still dropping telltale rice out of my clothes, shoes, and hair in a Boston hotel. We then rushed to our taxi, and the driver had to skirt some piles of dirt and upturned pipes on Church Street, and he bumped us terribly. The taxi threw me to the ceiling, and my head bumped the roof of the car. I consequently suffered a severe headache. We were then driven to the boat at Sewell's Point Pier and

Marrow's sister, Flora Stuart Garmany, circa 1919 (Courtesy of Olivia Stuart McFadden).

went on to the Hotel Chamberlain for lunch. I remembered Mother's sad look at the church ceremony, so I hastened to call her and told her we would soon leave for Boston by boat. I also indicated that I was alright and happy, and told her to "please take care of yourself." Father had to hurry back to his position at the Texaco Company in New York. Shortly thereafter, Mother, Flora, Jo, and Elizabeth went to the University of Virginia—and J.E.B. III who was already there—joined the family. Mother set up housekeeping and boarded students. Also, Mother did not want Elizabeth to go to school in New York, and thought she could make it easier for J.E.B. III by giving him a home and his board. Mother's first home in Charlottesville was on Virginia Avenue, then some distance away from the center of activities. However, it is now in the center of University life and classes. Once she was situated in Charlottesville, Elizabeth attended Chatham.[11]

While my family prepared for their move to Charlottesville, Drewry and I embarked upon our honeymoon. For some time before the wedding, we had planned to go to Boston for our honeymoon. We had reserved a room at the Thorndyke Hotel, which overlooked the Common, and this was to be our pivotal point. So on June 14th we boarded the splendid *Merchants and Miners* boat for Boston. This trip furnished excellent meals with the ticket—but alas, I became too sea sick to even lift my head or venture from the stateroom. No one on that ship saw me, but Drewry went to all the meals and came back and reported on the fine quality of everything as well as the service. Drewry then steered me off the boat and checked my baggage after the others had gone ashore. At the Thorndyke I remained in bed for another twenty-four hours. I could still feel the motion of the ship, and I was exhausted from ending my school career on June 12th and getting all my reports in along with preparing for the wedding. There was also a certain emotional upset because Mother and Father were so disturbed in their plans. I recovered shortly thereafter and we had our first dinner in Boston of squab on toast—and it was so delicious.

During the following two weeks we went to Lexington, Bunker Hill, Concord, Plymouth Rock, Magnolia, Annisquam, Old Salem, and many other places. We also explored Old Boston. Each night we returned to our hotel, except when we went to Annisquam. We hired a horse and buggy at Magnolia and drove around through beautiful sections of shade trees in the little town. During our trips we saw Louisa M. Alcott's home and the House of Seven Gables at Old Salem. I bought a brass candlestick from the shop in the house, and Drewry bought me the book by Nathaniel Hawthorne on the old home. We found the people in and around Boston to be very charming and very much like Virginians. They went to no end of trouble to help us in giving directions for our wanderings and exploration. The conductors on the trolley cars were also polite and offered many suggestions. We stayed a few extra days. However, our tickets then called for a return by the *Merchant and Miners*. I ate lemons and stayed in the air, and made the trip home without too much inconvenience.

We arrived home at the same little apartment and found Sakakinny had not brought our furniture. Mother had given me ten pieces of beautiful old walnut that Grandma Stuart had once used at Stuart Hall. Mother always said that the furniture would go to the girl who married first—I was lucky! I had Sakakinny make the old walnut wardrobe into a chest of drawers, and make a shaving mirror to go on it. There was a double bed, a bureau, a washstand, a bookcase, a desk, and four chairs. Sakakinny made a large footstool out of scraps of walnut, and used a tapestry-covered cushion that was adjusted on top. When we returned from Boston to Norfolk it was late in the day, and we had to telephone for our furniture, which came immediately. Drewry had also ordered a Beauty Rest mattress and springs from some wholesale place, and that was also sent promptly. Aunt Lou Phillips had given me an old San Domingan mahogany table that she had purchased for one dollar. It was full of ink-stains and had newspapers stuck to it because some servant had ironed on it. I later had the piece cleaned and scraped, and also had the ink-stains taken out. It was a beautiful piece. I later gave it to my son (Drewry Jr.), and it is now in his home in Santa Monica, California.

So we started housekeeping in our small apartment—four rooms and a bath. There were pink geraniums and trailing vinca in the dining room—and my lovely silver in the LaFayette pattern along with some quite nice prints and books. We had to buy rugs, an icebox, and a folding day bed in case any of the family came to visit us. Many friends came to see us and said that they thought everything was very charming. I also experimented on Drewry's diet and succeeded in getting him in good shape for his nerve-wracking office work. [*However, Marrow and Drewry's time as a newlywed couple was short as they soon had a small addition join their family.*] Drewry Jr. was born at Norfolk Protestant Hospital at buttercup time–April 18, 1917.[12] He came into the world when the seven o'clock whistles were blowing and the night shift of nurses was leaving as the day shift was coming into work. The interns and Dr. Baker were also there.

Drewry Jr. grew from crawling on his large cotton quilt to walking—from uttering a word or two to forming his thoughts into sentences. I held him in front of a framed print of Raphael's *Madonna Gran Duca*, and he said "Babee" with ecstasy—his first word. He walked perfectly at eleven months and showed confidence and daring. He lived in the sunshine each afternoon, generally at the park with friends meeting us there. The mornings included breakfast, a bath, a nap, and nourishment again—all on a strict schedule. The afternoons were enjoyed with great activity in the park. I cooked his oatmeal gruel every other day and strained it, along with making his applesauce, straining his spinach, and fixing his bottles. During that period, there were no timesaving baby foods on the market. He went on cow's milk at nine months and drank from a cup. Also, Drewry Jr. tripled his weight at nine months—to twenty-one pounds. He was the picture of health and happiness. I used the infant care booklet that the government printed as my guide, along with my previous knowledge of psychology.

The summers were sultry and hot in Norfolk, so Drewry Jr. and I went to visit Mother at the beautiful University of Virginia during July 1917 and August 1918. We also visited from April through August 1919. At the time, Drewry Sr. worked for the Roper Lumber Company and then for its associated company, the Norfolk Southern Railroad. He therefore had railroad passes and came to see us each weekend. His train pulled in at midnight with a shrill whistle as it passed in the valley below Mother's house, and he appeared fifteen minutes after that. I was exhausted from constant care of a very active youngster. We also had that dreadful "flu" during the winter of 1918, and I was left with a bad heart condition. Meanwhile, as war raged in Europe, Drewry Sr. had not been drafted for the war because of the birth of his son. In his words, "my son was my exemption from fighting in World War I." When he left the Roper Lumber Company, he took a position at the Norfolk Navy Base.[13] He served as secretary to Mr. Louis B. DeWitt, general superintendent for the Pacific Coast contractors Porter Brothers, who were building the Navy base and the great Navy base piers.

That year, the influenza or "flu" epidemic was raging and even strong men were stricken and died within a few days. Doctors did not know how to cope with this new virus. Drewry Sr. had it, and called for tomato juice. Then, our baby was ill and wanted only orange juice. I nursed them and they recovered, but finally I had the worst case. I could not go to bed on account of the baby, and I did not care to eat. If I did eat, I immediately suffered with nausea. We found a practical nurse that helped some. However, she had to go to an even more urgent case and quickly left us. Later, Cousin Lizzie came to help me. Finally, I left with a weakened heart to rest at Mother's in Charlottesville. Dr. Davis from University Hospital said that I had a flabby heart, very low blood pressure, and valve trouble. Consequently, I had to rest one hour before and one hour after meals. I eventually had to consent to a nurse for Drewry Jr. Also, Mother found Virginia, a little colored girl of about fourteen years, to look after him. She walked Drewry Jr., much to his delight, over to see the skeleton of the big mammal at the Science Hall of the University of Virginia. One day, he independently walked out of the house with Mother's fire poker, and some neighbors saw him and quickly let us know.

*Drewry McRee Smith Sr., circa 1920
(Courtesy of Sharon Stuart McRee).*

[*During Marrow's recovery, she and Drewry Sr. began pondering a move to a new home in Norfolk.*] Finally, when Drewry Jr. was two and a half years old, we moved from the Kirkwood Apartments to *our very own house* on Dunkirk Avenue. I had said that if I could only own a small place, I would be willing to go into a hen house. This was our second home, and it was a very comfortable five-room cottage or bungalow in the California style. There was a large, 13' X 18' sitting room with eight English casement windows, a glass entrance door, and a chimney. This room entered into a small hallway. On one side there were two bedrooms, and on the other there was a bathroom and a breakfast room. The hall then terminated in the kitchen. Therefore, from the front door one could look through the back door into the back garden. Altogether there was plenty of light and sunshine, as there were twenty-three windows to keep clean. A young architect, Gilbert Underwood, had planned this cottage as an experiment, and he priced it high. If it had not sold he would have moved into it himself. We quickly began to desire more than the lot upon which the cottage was built. We were carrying a large payment each month, but we undertook to pay gradually for the south lot that was owned by a North Carolinian. Next, we wanted the north lot adjoining our home, but the owner said that she wanted to sell her two lots for cash. So somehow we managed that. I put up my precious diamond ring and met some heavy payments.

We now had a house and four lots. Although I saw the necessity of a vegetable garden, I knew nothing about such things. I sent to the agricultural department and I studied every pamphlet they sent me. I bettered my soil, and had an outstanding garden. I raised cabbages, onions, snap-beans, lima beans, cucumbers, beets, carrots, chard, turnips, sweet potatoes, egg-plants, celery, and bell peppers at various times. Also, I had a Betchel crabapple that yielded three bushels of small apples one year. I made jelly and canned fruits and vegetables at night when Drewry Jr. was tucked into bed. We had a pecan tree, fig bushes, strawberries, ever-bearing raspberries, and artichokes that I pickled. One year I even raised some Irish potatoes. I often shared the garden surplus with the neighbors. I produced so many peppers that I was glad to find a recipe for pickled pepper mangoes. Those, along with strawberry preserves, made fine Christmas gifts. This hard work in the open air restored me. I was happy in our freedom of life and in possessing our very own home and garden, which was quite a show place. One day Miss Lane came to visit and asked me to please join the LaFayette Garden Club, as she thought that I could win a prize on our place. I did this to please her, and the ladies gave me first prize on landscape gardening. I also wrote an essay on "Our Little Place" that won the first place in the Society of Arts essay contest. However, life did not offer me much more in the form of cultural outlet. My neighbors lived close to their practical problems of everyday living–washing, ironing, house cleaning, marketing, cooking food, and sewing. In the schools we said, "food–shelter—and clothing."

Meanwhile, Drewry Jr. played with various neighborhood children, and I supervised this play. One summer day he came to the front door nude and spattered with mud with his sandals and clothes in a bundle under his arm and a big boy unknown to me standing behind him. The boy asked me if I was going to beat my son. I said, "Drewry, come inside the house." Then, I thanked the boy and told him goodbye. I placed Drewry Jr. in the tub and asked him what had happened. He said, "the boy told me to take off my clothes and wade in a mud puddle." I asked him if he was going to go through life letting others tell him what to do–and not think for himself. I then said, "you must think for yourself about what is right and what is wrong." Another time when Drewry Jr. was about three years old, he sat on the floor and made a marvelous design with his colored kindergarten sticks. I raved over it and asked him to tell about it. He said, "this is Mr. Hinkley's store on the corner; and this is the path; and these are the trees." I thought that I must keep this forever, but the sticks were soon scattered, and when his Daddy returned at night I could only describe his son's creation. Drewry Jr. came home one day with his pockets and hands full of interesting beans that he had found on the street. He planted them at the back door, and then moved them to more cultivated soil. They came up beautifully and produced string beans. He seemed to be conscious of growing things. At this time, Drewry Jr. attended kindergarten at John Marshall School, where he loved fine music and building with his blocks. He had to go on the streetcar and handle the ticket each way.

In 1919, Drewry Sr. went into the new Joint Stock Land Bank business to help Mr. F.W. McKinney. He had been polite to Mr. McKinney when Mr. McKinney came into the Roper Lumber Company office. So, when the Virginia Carolina Joint Stock Land Bank was organized, Mr. McKinney employed Drewry Sr. as assistant secretary-treasurer. The land bank was a subsidiary of the Guaranty Title & Trust Co. This work pleased Drewry Sr., as the government lent money to the farmers and certain legal papers had to be drawn up. He took us to Staunton for six months while he worked at a land bank there that he helped to organize. Mr. William Sproul was the chief promoter of this bank. We rented our Norfolk home, furnished, to the Lanes. Miss Bessie Lane was a primary teacher and her aunt, Miss Elizabeth Lane, lived with her. At Staunton we rented a furnished apartment. The Staunton people were so kind to us and showed us much attention—taking us for drives, having us to dinner, making calls, and bringing us Christmas syllabub. I had been born in Staunton and spent summers there with Grandma Stuart. I had also returned for a boarding school session and then visited the town as a young lady. Now, I was staying as a young married woman. Drewry Sr. had told dear Mr. Stott that I was very nice but not good-looking. So, when we went to dinner at the Stotts', Mr. Stott rushed Drewry Sr. in a corner and said, "you told me your wife was not good looking–and she is beautiful!" After several months in Staunton where Drewry Sr. was helping the land bank get organized and started on its loans to the farmers, we returned to our Norfolk cottage and the Lanes had to leave. They later bought a home near us. The land bank business next took Drewry Sr. to Elizabeth City, North Carolina for a short stay, and we boarded at that time. There was quite a flattering offer to Drewry Sr. to stay there and help to carry on the land bank, but we felt we liked a larger place.

On May 12, 1923, Grandma Stuart's great spirit passed on—she was eighty-seven years old. Prior to her passing, she had spent her days in her front room upstairs at Uncle Page Waller's. She came downstairs for her meals, and after supper remained upstairs until the Navy Yard's nine o'clock gun went off. Then, the basket of family silver was carried upstairs each night. Grandma was charming, bright, interested in everything, and mellowed by human sympathy and outgoing love. I usually went to see her with Drewry

Jr. once a week. She kept up with politics and with what young people were wearing. Before we entered the rather dark house, I would say to Drewry Jr. words like these: "Your Grandma loves you and is proud of you as her first great-grandchild. Please behave and act well, so your Grandma may always love you." He did. Drewry Jr. kissed her and then went to a window and quietly moved the shutters open and closed them—and repeated this–first closing and then opening them occupying himself while we talked, and after fifteen or twenty minutes I took him home. Grandma always said, "My daughter, your visits are so short. Why not stay longer?" I would say, "But Drewry Jr. must get his fresh air and work off his energy."

Minnie, our cleaning woman, came one day. She left by a door different from the one she came in–and remarked, "That is bad luck, Mrs. Smith." I recalled her comment when word came of Grandma's fall down four stone steps at the front porch. She had tried to pick up a toy dropped by a great-granddaughter—small Theo Page Waller. She struck her head and was unconscious and lingered on for four days. This was the way she wanted to go. For years her prayers were "to go suddenly and not be a care to anyone–not to be helpless–not to lose my senses." My grief was profound. Drewry Sr. and I went to the funeral at the home of Uncle Page. Father and J.E.B. III came in from New York while Cousin Maria Cooke took charge. The services were impressive, with the Rev. Myron B. Marshall (rector of Saint Andrews Episcopal Church in Norfolk) officiating. He was assisted by Bishop Robert Carter Jett of the diocese of Southwestern Virginia. Bishop Jett came from Staunton, and he and Grandma had already had a long association in church work when they established Emmanuel Church in Staunton as well as the religious undertakings at Stuart Hall. The Rt. Rev. B.D. Tucker (Bishop of the Diocese of Southern Virginia) and Rev. R.A. Benton also attended the services, the latter at the grave. The pallbearers were neighbors, such as Edward May, George H. Lewis, W.W. Gwathmey, Edmund S. Ruffin Sr., and L.P. Roberts, or business associates of Uncle Page, such as T.M. Bellamy, H.W. Hough, and R.S. Spindle Jr.

Governor E. Lee Trinkle[14] acted as representative of the state and military escort and had with him several members of his staff, including Col. Hiram H. Smith, Col. Clyde Ratcliffe, Col. John W. Williams, Col. Hill Montague, and Col. M.B. Rudd. Members of the local alumnae of Stuart Hall attended the funeral in a body. Also present were representatives of the Pickett-Buchanan Camp of Confederate veterans. Cousin Mary MacGill Chapin was devoted to Grandma, and she came from Pulaski. Cousin Mary's brother and sister-in-law also attended. Also present was Cousin Kate Harrison (Mrs. Carter Harrison of Charlottesville–she was the former Kate Duval of Staunton). Ex-Governor Henry Carter Stuart and his brothers Dale and John (all nephews of

General Stuart) along with young John Stuart of Richmond (a great nephew) were also present. The large home was crowded to overflowing. Three large rooms and a spacious hall were used. The Wallers sat on the stairs leading to upstairs, and much to my sorrow, we were ushered to the center of interest in front of the coffin and in full view of everyone.

As Father was the son our carriage followed the hearse. The funeral cortege left the Waller house on Warren Crescent and went on to the C. & O. boat, and at Newport News transferred to a train for Richmond. Many, many dear relatives and friends stopped at my seat on the train to offer sympathy to me. However, with my tear-stained face and grief I was not in any mood to have so many social contacts. On the boat, Father left us to guard the remains. The expenses of taking care of this large funeral group were deducted from Grandma Stuart's estate. At Richmond, a delegation of Confederates met the train and went on to Hollywood Cemetery. Our group had lunch at Cousin Rachel Cooke's (Dr. Baskerville Bridgeforth's), and we were joined by Cousin Di Duval and other cousins. The Wallers went in another group to other Cooke cousins. The Cooke nephews and the husbands of Cooke nieces served as pallbearers in Richmond. At the train silent tribute was paid to General Stuart's widow as the body was removed from the train to the street below and the waiting hearse. Various delegations formed lines on each side. Among these were the women of the United Daughters of the Confederacy and the Confederate Memorial Literary Society. There were also chapter representatives of the United Daughters of the Confederacy from Norfolk, Richmond, and Goochland, as well as from West Virginia and Maryland.

Scattered among the group at the station were several men in gray–some of them had served under the famous cavalry leader and had come to honor the woman who had added to the fame of her husband by her own service. These included George K. Roper (Commander of Robert E. Lee Camp No. 1), A.C. Peay (Adjutant), A.W. (Tony) Miller, Capt. R.S. Hudgins, R. Werth, and Gen. Tyler Johnson. More than a score of Confederate veterans (as representatives of the soldier's home) were brought to the burial ground. These included some who had served under Grandpa Stuart. One veteran on crutches, George L. Christian,[15] had served under him, and his companions were Capt. John Lamb,[16] W.B. Lightfoot,[17] and W.S. Archer.[18] Relatives and friends gathered around the open grave in a partial circle. Men in gray along with representatives from loyal organizations (including the Oakwood Memorial Association, the Lee Camp Confederate Veterans, and the Lee and Jackson Camp sons) all stood in solemn and loyal attitudes of great respect. Amid beautiful flowers a short grave ceremony was solemnly spoken–and the peace of Hollywood enveloped the scene. Nearly sixty years had passed since Grandma Stuart's gallant husband had been laid to rest.

NOTES

1. Born in Lewes, England, James Iredell (1751–1799) was appointed to the U.S. Supreme Court by President George Washington in 1790, and served until his death in 1799. Prior to the appointment, he served as North Carolina's attorney general from 1779 to 1781.

2. Born in North Carolina, James Iredell Jr. (1788–1853) was the state's 23rd governor, serving from 1827 to 1828. He represented North Carolina in the U.S. Senate from 1828 to 1831. Iredell's uncle, Samuel Johnston (1733–1816), was North Carolina's sixth governor, serving from 1787 to 1789. In turn, Samuel Johnston's uncle, Gabriel Johnston (1699–1752), served as a royal governor of North Carolina from 1734 to 1752.

3. Griffith John McRee (1819–1872) was an 1838 graduate of the College of New Jersey (now Princeton) and passed the North Carolina Bar in 1841.

4. Dr. James Fergus McRee (1798–1869) was a son of Lt. Col. Griffith John McRee (d. 1801), who served in the Continental Army during the American Revolution.

5. William Henry Hill (1767–1809) was a North Carolina attorney who served in the U.S. House of Representatives from 1799 to 1803. President John Adams appointed him to be a U.S. District Court judge near the end of his term, but President Thomas Jefferson later withdrew the designation.

6. Eliza Ashe Hill was a daughter of John Ashe (1720–1781), who was educated at Harvard and served as speaker of the North Carolina Assembly from 1762 to 1765. During the American Revolution, he joined the patriot cause and served as a brigadier general in the North Carolina Militia.

7. Asheville, North Carolina is named after the younger brother of Brig. Gen. John Ashe (1720–1781), Samuel Ashe (1725–1813). Samuel Ashe was North Carolina's ninth governor, serving from 1795 to 1798.

8. Zebulon B. Vance (1830–1894) was a prominent North Carolina politician. He served as the state's governor from 1862 to 1865 and again from 1877 to 1879. Vance also served as a U.S. senator from 1879–1894. During the Civil War's early stages, he served as a colonel in the Confederate Army.

9. *Lohengrin* is a romantic opera that was written by Richard Wagner (1813–1883). The most recognizable part of the opera is the "Bridal Chorus," better known as "Here Comes the Bride."

10. German composer Felix Mendelssohn (1809–1847).

11. MSS is likely referring to Chatham Hall, a private all-girls school in Chatham, Virginia founded in 1894.

12. From this point on, "Drewry Sr." will refer to MSS's husband and "Drewry Jr." will refer to her son.

13. Naval Station Norfolk is now the world's largest Naval base.

14. E. Lee Trinkle (1876–1939) was Virginia's 49th governor, serving from 1922 to 1926.

15. George L. Christian (1841–1924) had served as a sergeant in the 1st Regiment, Virginia Artillery and the Richmond Howitzers during the Civil War. In 1864 he was

severely wounded, losing one foot and part of the other. Following the war, he briefly attended the University of Virginia and later became an attorney and judge. Christian was also very active in Confederate veterans organizations in his later years.

16. John Lamb served as a captain in the 3rd Virginia Cavalry during the Civil War.

17. William B. Lightfoot served as a private in the 9th Virginia Cavalry during the Civil War.

18. This was likely the William S. Archer who served as a second lieutenant in the 38th Battalion, Virginia Light Artillery during the Civil War.

Chapter Seven

An Art Career

[*Following her Grandma Stuart's funeral, Marrow had to undergo more transition brought about by Drewry Sr.'s evolving career*.] My husband was very competent in office work, English composition, spelling, shorthand, typewriting, and law. Therefore, he had no difficulty in finding positions. He now made a change to Franklin, Virginia, to be secretary for a very ill and rich Mr. P.D. Camp.[1] He tried out the job and accepted it, so we rented our Dunkirk cottage, had our pieces of antique furniture crated and shipped, and Drewry Jr. and I followed. The Franklin people were extremely kind. We fitted into helping with church bazaars because I knew a Stuart Hall classmate living there—Sue Pretlow McCann. She found for me one of the old Smithfield hams that excelled in flavor and quality of meat any ham I have ever eaten. When it was cut its fragrant aroma permeated our home. We fitted up the apartment beautifully and paid one hundred dollars for an oil stove. I stained and waxed the floors and bought nine washable shades for all of the windows and marquisette curtains. After three months, Drewry Sr. left the job—the old man died shortly afterwards.

Christmas was now coming and Drewry Sr. had no new job in sight, but we had a few dollars in the bank. We decided to leave our apartment in Franklin and go to Norfolk and stay at a hotel. The Norfolk city lights looked so beautiful and we felt free and happy. The shops looked magical—even the barbershops were interesting. We walked up and down the crowded streets with the passing throng. I found a lucky penny on Granby Street and we laughed over that. We then ate supper at Child's Restaurant, and our special waitress gave us every attention. Later, we went to the Monticello Hotel to hear the choirboys of Christ Church sing Christmas carols. They marched from the stairs singing as they formed around a huge, tall tree—all lit in splendor—in the downstairs lobby. The carols of "Come All Ye Faithful," "Oh Little Town of

Bethlehem," "Rejoice Ye," "We Three Kings of the Orient," and the breath-less "Holy Night," lifted me out of the worldly. Then they trailed away, leaving me numb with religious fervor. About then, Mrs. Northern and Claude Northern found us and invited us to have Christmas dinner with them—and we accepted. It was a great Christmas of Christmases—of loosening all shackles—of great faith—of trust in the Lord. During the Norfolk visit on one Friday I met Miss Bell Irvine, who was art director of the Norfolk Public Schools, on Granby Street. She asked me if I was available for teaching art. I said, "Yes, I am." She then asked me if I would start Monday at the new Blair Junior High School.[2] I said I would report at nine o'clock on Monday. This started again my art teaching and supervising, and added to my six previous years of teaching, which developed finally into thirty-two years of dutiful and responsible service.

As the tenants had a lease, we could not get into our little Dunkirk cottage, so Drewry Sr. signed a lease for a very dirty, abused and old-fashioned house on old Yarmouth Street. Drewry Sr.'s tailor, Mr. Maynard, was our landlord. Since we were over the soft coal furnace, it was impossible to keep the place clean from this black dust. Big rats also ran in and out of the house.

We got rid of all but one of the rats. This great-grandfather rat was a crafty, stubborn, and aggressive creature. Although I put all of the food away, he still visited us and would knock the top off of the cocoa box. One night we spied him gallivanting around in Drewry Jr.'s room, and I shut the two doors and told Drewry Sr. to go in and kill him with a broom. There was a fierce battle and loud squeals from the rat when he got cornered. The rat then jumped under the bed and clung to the springs, and Drewry Sr. could not aim a good whack at him. Finally, Drewry Sr. was worn out and said he would give up. I said, "no, do not come out of that room until you get that rat." The battle continued for another half hour. The cries of the rat were death cries of fear and rage. Finally, the rat was not so alert and allowed himself to become vulnerable. Drewry Sr. ended his misery with the broom, which by then was completely ruined. The next morning all of our neighbors came over to find out what had been the matter the night before!

By February 1924 we had settled into the very normal life of old Yarmouth Street. My boy went to the Robert E. Lee School[3] and had the wonderful teacher Miss Sally Holladay, who was a real lady and a cultured person from old Portsmouth. Drewry Jr. entered the higher first grade, as he had had Miss Bell for the beginning first grade at Franklin. Miss Bell had taught school for forty years. She had loved Drewry Jr., and had praised him and spoiled him. She said he was very bright—the best pupil she had. We also became neighbors with some of the old families of Norfolk—the Albert Ropers,[4] William Ropers,[5] William Shields, Robert Johnstons, the Bowdens, Admiral Burrage,[6]

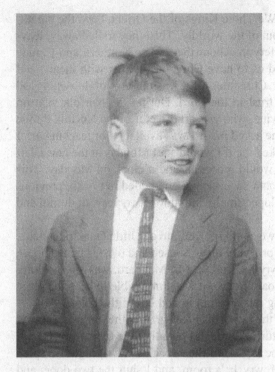

Drewry McRee Smith Jr., circa 1925 (Courtesy of Sharon Stuart McRee).

the Richard Ketners, the George Foote family (he from North Carolina and she from Georgia), the mother of Morris Hawkins (president of the Norfolk Southern Railroad), and the McClennans all lived on the same block.

After six years of taking care of Drewry Jr. and giving him the most thoughtful and unremitting care, I began now to build my career in art education and in my painting profession. I found conditions at Blair Junior High School very demanding. There were always five classes each day, and sometimes six classes. After school, there were also long talks with wayward students and hours devoted to constant care of children's painting materials and drawings. Along with posting work on the bulletin boards, I also helped students with poster work or drama projects. I also had teacher meetings every Monday and reports to complete for five hundred students every six weeks. I never left school until about five o'clock, and often had to feel my way into the dark halls and through the engine room (as all the other exits were locked). By this time, Drewry Sr. worked for the second time (1925-1932) at the Norfolk Southern Railroad (1918-1919 was the first period). At home, I had a good maid who looked out for Drewry Jr., and he had his house key fastened on a chain to his belt. We often had our dinners at the Y.W.C.A.

located a few blocks away at the corner of Freemason and Yarmouth Streets. Drewry Jr. attended Robert E. Lee School in the morning, and played with the little girls on Yarmouth Street in the afternoon. He often brought a congenial playmate, Hugh Fallin, home with him, and they experimented with electric trains and hanging around the Hague banks.

In 1925, on request, I gave a series of lectures on interior decorating at the Y.W.C.A. classes. In 1926, I won the Norfolk Society of Arts prize for my English essay, "Our Little Place." In addition, I started to do creative painting, and I entered a watercolor in the 1927 Society of Arts Exhibition. [*Over the next few years, Marrow was also privileged to win a number of other awards for her work. These included*:]

1. I won the W.B.G. Still-Life Award—a first prize on a study called "From an Old Cupboard."
2. In 1928, I again won the W.B.G. prize on a still life, "The Proud Pitcher on Parade." This painting later was sent to the Society of Independent Artists at Grand Central Galleries in New York (1930).
3. In 1929, I was awarded first prize for figure or figure in pastel—a group of puppets called, "Drewry's Marionettes."
4. In 1930, the May Barrett Prize for flower composition in oil, "Calla Lilies," came to me (our fire in 1948 burned this dreadfully). In 1931 I entered no entries.
5. In 1932, the Anna Cogswell Wood Prize for figure composition, "Paxton," took the honors.
6. In 1932, the Matilda McCord Roper Prize for the pastel portrait, "Anne"— given to little Anne James,[7] age six, because she posed so beautifully. I gave her crayons and sketched her as she looked up. Her eyes were bright with joy. She did not keep still long, so I had to memorize her.
7. In 1933, the C.D.S. Prize for landscape or seascape—"Watermelon Time on the Docks."

The competition for these events was very keen and I tried to find unusual subjects and unusual treatment. This all stimulated me to new progress and brought me excellent publicity. In 1929, we three took a trip by train to old Edenton and stayed for one night at the hotel. While there I wrote an essay on "The Romance and History of Old Edenton." This essay tied for third place in the Norfolk Society of Arts spring festival. Meanwhile, Drewry Sr. won three first prizes in succession on his essays "On Books," "Tolstoy," and "Thomas Hardy." He went to the library and did much reading and brought home several novels by these writers. He then just sat down and wrote these appreciative essays—typing and retyping until he had beautifully organized

"Drewry's Marionettes," by Marrow Stuart Smith (Courtesy of Sharon Stuart McRee).

papers. Drewry Sr. became quite an idol at the literary sessions of the group. Then, he said that he was tired of winning and wished someone else would win. Finally, poetess Mrs. Mary Sinton Leache won the prize, and she was excited!

Drewry Jr. seemed to catch the spirit of creation, too. He made some very interesting and glamorous puppets. He kept trying to cut them in wood and join the head and limbs with screw eyes and cloth. I did not seem able to help him, but he did have one magazine article from the *Ladies Home Journal* to use as a reference. I painted the faces and hands for him, and together we made the costumes. He wrote a play with all male characters in it, and he did the stage scenery to go with it—all assembled in a large dry-goods box. There was "Don Juan," the "Chinaman," the "Dutchman," and the "Indian" in that play. Later, "Gretchen," the little Dutch maid, was added to the group. The first scene was in California, and then the players or actors went to Holland. There was then a weird attic scene with cobwebs painted in the scenery. If anything went wrong, like a string breaking or getting tangled, he improvised, and he certainly did fill in cleverly with great composure. Drewry Jr. persevered in making wooden puppets, and I helped him with the sewing of the costumes. He made a man to open his mouth as if in singing, and he also made a very good horse. Drewry Jr. wrote all his plays and gave delightful performances. Drewry Jr. would gather a group of children on our steps and make up stories—the children seemed to be held spellbound. We often allowed him to entertain our dinner guests.

During this time, we had superb records of classical music, some of which we had acquired at the Dunkirk home, and we added to our collection constantly. At night we enjoyed playing these on our R.C.A. Victrola.[8] Drewry Jr. especially loved these, and he loved his growing collection of fine books. By this time he possessed about two hundred books with his bookplate. It was during these years that he wrote some lovely poems. When he was nine years old we went to Virginia Beach quite often. On these occasions I painted, Drewry Sr. read his newspaper or a book, and Drewry Jr. played in the sand. This poem followed one of his trips:

> While I was down on the beach,
> The waves came up unto my reach,
> And the gorgeous sun shone down,
> And made them seem a sparkling town!
> And as I was dreaming still,
> The little ships came in until,
> They filled the harbor wide,
> And stood, like soldiers, side by side.

We played the record of Schumann-Heink[9] singing the slumber song by Brahms,[10] his "Lullabye." As Drewry Jr. was drifting into sleep he composed this poem:

> To Slumber Town—to Slumber Town,
> Hear the crier call:
> This is the land, the open land,
> The land that is free to all:
> Come this way, come this way,
> Where the moonbeams gently sway!
> Now we're here, let's quietly sing,
> And the bells will softly ring.
> And we'll all be leaving here.

On one very snowy day, Drewry Jr. had a slight cold and was not allowed to go out. He did not like staying in and not playing in the snow, but he stood pensively at the window—and out came this poem that I just love, called "Snow Flakes":

> *One day, as I looked out the window,*
> *There fell upon my gaze,*
> *Tiny little snowflakes,*
> *In the queerest kind of maze!*
> *So I watched till the ground,*
> *Was covered with white,*
> *And never a dark spot met my sight,*
> *When Mr. Wind got up to play,*
> *And he piled the snow in any old way!*
> *And now the poor trees had their chance,*
> *Dressed all in white, as if going to a dance!*
> *But the poor birds—what could they do?*
> *I threw them some crumbs—then away they flew.*

These expressions are all from Drewry Jr.'s environment and his personal experiences. His vocabulary seemed to me excellent for his age, and his sensitized feeling was remarkable.

[*While Drewry Jr. was busy writing poetry, Marrow was occupied with expanding the number of cultural outlets available in Norfolk.*] The Norfolk Museum, at the entrance of The Hague and old Yarmouth Street, was not yet built.[11] The site for it was part of Smith's Creek—and old gas stoves, old tires, brickbats, and junk was constantly dumped into the creek to make the necessary fill. While this land was now in the process of forming, the eyes were treated to a dilapidated scene and the nose treated to moldy and disagreeable smells. However, the vision of the beauty of art was there, if one used the imagination. I worked hard for the encouragement of this project. I constantly told the five hundred Blair art students who I taught about what joys could be derived from such a project. I gave talks on art appreciation at school and at the Society of Arts, and wrote articles on art that were published in the newspapers, art pamphlets, and educational magazines. I also took large groups of pupils in busses to see the worthwhile exhibitions at the Wainwright Building. Further, I had the students' work displayed in large exhibitions in Norfolk.

Meanwhile, Father thought that he would retire and he visited us while we were living on Yarmouth Street. He had led an active career since the appointment by his old friend Theodore Roosevelt as customs collector for Newport News. In 1911, he had joined The Texas Company (now known as Texaco) in New York, and became an expert statistician in oil. Grandma Stuart's friend from Portsmouth, Mr. Thompson, had assisted in this appointment. While with this company, Father was sent to South Africa to straighten out some oil matters. During the First World War, he served in London during the terrible bomb raids, and helped the ladies from bombed hotels. Father also served in France with the supply department and wore a U.S. uniform with a dog tag. However, he was rated a civilian in the American Expeditionary Force, and he remained overseas in that capacity for eighteen months. After the war ended in 1918 he came to visit us in our small apartment home. Father could not sleep at night and just read and read detective stories, and he had terrible dyspepsia. His fare in France had ruined his once rugged digestive system, and his nerves were very jumpy. Father later returned to New York and resumed his work with Texaco (I think they found a place for him), retiring around 1927.

While visiting us in Norfolk on Yarmouth Street, Father had various friends and he went out to play bridge nearly every night, always sleeping late the next morning. Drewry Sr. did not like cards and I was far too busy with home and school duties, or too exhausted at night to indulge in any social life. So, Father kept a list of bridge players on the telephone stand and checked off the players each night. He played cards with the three Jordan girls (then living on Manchester Avenue), with the McClannan ladies across the street from us, with his friends Mr. and Mrs. Braden Vandeventer,[12] and with others. I worried about Father, who was nearly seventy, going about on our irregular sidewalks at eleven or twelve o'clock at night. Prior to the visit, he had complained of a pain in his shoulder and thought that a fall on the ice in New York had caused the injury. Nevertheless, he used a cane and felt his way through those rugged sidewalks every night. He loved it! Mother came to visit us too, and she and Drewry Jr. enjoyed playing backgammon. They argued and fussed like children!

I remember that Father brought his Spanish-American War uniform and some blankets and asked me to keep them for him. The uniform included the coat and cap. Later, he returned to New York and was scheduled to march in a big political parade. He wrote and asked me to send on his uniform, but I could not find it. We had moved, and I had put the coat and cap in our large old sideboard, and that had been stored as it was too large for our apartment. I concluded that I did not have them, but that I believed he did, and I wrote Father to that effect. I know he was disappointed not to have these articles. I wonder if he paraded without the uniform. He and I both had failed to remember, or maybe he remembered and I did not remember the trust. It does worry me now. Mother later told me that J.E.B. III found the trousers in Father's trunk, and I had Father's cane as a memento.

Around this time, Drewry Sr., Drewry Jr., and I went to old Williamsburg. We stayed at the old hotel there and Drewry Sr. used the washbasin in our room. It did not seem clean to me. Then, he went to the graveyard and looked over tombstones and went to the library to indulge in inspecting some very old books. Somewhere he caught a germ—maybe poison ivy or a cinder from the train got in his eye. Regardless of the cause, he had a corneal ulcer, and it became so bad that I was afraid he would lose his eye. One Norfolk doctor thought it was from his teeth and sent him to the hospital to get his teeth x-rayed. The sore did not heal under the treatment of Dr. Burke, so he went to another specialist, and another. He could not work because the doctor told him to not use the eye. Finally, I borrowed money from Flora and J.E.B. III and sent Drewry Sr. to Johns Hopkins Hospital in Baltimore. Here he was put to bed and they gave him every test. Nurses gave hot, wet applications to him, and after a week or so he came home. He told me that so many patients were losing their eyes from tuberculosis or had cataracts, and he felt that he was so lucky to only have a corneal ulcer. He therefore forgot his pain when he saw the suffering of others. All of his treatment and examination by the finest specialists hardly cost anything. However, the Norfolk bills from doctors and hospitals piled up and were terrific, and before I could pay them the dues came in.

[*While Drewry Sr. recovered from his eye problems, Marrow's father continued his visit.*] I remember how Father enjoyed the fresh Hanover salad we had, and he asked me what it was. I said that I believed it was a cross between spinach and turnip greens, and kept on having it with loin lamb chops and rice. Father often washed the spinach so when I came home from school, it was already fixed in the icebox and it did not take me long to get a good dinner on the table. Pineapple salad, coffee, and dessert finished the meal, and Father always enjoyed our cuisine. However, he became restless and longed for the excitement of New York. There were no ball games on Sunday, and Father missed his friends. He said we "might as well be buried alive as live in Norfolk," and returned to New York.

[*Following her father's departure, Marrow and Drewry Sr. had some major decisions to make about Drewry Jr.'s education.*] One day on the C. & O. boat I met Mrs. Cosnahan, a quite experienced professional who was Drewry Jr.'s second-grade teacher, and she told me it was a joy to teach him. She said she did not like to brag, but Drewry Jr. was the best student she had ever taught–and that he entertained the whole class in the afternoons by spinning stories. She asked him if they were true, and he said, "yes ma'am." Well, that second grade was crowded, and the principal decided to skip four boys to a higher grade. My son and Henry Abbit were two of the four selected. Miss Banner was the debutante who now taught him, and he thought that she was very pretty and nice. Drewry Jr. could do the work with ease, but all the boys were larger and he was the shortest, so he was always put at the end of the line. In this second grade slot, he would now be with the repeaters and graduate in February instead of June, and his classmates would always be taller and heavier than he. Years later, he said to me, "Mom, there is only one thing that I hold against you." I said, "What is it?" He said, "my size—why am I not taller!"

Drewry Jr. did not like being 5'6'' tall, and took all kinds of exercises on a gymnastic bar, along with pole-vaulting at home and tumbling and relay racing at Blair Junior High School. He also played basketball on the second team at Maury High School.[13] He talked for hours with Mr. Fletcher (the gym teacher), and tried to get on the first team of basketball, which had boys who were six feet and taller. Drewry Jr. did not realize that God never gives one everything. He was so agile and quick, and all around developed and healthy, and never had any trouble with his lessons. He won a pennant banner at Blair on running, which made him feel better, and he was selected with about a dozen boys to demonstrate on mats at Blair auditorium. He also was one of four to belong to the harmonica group, which visited other schools and gave performances. By this point, I realized that Drewry Jr. should go to another school, as the neighborhood seemed to be going down. So, in order to place him at Taylor School, we moved in 1929 to the Weyanoke Apartments on Colley Avenue and Princess Anne Road. It was a small, more modern apartment in a progressive neighborhood, and Drewry Jr. was then enrolled in sixth grade at Taylor School near us.

The apartment had only two bedrooms, and in fact one of these was an enclosed porch that projected among the branches of the luxuriant sycamore trees. There was a living room in the center of the plan, and down the hall in the back was a large closet and kitchen. The bathroom had to be concealed as it opened into the large living room. The living room in turn entered the master bedroom, which had folding doors, and it also entered the hall and porch. I had to store many things. We paid sixty dollars a month for these three rooms, a porch, and a bath. Minnie, the maid, came twice a week to clean the place and iron—and often made us a lemon meringue or mincemeat pie. She also stayed, cooked, and served a delicious dinner if we so desired or if we had company.

Father came from New York to visit us at the Weyanoke Apartment. He was given Drewry Jr.'s low, four-poster maple bed to sleep in, and his grandson went on a studio couch in the same porch room with windows on three sides and surrounding trees that made a screen. After dinner, Drewry Jr. brought out his books to study. While he was working on his Latin, he had to dig out some special tenses. To my amazement, Father (without looking at a book) could reel off the verbs. I said, "Father, I had Latin for four years in high school but cannot remember it like that." Father said, "but you did not learn your Latin with a hickory stick!" Drewry Jr. also had a pet white rat named "Felix" who usually slept in his box in the kitchen. However, for this special occasion, Drewry Jr. decided after we went to bed (as a special favor to his grandfather) to include Felix with the distinguished guest. Poor Felix was cold and upset, and spent the night tearing up paper to keep him warm, while Drewry Jr. slept on. The next morning, I asked Father how he had slept, and he said, "that damn rat kept me awake all night!" I said, "He was in the kitchen." Father then responded, "No, he was on the porch!" We all enjoyed this short visit of Father's. He seemed so mellowed and so glad to be absorbed into our family picture. He also enjoyed smoking his cigars—I still have the small cigar-box that he used that night.

That was the last time I saw Father. He then went back to New York to J.E.B. III's home at Manhasset, Long Island, and packed his trunk for Florida. The doctor had told Father that he should move to a milder climate, I had offered Father our Dunkirk Avenue house and Minnie to help him until we could find a larger apartment—or we would rent a room in the building for him and have all of our meals together. However, he took Drewry Sr. out to have oysters on the half shell and asked him to say truthfully if he had any debts. Drewry Sr. said, "yes," and Father decided not to add to our expenses. On November 25th, 1930, he passed away at Sebring, Florida, where he had bought a small farm to try and raise chickens.[14] He choked to death and was gone in ten minutes. When Mrs. Deane came in to offer help, Father's last words were, "too late." There were no clues found as to members of his family who should be notified. However, he was working on some tax papers for Mr. Lynch of New York, which enabled the Deanes to write to Mr. Lynch, and through that means my brother was notified. It was around Thanksgiving at that time, and I had attended a teachers' convention in Richmond. I had finished a talk before the Virginia Art Association on "modern trends in art" at the Richmond Hotel, and I was starting to a reception at the governor's mansion when the telegram with the shocking news was handed to me. Mrs. Baldock, one of the Norfolk art teachers, was so kind and sympathetically escorted me back to Norfolk.

A soldier escort brought the remains to Arlington National Cemetery, but as it was Thanksgiving there were delays in carrying out plans and promises. We in our confusion went to different hotels. Drewry Sr., Drewry Jr., and I selected the National Hotel on Pennsylvania Avenue where Abraham Lincoln had once stayed. Millionaire Indians came tramping through the corridor in blankets. Flora and Jo stayed at the Willard with their husbands, and Elizabeth, J.E.B. III, and Mary (J.E.B. III's wife), went to the Mayflower. J.E.B. III and Mary had married on November 17, 1928 in Tazewell, Virginia. We had attended the wedding and stayed with the Peerys. J.E.B. III later brought his bride to visit us one summer, and we enjoyed his devoted ways. Going back to the funeral, Mother had had a fall, and was advised by Flora not to attempt the trip to Washington. The slow hours moved on and arrangements could not be worked out. Sinclair Phillips came from Newport News to our hotel to offer sympathy. I later went to the station and found that the coffin had arrived. I placed my pyracanthus wreath on the top to show that I had been there and cared. I prayed for some help to bear my great sorrow. Then, I saw the sunrise on the Washington Monument and this obelisk pointed skyward and was glowing in rosy light. It seemed a great symbol of truth, courage, steadfastness, and stood with exquisite beauty and uplift. I read this meaning into my father's life. At the graveside in the Spanish-American War veteran's section there was a soldiers' salute and "Taps," and the flag-draped casket was lowered. But overhead, the circling airplanes drowned out the chaplain's words. A group of Father's friends came from New York and gathered with the relatives. Father's loyal friend, Mr. Pouncey, from New Jersey, was also there. I returned with my husband and son to a dreary, dark hotel room, unable to eat and suffering from shock and such fatigue that I could hardly walk.

[*After losing her father, Marrow found solace in spending time with family and friends*.] Back in Norfolk, Drewry Sr.'s sister (Margaret) and her husband (Roy Jeter) came from Cameron, Texas to visit us. We gave up our room to them. Roy dressed in white linen suits and so did Drewry Sr. We all went to old Jamestown and Williamsburg. We were shocked at how a tobacco company was using the tomb of Princess Pocahontas to advertise tobacco. Shortly after the visit, I came home one day from school and found a friend, Marguerite Cove, there. Minnie had made her at home, given her a cup of tea, and had allowed her to rest on the bed. During this time, I also often asked Lillian Banks and her sister, Marian, for lunch. Then, in the afternoons Lillian used her car and took us for drives to sketch and paint. Drewry Jr. liked Marian and teased her, and I had to quiet them down. Years later I did a portrait of Marian.

It was during this period of my life and a few years later that I did my most creative work and was quite prolific in my output. The Maury students inspired me, life at home was easy, and I received good publicity at exhibitions in Norfolk, in many parts of the state, and in other parts of the country— Washington, D.C., Ogonquit, Maine, and New York. Somewhere in these years William Simpson,[15] the young sculptor who won the Prix de Rome[16] in 1930 (at age twenty-seven), often came to see us. He would see our light burning when he took a walk at night. This was after he closed his old cotton warehouse studio after intensive sculpturing. There would be a rallying game of checkers with one of the Drewrys, and sometimes the game was played on the floor. I later gave a nice dinner party to William and Polly Baldwin, one of my talented high school students. There were also picnics at Cape Henry Beach. At one point, William was invited to give a short talk at the advanced art class at Maury. He asked Lindsey Ocheltree, an art student, to pose for the hands of St. Francis. Finally, this fine piece of work was finished, and we all went on a certain open house day to the studio to see the masterpiece. It did possess originality and freshness, and a fine spirited quality! It was cast in bronze and sent to be judged, and won the Prix de Rome, which entailed chiefly academic work in Rome with a side trip to Sweden.

Years later, there were other creations of importance from his hand. Symbolic grills decorated the entrances to army headquarters in Honolulu and brought William Simpson a much cherished commendation ribbon and citation for meritorious service. Also, he created many carefully executed busts to decorate the halls and library of his alma mater, Virginia Military Institute. He was later given several sculpture commissions, which included the design for the Norfolk commemorative half dollar issued in 1936, and the Roanoke Island half dollar issued in 1937. He created these coin designs while serving as director of the Rinehart School of Sculpture in Baltimore. I really think William found a congenial atmosphere in our home, and I had an understanding of the creative urge and encouraged him whenever I could. Years later, he came back to Norfolk. He and his wife were divorced, and the Rinehart School of Sculpture ceased because of the war's demands.[17] So William then returned to live with his quiet, old widowed mother on Grayden Avenue. He taught at the Norfolk Museum and asked me to help him secure a position as art instructor at Maury High School, which I did. The classes were delightful with him.

I have already mentioned "Felix" in connection with our life at the Weyanoke. How did we find him? Just before a family trip, Drewry Jr. paid a quarter to Luther Upton for a rat not yet born. When we returned, Drewry Jr. rushed to see the litter and claimed a nice one. He built a comfortable box with two stories and also studied in the encyclopedia what was good food for a rat–lettuce and milk were important foods. One time when I returned from school, I discovered that Drewry Jr. had the bathtub filled with water and said he was giving Felix a bath. He was also dipping a large bath towel in the tub so the rat could have something to which to cling. Then, Drewry dried him and used my French perfume on the pet. Felix was very unhappy over the treatment, but looked snowy white and pink afterwards. Drewry Jr. later taught this rat to climb a broomstick and do numerous things, and he often tucked him into his sweater for a visit to school. One day I rushed home to go to a principal's dinner—and Drewry Jr. looked miserable. He had experimented with the rat and tied a string around a paw, and every time he tried to remove it the rat bit him. Felix was in pain. I had to stop and put on gloves and take the manicure scissors to cut the binding string. Drewry Jr. and I then had a talk about being kind to helpless creatures. There were many other adventures, and Felix lived for three-and-a-half years. He was buried in Mr. Killiam's garden with an epitaph that was beautifully composed by Drewry Jr. and placed over the mound. We all had tears in our eyes.

During our stay at the Weyanoke, I felt free of housekeeping and painted every weekend. I taught two or three adult art students on Friday afternoons, and that left me Saturday and Sunday for my own creative efforts. At one point, I painted Drewry Sr. on the open porch reading his *New Republic* magazine. He was looking down and had a cynical expression on his face. I also painted some white roses that Mrs. Riley, from the Albright Florist Shop, gave me. These were done in pastel while beautiful cathedral music was being rendered on the radio. Drewry Sr. made me coffee and I just painted and painted. I also painted those same roses in oils. I have since refused to sell either of those paintings. Meanwhile, in 1930 Miss Irvine died and I became art director for forty-two schools. In the summer of 1931, I taught art at the Atlantic University, which was largely a course in art appreciation.[18] Alice Saunders provided me transport to class in her car. However, I had some

"Drewry McRee Smith Sr.," by Marrow Stuart Smith (Courtesy of Sharon Stuart McRee).

difficulty in ever getting any salary as the institution failed. After the work was over, Drewry Jr. and I went to Wytheville and he enjoyed swimming in a pool while I painted.

While we were living in the Weyanoke, U.S. Marine Captain John W. Thomason Jr., a World War I hero, called on us.[19] He wanted to check certain facts, and obtain photographs and personal information as he was working on a book about my grandfather, called *J.E.B. Stuart*.[20] He did not use the photographs but made sketches for his book instead. During the meeting, he was very modest and polite. We later returned this call at his Washington home and met Mrs. Thomason. After our visit, Captain Thomason took us for a lovely drive around Washington. We liked his book, which Charles Scribner & Sons published in 1930. Along with the book about my grandfather, Captain Thomason also won fame with his books, *Fix Bayonets*[21] and *Red Pants*.[22] He later served several tours of duty in Washington, D.C. and at Quantico, ultimately becoming a lieutenant colonel. He died on March 12, 1944 in San Diego, and his widow later lived in Terrell, Texas.

After ending our visit with the Thomasons, I wished to see the art at the Phillips Gallery,[23] and then the art at the Corcoran Gallery of Art.[24] It was a bitter cold day, and I had on my fur coat. Drewry Sr. insisted that we walk from one gallery to the other. I was so cold–I could hardly walk. When we came to the Corcoran, I fell on the sidewalk, sprawled out in front of it, and exclaimed, "Thus do I prostrate myself before art!" Well, men were running to help me and asking if I was hurt. My bag had the handle torn off, and when I came up on my feet I discovered that I had two immense holes in each stocking. I therefore went into the Corcoran and bent myself forward to try and hide the holes!

In 1932, we moved from the Weyanoke to a larger and very attractive apartment next door–The Brandon. We now had three bedrooms, and this allowed Mother to visit us and gave Drewry Jr. a larger private back bedroom looking out on a garden. We also had a living room in the front of the apartment, a large dining room, and a concealed kitchen. There was then a passage toward the back along a hall to the three bedrooms and a bath. I regret that Drewry Jr. had no social space to ask his friends in to play. Since I was seldom home, he went to the homes of Tony Burke, Pryor Worthington, and Jack Norton. At Tony's he rode a pony, and at Jack's he played golf. Sometimes, Mr. Worthington allowed the boys to shoot. I did not know of this until Drewry Jr. told me about a shot ricocheting back at him. Drewry Jr. knew and loved that pony and made a wonderful piece of soap sculpture of him. He carved so carefully for days, and did not cut away without thinking and thinking. I thought it looked like a miniature Greek statue, so I took it to the Academy of Arts meeting to show the ladies. Unfortunately, Miss Helen

Rodgers dropped it and it broke into two parts. Drewry Jr. could not make it stick together after that. I painted on weekends and on holidays, while Minnie kept the apartment in splendid order. Along with teaching my three talented students on Friday afternoons, we had friends in for dinner quite often.

[*While Marrow's career was steadily progressing, her sisters were undergoing extensive changes in their own lives.*] Elizabeth, my younger sister, had obtained her divorce from Rorer James Jr.,[25] and small Anne and her little fox terrier, "Topsy," stayed with us while her mother attended court in Danville. After the divorce was granted, Elizabeth had a small home built in Virginia Beach. Mother had lived with Elizabeth in Danville, and she now lived at the beach with Elizabeth and her two girls, Stuart and Anne. Before this she had a home on Mallory Court in Norfolk. Around the same time, following the death of her husband, Luther Prescott "L.P." Grover[26] (at the early age of thirty-eight), Jo also came to live on Mallory Court. She had two boys, Fred and Stuart, and a girl named Josie. They had lived previously in Nashville, Tennessee and Rutherford, New Jersey and they soon left Norfolk and moved to Alexandria, Virginia.

Marrow's sister, Elizabeth "Lib" Stuart James, with her daughters E. Stuart James (left) and Anne Wilson James, circa 1938 (Anne Wilson James Hundt Papers).

By this time, I was extremely interested in painting harbor scenes and the men on the docks. I tried to catch the quick movement of their figures as they trundled freight or as they unloaded the cargo from a ship. Sometimes there was a steady, fast procession of men that almost made one dizzy. Some men were tall, some heavy set, each having individual characteristics while managing to avoid each other. I had some difficulty getting permission to sketch, as the Old Dominion Steamship Line was afraid of injury or lawsuits. One woman had just sued because she had caught her high heel in between the floor planks and fell. I told the man in charge of the docks that I would find a place and sit in that spot and not get in the way. Drewry Sr. was with me of course and acted as a chaperone. When the noonday rest and lunchtime came I watched the men group about and eat their lunches. They usually ate something sweet like Coca-Cola and pie, and not the heavy meats that I expected they would eat.

One day one man climbed the rafters supporting the roof of the pier. It was so dramatic as everyone watched and yelled advice. Finally, he stopped at a pigeon's nest and put two squabs into his gray-blue denim coat and carefully lowered himself from bar to bar, and finally slid down a support. The others showed admiration for his bravado. I did not sketch this, but I made numerous sketches of just how a man looked in motion pushing his hand-truck. At home, I developed these sketches in oil-painted compositions. No one worried me by looking over my shoulder or asking silly questions, and in fact what I did on the docks was really the shorthand of it. Drewry Sr. was so interested in labor, and he called these paintings "your labor pictures." I was also interested in what was shipped through the Port of Norfolk. There were bales and bales of cotton sent to New England to be manufactured into cloth, and crated furniture came from the North Carolina factories. However, most interesting to me was the shipment of the plant "deer-tongue." I had never heard of this, so I asked the head pier man. He said that the deer-tongue was used to dilute tobacco.

One Sunday I went on another pier to paint a small composition of the large boat tied to the pier. The captain appeared and invited Drewry Sr. and me to have a fine dinner on the ship with him. I wanted to paint and not to eat, and I had trouble tactfully telling this jolly captain that I needed to make that painting for an exhibition. He came back later and insisted again–it seems that this is a rule of the seas. On a Saturday, Mr. Henry Ball came to paint from my model and stayed to lunch. Mr. Ball came from a little town somewhere near Tazewell, Virginia, and he had attended Columbia University and obtained a master's degree. I had later made him instructor of art at Maury High School. He was a delightfully pleasant person, very sensitive and tactful, and earnest in his teaching. One time, we started to paint "Paxton," one of the apartment

"Paxton," by Marrow Stuart Smith (Courtesy of Sharon Stuart McRee).

Negro janitors, who came from the fields of North Carolina. Paxton sat immobile for about two hours, and then insisted that he rest. He left his hat and went out and did not return. Days later I found out that other janitors told him, "Mrs. Smith would make his picture and have the goods on him, and he would be put in jail." The simple soul believed them and never came back for his hat. So Mr. Ball and I worked on from memory and our inner interpretations. Mr. Ball portrayed him sitting in a church, looking inspired. I painted him very passive, and sitting resignedly idle in a kitchen or eating place.[27] Mr. Ball taught for about two years, and at Christmas went back to New York to recharge himself. He caught a dreadful cold and died of pneumonia. I was greatly affected by the loss of such a fine teacher and agreeable person.

On another occasion Miss Effie Rogers, an elementary art teacher, came on a Saturday and Lillian Banks posed for us. Effie was a graduate of Columbia University, and was very creative and prolific in her work. That day, the telephone rang incessantly and the newsboy came to collect. The groceries also came at the back door and Drewry Jr.'s friends came to look for him. It seemed to me that I jumped up from my work every five minutes. I finally said, "I am not answering anything after this, and I am doing this study or I'll bust." Effie was now all upset by my many moves, and could not recover enough to get a worthwhile study. However, I did an excellent pastel portrait of Lillian.

In 1933 we had a dreadful hurricane.[28] We were in our Brandon apartment and felt safe, but the storm lashed and lashed. Electric wires fell all around us. Water also poured and rushed through the streets, and the Norfolk drainage system could not take care of the downpour. The storm raged on as our Frigidaire and our lights went off. We were also afraid of the live wires down all around us. Elizabeth came from the beach and deposited Jo's two boys, Fred and Stuart, who had been visiting her at the beach. She told me that Virginia Beach residents had been told to evacuate. Elizabeth kept her Anne with her while I watched the boys. They were quite restless and highly excited, so I started a poker game with four of us playing with chips, but they soon grew tired of that. I did not know what to do, and Fred had a terrible bronchial cough. I asked what I could do for him, and he said, "Just let me have a wet towel." He wrapped this around his throat and stopped coughing for a little while, but later coughed all night. Drewry Jr. put boots on and went out to see what the storm was doing, while I was thinking that I could not hold the Grover boys for much longer.

On the next day we learned that cars were stalled all over the city and that three thousand large trees had fallen. The city had a desolate, disorderly appearance. Great truckloads of butchered trees and limbs went to their funeral end. Salt water also came upon the land and ruined many gardens, while boats were wrenched from their moorings. We learned that Elizabeth's antique maple chairs were swept away to sea from her front porch at the beach. It appeared that they had floated back to the shore and were appropriated by storm collectors, but she later claimed them without any trouble. Elizabeth also had some books once owned by General Stuart that were water-stained. As such, they had to be rebound. She gave one afterwards to the Virginia Military Institute when I gave my copy of *Court Martial Law* along with an enlarged photograph of my grandfather.

Following our recovery from the hurricane, we learned in spring 1934 that Mother was far from well. She came from the beach to visit us and to receive treatments from Dr. C.J. Andrews. She often rested on the bed throughout the day and occasionally played Parcheesi with Drewry Jr. I moved her into the sunshine at the back part of the house so she could enjoy Mr. Killam's garden. A redbird came and stayed there on a branch near the window-seeming to communicate with Mother. It cheered her, but I almost felt that it was an omen and message from another world. When she went to Dr. C.J. Andrews' office, I usually took her. Mother finally gave up and went to bed. Elizabeth employed a trained nurse and called in Dr. Mallory Andrews. He called regularly but did not help Mother. Although I begged him to tell me about Mother's condition, he would not say whether there was hope.

Mother got it into her head that she wanted to go to Flora's at Port Washington, New York to see Flora's father-in-law, Dr. Jasper Garmany.[29] He was a prominent New York City surgeon, and she hoped that he could help her. Mother also wanted to see J.E.B. III, who could not manage to make the trip to Norfolk. Perhaps she thought that I would soon be busy with schoolwork. Conversely, Flora was at a nice home and could give Mother every attention. Elizabeth also decided that Mother should go, and one day informed the nurse that she was going to move her whether the doctor gave his consent or not. I think Dr. Andrews ultimately said that Mother could be moved. Mother was lifted-seated in a chair-to a waiting car, and I was so overcome that I do not know what I did. I rushed out into the fields and walked and walked. I felt it would be the last time I would see Mother. She was getting weaker and weaker. Each day, I studied her and she seemed not to care to live. I think Elizabeth later regretted moving Mother, as she was in such pain that she could hardly make the trip, even though she had a drawing room on the train. In New York, Elizabeth engaged an ambulance to take Mother to Port Washington. It had to move very slowly and Mother was given pain pills to endure the trip. In all there were five months of dreadful suffering.

I later received a telegram from Flora saying that Mother had had a stroke. I was allowed a leave of absence, and Drewry Sr., Drewry Jr., and I went to Flora's at Port Washington. I telephoned J.E.B. III at the station. It was a beautiful Sunday morning at the beginning of October. J.E.B. III said that he could not come to meet us, and instead told us to "just follow the sign on the road and you will be there." The sign had been knocked down and hidden in the grass, and we just walked and walked. Finally, I stopped at some house and asked for directions. A lovely lady put us in her car and took us to Flora's. Mother had not been given her pain-killing drug that morning and was suffering all the time we were wandering over the roads. Mother gave me a penetrating inspection–her words were few. She soon lapsed into unconsciousness. The next day, when she was hardly conscious, I asked her if she wanted a minister, and she did, but we had trouble finding one, as they were all out of town on their vacations. Finally, Flora found one and I took him to the room and asked him to make his prayers very brief. His words, "God is love," were very comforting. Mother lapsed into unconsciousness and passed away during the night—on October 5, 1934.[30] I think all five of her children were at the graveside in Arlington.

[*Meanwhile, Drewry Sr. was suffering from his own health problems.*] His hands and the nerves in his hands were giving away–he was in poor health. Drewry Sr.'s nerves also affected his stomach. The doctors said he had neuritis or an occupational disability. Drewry Sr. was working too hard over an invention he had made—a desk appliance that would manage documents for a typist. The government had granted him nine counts on it, and he had already paid the patent lawyer in Washington some money. Mr. Sapper, the shop man in Norfolk had also made many models. Finally, when we had to send the last twenty-five dollars to the patent lawyer to fix the patent, Drewry Sr. said he was no longer interested because he had already improved the process. Consequently, he did nothing to cinch the invention with a patent. However, I know the hours and hours that Drewry Sr. spent on just thinking about the thing, and I was disappointed. He also invented a scale to use in lining up and spacing several columns of figures. These columns would be indicated on a "rough sheet" first, and then this scale (an adaptation of, but not the one attached to the typewriter) would be used. When applied to the columns indicated on the rough sheet, it enabled the typist to make an effortless and exact column line-up in whatever tabulation work in which he or she might be engaged.

Over time, Drewry Sr.'s hands became worse, and he had to give up his work. He did not seem willing or able to attempt another type of work. Consequently, for the years 1933 to 1941 (covering the Depression years), and 1944 to 1951, he was out of work and at home. In the interim, he worked for three years at the Naval base filling orders, with the assistance of two young and frolicsome Negro helpers, for various government ships and activities from the vast stocks of heavy steel, bronze, brass plates, etc. This made matters difficult for me. Supporting a household and not having a salary in the summer months forced me to go into arrears on our rent. I finally asked the landlord to let me leave without holding my furniture, and I gave him a bank note. We then moved back into our Dunkirk cottage. All of this trouble affected Drewry Jr., since he had such admiration for his father. Our difficulties gave him a terrific inferiority complex, but they also developed his manhood. He, without my knowledge, took his new bicycle to a man and raised some cash for his thirty-five dollar "wheel." Next, I went to Groves and asked for credit on groceries from September to October 1st. This allowed us to live independently, and I faced up to our obligations in the fall. Courage is facing up to responsibilities and obligations without flinching.

NOTES

1. Paul D. Camp (1849–1923) was a founder of Camp Manufacturing Company in Franklin, Virginia, which was a highly successful lumber company. Paul D. Camp Community College was later named in his honor.

2. Blair Junior High School opened in 1922 and was named after James Blair (1656-1743), a Scottish clergyman who founded the College of William and Mary. It was later renamed James Blair Middle School in 1985.

3. Robert E. Lee Elementary School no longer exists.

4. Albert L. Roper (b. 1879) was a prominent attorney and business executive in Norfolk.

5. William B. Roper (b. 1870), an older brother of Albert L. Roper, was a prominent businessman and civic activist in Norfolk.

6. Vice Admiral Guy Hamilton Burrage (1867–1954) served in both the Spanish-American War and in World War I. He also served as commandant of both the U.S. Naval Academy and the Norfolk Navy Yard. Admiral Burrage was arguably best known for bringing back Charles Lindburgh (1902–1974) and the *Spirit of St. Louis* from Paris, France following Lindburgh's successful trans-Atlantic crossing in 1927.

7. Anne Wilson James (1925–1994) was the youngest daughter of MSS's sister, Elizabeth Stuart James (1901–1982).

8. Designed in 1906, the Victrola was a phonograph (record player) that was tucked away in a wooden cabinet. The intention was for the phonograph to look less like a piece of machinery and more like a piece of furniture. Victrolas quickly became the most popular home-based phonographs and sold in large numbers through the end of the 1920s.

9. Noted opera star Ernestine Schumann-Heink (1861–1936).

10. German composer Johannes Brahms (1833–1897).

11. Founded in 1933 as the Norfolk Museum of Arts and Sciences, the institution later became the Chrysler Museum of Art following the donation of automotive heir Walter P. Chrysler Jr.'s (1909–1988) extensive art collection in 1971. Today, it is considered one of the major art museums in the Southeastern United States.

12. Braden Vandeventer (1878–1943) was a Norfolk attorney who instrumental in developing the law firm known today as Vandeventer Black LLP. His son, Braden Vandeventer Jr. (1921–1998), was also a partner in this firm.

13. Named after famed oceanographer Matthew Fontaine Maury (1806–1873), Maury High School opened in 1911 and was later renovated in 1986. Today, it is one of five comprehensive high schools in the Norfolk Public School System.

14. Sebring is the county seat of Highlands County, Florida.

15. William Marks Simpson (b. 1903) was a noted sculptor who did engraving work for the United States Mint.

16. The Prix de Rome was a scholarship for arts students, particularly in the realm of painting, sculpture, and architecture, which was awarded annually between 1663 and 1968.

17. The Rinehart School of Sculpture is now part of the Maryland Institute College of Art.

18. Atlantic University was founded in 1930, but closed two years later due to the effects of the Great Depression. It reopened in 1985 and offers graduate coursework in such areas as transpersonal psychology, dream interpretation, and alternative healing. Its curriculum is closely aligned with the teachings of self-proclaimed psychic, Edgar Cayce (1887–1945).

19. Lt. Col. John W. Thomason Jr. (1893–1944) was the grandson of Capt. Thomas Jewett "TJ" Goree, CSA (1835-1905), who was an aide to Lt. Gen. James Longstreet, CSA (1821-1904). The U.S. Navy destroyer USS *John W. Thomason* (DD-760) was named after him.

20. See J.W. Thomason, *Jeb Stuart* (Lincoln, NE, 1994). Multiple versions of this book have been published since the 1930s.

21. See J.W. Thomason, *Fix Bayonets! And Other Stories* (Quantico, VA, 1991).

22. See J.W. Thomason, *Red Pants and Other Stories* (New York, NY, 1927).

23. Located in Washington, D.C., the Phillips Gallery is now known as the Phillips Collection.

24. Founded in 1869, the Corcoran Gallery of Art is the largest privately supported cultural institution in Washington, D.C.

25. Rorer A. "Buddie" James Jr. (1897-1937) was a member of a prominent Danville, Virginia family. His father, Rorer A. James (1859–1921) served in the Virginia House of Delegates (1889–1892), the Virginia Senate (1893–1901), and the U.S. House of Representatives (1920–1921). The family was best known for its ownership of the *Danville Register & Bee* newspaper from 1899 to 1996, when it was sold to Media General, Inc.

26. A native of Burlington, Vermont, Luther Prescott "L.P." Grover (1895–1933) was a 1917 graduate of Harvard University. He is buried at Mount Auburn Cemetery in Cambridge, Massachusetts, along with his wife, Josephine "Jo" Stuart Grover (1892–1966).

27. This painting is now owned by MSS's grandson, Drewry McRee Smith III.

28. This was likely either the Chesapeake Potomac Hurricane of August 23, 1933 or the Outer Banks Hurricane of September 15, 1933.

29. Dr. Jasper Garmany (1859–1947) was a well-known New York City physician who was on the medical team that treated wealthy industrialist Andrew Carnegie (1835–1919) prior to his death. His son, George Mackenzie "Mac" Garmany (1890–1957), served as a lieutenant in the U.S. Army Engineering Corps during World War I. He was also the husband of MSS's sister, Flora Stuart Garmany (1890–1975).

30. Josephine Phillips Stuart's date of death is listed in other sources as October 4, 1932.

Chapter Eight

Memories of Drewmar

[*For Marrow, the years between 1933 and 1948 were wrought with both challenge and opportunity.*] These were the years of greatest accomplishment in my career, but also the years of my greatest anxieties. Drewry Sr. was far from well, unemployed, and very depressed. He also did not like that a woman was the breadwinner of the family. Drewry Jr.'s terrible inferiority complex developed further over the course of his Daddy's breakdown, and it seemed that I could not find any way to meet the situation. Nevertheless, Drewry Jr. graduated from Maury High School in 1935 and then attended the William and Mary College at Norfolk[1] for two years. He then went to the Virginia Polytechnic Institute (V.P.I.) at Blacksburg, where he received his degree in electrical engineering in 1939. We had bought a Chevrolet car about six years before that helped us considerably.

My garden was a joy. The place did not look as trim as when we lived there, but the trees and shrubs had grown and there was a great privacy and soul stirring beauty from the wise plantings and arrangements. Our lovely garden setting also allowed Drewry Sr. to enjoy the outside nature world along with its restoring effects and desired seclusion. In the spring the crabapple tree, several white dogwoods, masses of camellias, forsythia, various spireas, weigelia, and cydone Japonica were in full glory. Also, Darwin tulips and daffodils offered splendor and accents. The iris of every color came next, and the old fashioned day lilies, the masses of heavenly blue larkspur under the fragrant small locust lured, and the honeysuckle hedge gave whiffs of haunting enchantment. Our large pecan tree produced large quantities of paper shell nuts in the fall. There were also less dramatic flowers—like blue phlox, zinnias, spider lilies, Rose of Sharon (althea), and Peruvian lilies for after summer bloom. Drewry Sr. spent hours in this retreat, and I would come home for lunch to enjoy a few minutes of this beauty and enchantment.

I now began to supplement my income with teaching classes after school hours at the Norfolk Division of William and Mary College (1937-1939). I taught history of art and art appreciation. For one term I also taught appreciation of architecture and took the class on tours to see some of the old homes in Norfolk and Princess Anne County.² I painted when I could on Saturdays and Sundays. However, I often had to shop, put the house in order, or study instead. At one point, the Academy of Fine Arts in Richmond, Virginia invited me to have a one-woman show of my paintings. Mr. Thomas Parker, director of the academy and architect, came to see us and selected a group of my paintings. The show (or exhibition) was held for two weeks beginning on March 21, 1934. It was held at the old Academy Building, facing Capitol Square and the governor's mansion. Mr. Parker insisted that I come to the reception on the first day of the showing, and he telephoned my friend Mrs. Fred Barrett and told her to bring me. There was a snowstorm on that Sunday and we could not drive, so Mrs. Barrett and I went on the train and we stayed at the Hotel Richmond. The reception was lovely and I received excellent publicity.

During this period I was president of the Norfolk Artists Group and we were allowed to use a fine store in the Selden Arcade for our exhibitions. We bought monk cloth and I—with the help of Polly Baldwin, Lillian Banks, and two of the students in my art class at Maury—paneled the walls. We had some excellent exhibitions in the heart of downtown Norfolk. Every artist was working to do his best paintings for display. From time to time I had also assembled some stunning artwork of children from the Norfolk Public Schools at various places—the Wainwright Building, the Norfolk Museum, and at the schools. In 1935, I was told by the Norfolk Education Association that the schools should have a large exhibition of children's work at the Norfolk Museum. This celebration was to commemorate the two hundredth anniversary of Norfolk (1736-1936). While I thought that this event was very important, I did not wish to go through the difficulties of gathering up work, hanging the display, hostessing, making a catalog, and managing the publicity of such a large affair each year under the restrictions imposed by the museum. Furthermore, the undertaking took so much time from teaching—work had to be selected, carefully mounted for display, properly coordinated, and I had to haul it in my car unless some school would offer to take its share. Maury High School generally took their ceramic creations. So what would I do?

I thought and thought, and finally suggested that having a historical pageant would be a fine way. I had to do all the research on Norfolk and show how we could take each event and dramatize it. Well, I had to do much talking and I finally persuaded the school administration that I could really put the show on wheels, and at little cost. They had grave doubts quite often and called a meeting at the school board office of all the principals and supervisors. The manual training director fought the idea, and kept saying that the children would fall off the trucks. I told him that I would glue the children on! I later went to the Chevrolet factory at Campostella and asked them to please lend us some trucks. They promised to lend thirty new trucks, to furnish drivers for each vehicle, and to put five gallons of gasoline in each. This was beyond my expectations. At the factory, I was also allowed to make a drawing of a truck to know what space there was, where I could fasten material, and where I could place children. I later had this sheet of measurements and details mimeographed to give to the art teachers or anyone else who needed it. Finally, after many doubts on the part of the school administration and directors, it was decided to go on with my plans and the Pageant of Norfolk. So, I planned "The History, Tragedy, Romance, Industry, and Progress of Norfolk," from 1607 through 1935, and it was catalogued under the Norfolk Education Association.

The starting event of the historical milestones we planned to commemorate was the "Planting of the Cross at Cape Henry" on April 26, 1607. In 1621, Adam Thoroughgood came at the age of eighteen and settled on his English grant of 5,350 acres of land that fronted on the Chesapeake and Lynnhaven Bays.[3] It was his reward for bringing in one hundred and five new colonists. Before 1640, he built a home of such enduring sturdiness and beauty that it still stands for our admiration as one of the oldest homes surviving from the days of the first English colonists. Colonial Norfolk later received the priceless gift of the famous Silver Mace in 1754—a badge of royal authority from the Honorable Robert Dinwiddie, "His Majesty's lieutenant governor and commander-in-chief in this Dominion."[4] There is said to be only one other such mace in this country—that of the State of South Carolina—in the state house at Columbia. Other major events were the Revolutionary War's Battle of Great Bridge (December 9th, 1775), the Burning of Norfolk in 1776, the construction of the nation's first lighthouse at Cape Henry in 1792, a lamplighter of old Norfolk in 1811, the Civil War's Battle of the Ironclads in 1862, and so on to the peace and prosperity of a Greater Norfolk.

I was determined that this undertaking would be a success. I won the complete support of the art teachers, and I told them that they could telephone me at my home, or any place, at any hour if they needed help. I then lived through a period of eating my dinner at the telephone. I generally talked from dark until nine o'clock in trying to iron out difficulties, and I went from school to school boosting the construction or acting for the tableaux. I urged the school people to study the history of Norfolk, and I assigned each school a part. I remember especially the float that showed the first American settlers planting the cross in 1607 because it was so troublesome. The art teacher was in tears over making the sand dunes. We finally used chicken wire, paper mache, and paint—upon which we threw sand. Principal Lucy Keeling later insisted on buying an expensive silk flag for the float when we could have taken a piece of cloth and painted the royal flag, with its Cross of St. George, very effectively. Then, we had to study all of the costumes from the 1606 period, including those worn by gentlemen, seamen, and laborers. We built a replica of the first Norfolk train (1834) and children delighted in riding on it. Also, the replica of Black Beard's pirate ship was so dramatic and breath taking as the wooden swords clashed.

Then came the catalogs, and I was told that the words must be counted and limited (this from the printing shop at the school). Our publicity was poor, so I went to the editor of the *Virginian Pilot* and showed him my manuscript (or draft) of the ceremony. The editor (Mr. Jaffee) later borrowed the draft. The newspapers took fine pictures of the floats, as they were assembled the day before the event, and the day of the pageant. These pictures covered pages of the morning newspaper. Therefore, we had an enthusiastic crowd on the downtown streets. The designated day, November 15, 1935, was rather cold with a threatening rain. However, after debating it was decided to go ahead. The pageant was superb! Only it moved too fast for a person to read the story of the event and see all the details at the same time. This was the fault of the chairman I had selected for the moving procession, for he decided the space between floats and the timing. I talked to him but could not budge him on the timing. Since it was cold I think he had stepped up the time.

The night of the event a dinner was given and praise was heaped on the Chevrolet Company, but not an art teacher nor I was present—we were exhausted. On the next day, two excellent editorials lavishly praised the Norfolk art department, but my name was not mentioned. I had asked Mr. Jaffee in advance not to feature me and focus instead on the historical events. Even today, the pamphlet is used by the Chamber of Commerce and is also studied in the schools. However, the Norfolk Wednesday Club noticed this accomplishment and I was voted unanimously to be a member. I received a letter, dated November 3rd, 1935, asking me to be a member of their group. This was a very learned literary club, composed of thirty cultured Norfolk women. I became a member and was assigned to write a paper on "Richardson: The Middle Class Spirit and the Novel." I read and reread his *Carisso Harlow* and some other writings. This was the beginning of the novel and it evolved from the form of the letter in style. The next year I was given the subject "Primitive Thought in Japan and the Gospel of the White Lotus." I went to the library to prepare and in time read thirty books. The ladies of the club were intelligent and gracious, but I just did not have the time to prepare papers on such subjects, and I in fact preferred to use my time for painting. Consequently, I resigned with regrets.

By this time, Drewry Jr. had developed many resources within himself. He made beautiful model airplanes, like the model of the "Winnie May" from purchased plans, and others that were creatively designed. He also set up an acting bar in the yard and chinned. Further, he made a sawdust pit and pole-vaulted. Meanwhile, the gym class at the school used him on the second team of basketball, as he was not tall enough for the first team. Drewry Jr. also made a fine rowboat in the back yard from plans. In the summer, he took a job as a truck driver at Groves Market, and he supported the family through the season on that salary. In the fall, he went to V.P.I. in Blacksburg, and Drewry Sr. and I made the trip with him. By this time, I wrote him letters while struggling to pay the bills for tuition, board, clothes, expensive textbooks on electrical engineering, and drawing instruments. When the Thanksgiving and Christmas holidays came, we went to the college in our car and Drewry Jr. loved to drive back to Norfolk. I remember I once sent him a check to pay for his return home by bus. However, the check was delayed in arriving and Drewry Jr. decided to hitchhike home instead. Eventually, an undertaker picked him up and offered him a big cigar. Drewry Jr. rode on with him and enjoyed chatting, but at Blackstone the journey ended. He then waited and waited on the road for some car to take him. Finding no success, he called me on the telephone that night and reversed the call. I was half sick with a cold, but I responded and went to the drugstore to buy some cold pills. I then drove off into the night with Drewry Sr. acting as escort. We finally found a very impatient Drewry Jr. at the hotel at Crews, Virginia, and he then drove us home.

In the autumn, the honeysuckle on the banks along the road offered all its fragrance, and coming forth in the night air gave a haunting, nostalgic mood. There were often heavy fogs, and riding the narrow roads with steep slopes was perilous. I would sometimes make the speed of five miles per hour at these dangerous places. We often made trips to Washington, D.C. during this time to see the art displays at the Phillips Gallery, the Corcoran, and at the beautiful National Gallery after it was built.[5] I especially studied the modern art at the Phillips Gallery. I always enjoyed Daumier, Cezanne, and Matisse. I also liked Renoir's vital and gay *Boating Party*, which combined landscape, portraiture, and still life in one with the gaiety of French life. We sometimes stopped at the George Mason Hotel in Alexandria, or often visited my sister, Jo Stuart Grover, at Jefferson Park in Alexandria.

On November 20, 1936, we went to the little town of Stuart, Virginia to witness the unveiling of a statue of my grandfather, General J.E.B. Stuart.[6] We three went and invited Frances Hogarth (wife of Lieutenant Commander Percy Hogarth) to go with us. We spent the night at a motel and started early to get to the ceremony in time. When about three miles before we reached the place, Drewry Jr. announced that the gas in the car was running out.

Unfortunately, we could not find a gas station. Drewry Jr. did manage to coast down the hills and reach the parking lot, allowing us to walk to the grandstand while the band was starting. Lt. Gov. James H. Price gave a splendid unveiling address.[7] The Stuart Junior Book Club had sponsored the undertaking and had received contributions from all over the state. A great pleasure to me was walking after the ceremony to the places where my grandfather had lived and made adventurous trips. The town of Stuart had been called Taylorsville, Virginia back in his day.[8] The road to Laurel Hill climbed the mountainside where the old Stuart home had been (it had later been destroyed by fire.) However, my great-grandfather, Archibald Stuart (father of General J.E.B Stuart), was buried there. As such, I knelt in reverence and offered a short prayer, gathered a few roots of vinca (or blue periwinkle) from the grave, and brought it home to plant around my door.

At the end of the summer in 1939, we attended the World's Fair. Drewry Jr. drove and we planned to stop at Flushing, New York to find accommodations and then make the trip by bus or taxi to the fair grounds. However, Drewry Jr. followed the arrow markers and before we knew it we were in the fair grounds. Our car was parked with thousands of others in the lot. As we were interested in different exhibits, we decided to separate and meet again at a certain place. Drewry Jr. was so interested in the new invention of television, and spent his time looking at the dots. Drewry Sr. sought out the aquacade and bathing beauties and watched them dive. I was interested in the contemporary art and the old world exhibitions. It was Labor Day as well as the fair's final day, and the crowd was immense. My body was quite sore afterwards from the bumping by the passing crowd. We later found our car after a search and started for home. We discovered the Howard Johnson restaurants along the way and found them to be attractive and elegant.

During these years I took night classes at William and Mary College at Norfolk. Miss Eunice Hall taught secondary education, Miss Ruth Livermon taught visual education, and Dr. Ferguson taught biology. I took all of these courses and made "A's" on all except for a course in German language under Mrs. Korn, for which I received a "B." Only one "A" was given, to a German girl. Then Charlotte Dadmun, a Norfolk school principal and friend, persuaded me to take a course in field guidance with her on Saturdays in Williamsburg under Dr. Helseth. We had to be in the classroom by nine o'clock in the morning, and that meant much driving and crossing Hampton Roads on an early ferry in the morning. However, the work was very interesting and I enjoyed the trips immensely.

My problems at school seemed to increase. Art teachers were difficult to find and while applicants usually had some art training, they often had no teaching experience and found a large city confusing. I was constantly told that I must "induct" them. I held meetings and demonstrated creative teaching. I also gave them books to read, and they later drafted reports for me. I would later go over their problems and advise them. Overall, I visited forty-two schools in the city. At the end of the school term in June I was always worn out. However, I was told one year that they needed me to teach at the teacher's workshop that was held at the new Granby High School for two or three weeks.[9] The art course was to be recreational and no credit was allowed. It was so hot, and I broke out with heat. Nevertheless, the teachers taking the class were so interested and made me feel like I was really helping them. However, I was shocked to learn that I did not receive any pay for this work.

Meanwhile, Drewry Jr. took our car and went to some dances of the Junior Cotillion Club at Norfolk, and he seemed to enjoy this pleasure. There was a Depression and he could not immediately find work following his graduation from V.P.I. He went constantly to see the Virginia Electric and Power Company and told them that he was available for a job of any kind. This company finally accepted him and gave him various tasks to teach him, such as measuring soft coal by measuring the cubic space. This was a dirty job! Next, he ran up and down steps to register the gauge on the pumps at the station. He then cleaned out dead crabs from the wire nets. This was smelly!

Drewry McRee Smith Jr., circa 1940 (Courtesy of Sharon Stuart McRee).

Finally, Mr. Rose passed him on to the main office. Once there, they sent him to the outlying districts on surveying jobs. Upon returning, this information was transferred to map making for new poles. Drewry Jr. then became very interested in designing a general truck with many compartments for different tools. He consulted all of the workers and made note of what they needed in space. Drewry Jr. went into this work with enthusiasm and zest.

Later, he bought a Johnson five-horse power motor on the installment plan for the rowboat he had built. Drewry Jr. was trying to decide where to place the boat. On one hot day in August I saw an ad about a waterfront lot on the Lynnhaven River in Princess Anne County. On a Saturday, I called the agent, Mr. Whitt O. Sessoms, and told him that I was interested and he said that he would show us the place. Drewry Sr. and I went with him and when we returned home I had made up my mind. I said that I wanted the place. "All right," said Mr. Sessoms, "just pay me one dollar and I will give you a contract of sale." So I did that, and in November I would have to produce some cash and sign a deed of trust for the balance. After paying the balance, Drewry Sr. said to me, "I would like to know how you could do that."

In the meantime, a Norfolk lawyer named Mr. Richardson (who had been looking at the place for six months and could not make up his mind to buy it) came upon us on Sunday as we were burning trash from our house, the servant's room, and the garage outside. Mr. Richardson asked me if I had bought the place and I said, "Yes!" However, I did not tell him that I only paid one dollar. Then, he asked, "Why did you buy this place?" "What do you see in it?" I frankly told him that the place was complete and had well water, electricity, screens, and a hot water heater. It was also in the heart of the country, it had beautiful trees, oyster grounds, and best of all, it was only a short drive from Norfolk (about thirty-five minutes). He went to Mr. Sessoms the next day and tried to break my contract. Next, he offered Mr. Sessoms five hundred dollars for me to turn my contract over to him. To that, Drewry Sr. said, "now you can make five hundred dollars without lifting your hand, why don't you do it?" This made me anxious because I wanted the place. I saw great possibilities in the undertaking, and I thought especially of Drewry Sr. and the peace of the place. Therefore, I consulted a lawyer and he said, "Just hold your contract, and on the day mentioned in November be sure to be there to pay as the contract stipulates. No one can take away your rights." So I did that, and I now have a beautiful place on the Lynnhaven River, all debt free, and worth many times more than what I paid.

The days at our new home, "Drewmar," on the beautiful Lynnhaven rushed by all too quickly. There were always the little demons pinching and poking me, saying: "Go to the bank—go for groceries—take your laundry—go to the spring for drinking water—go to the school board office—tidy the house—

get the car overhauled—take suits to the cleaners," and so on—a thousand petty duties that make the framework of daily living. However, around the corners was the magical plan of this place. Drewry Sr. and I spent a lot of time studying its leaves. We found Post Oak, Black Jack (or Scrub Oak), Chestnut Oak, Laurel Oak, Willow Oak, Scarlet Oak, White Oak, Live Oak–all on our acres. We also had the Black Cherry, Red Cedar, White Cedar, Dogwood, Virginia Bay, Red Maple, Hickory, American Holly, Swamp Magnolia, Scrub Pine, and maybe some others. This was part of Pungo Ridge and the tail end of the Dismal Swamp area. We also had lovely birds and wild flowers in the summers. The towhee often sang and fed near the porch. Small Mrs. Wren would establish herself in a basket of sticks and grasses in our garage, and often lay several gray-tan eggs almost in full view. The Day Lilies and Deep Garnet Petunias were always lovely during this time. I also had a victory garden of peppers, tomatoes, and okra. First, the brown rabbit would eat up the tender tops, and then the green grasshoppers would finish the business.

Meanwhile, after about a year or so with the Virginia Electric and Power Company, Drewry Jr. took a government examination. He was sick with a bad cold on the day the test went off but he went anyway. He returned saying that he was sure that he had failed—but remarked, "when I could not answer one problem, I moved on to the next, and the whole examination was timed." His engineering professor at V.P.I. told him that not any V.P.I. man had ever

Drewmar on the Lynnhaven (Courtesy of Sharon Stuart McRee).

passed, but he urged Drewry Jr. to try anyway. Well—Drewry Jr. made third place. Then a telegram came saying that a position was open at the Navy Yard and that he was third choice—would he accept? The position involved doing clerical work at the Navy Yard. Drewry Jr. wrote "yes," but an older friend of his named Simenson was first choice and accepted the offer. He had a fellowship at V.P.I. when Drewry Jr. was there and had also completed graduate work. A second notice then came saying that a position was open at Langley Field, and that he was in second place for the job. However, the first place choice, Drewry Jr.'s friend Thurmer Hazzard ultimately accepted the position. Drewry Jr. became quite restless and impatient, but during all this time he was being promoted to more responsible work at the Virginia Electric and Power Company. Then came the third notice, which was the best of all—a position at the David Taylor Model Basin at Carderock, Maryland.[10] Drewry Jr. lost no time accepting this offer—and he bought a pretty second hand Dodge Roadster and left us, also leaving behind his boat motor.

For the winter, we returned in late November to the Dunkirk home in Norfolk. Consequently, the deserted place on the Lynnhaven attracted thieves who broke a windowpane and unlatched the window to get inside the house. Upon later inspection, we found two birds that had entered by the broken windows. There was some disorder as the thieves had hurriedly searched the premises, and barefoot tracks were visible on the dusty floor. They took Drewry Jr.'s boat motor, which was standing in a corner of the kitchen. They also took four pieces of my grandmother's Queen Anne silver service (leaving me only two large pots for coffee and hot water) and an old Rosewood clock with Seth Thomas' works,[11] leaving the key on the clock shelf. In the sideboard they found wrapped up in several newspapers an old double-lined silver water pitcher with the two-headed James on the top lid. Drewry Sr.'s grandfather, William Drewry Smith of Fayetteville, North Carolina, had left this treasure to my husband and his namesake. With this token of affectionate remembrance gone, Drewry Sr. had only two little books handed down to him from this fine ancestor he never saw. The grandfather had married a second time and the last wife received most of his earthly possessions. Drewry Sr. cherishes a copy of the New Testament in very fine print and a wee copy of *Pilgrim's Progress*[12] as a precious link into the past and from his grandfather's possessions. The inscription in the much worn New Testament mentions "Hobah Grove" of Fayetteville, North Carolina as his plantation. However, Drewry Sr. was born in far away Texas and his grandfather never saw him.

[*Unfortunately, the thefts continued for Marrow and her family during this time.*] While we were staying at Dunkirk with a few possessions, Drewry Jr. returned from Washington to visit us at the Christmas holiday. I urged him to bring in his two suits and suitcase, but he left his car on the street with the trunk unlocked. During the night his technical books were stolen along with several pairs of shoes. What he loved most was also gone—his logbook of flying with every flying record signed, dated, and described. Drewry Jr. had paid for his lessons in Washington and had only to complete his solo flight. I always felt that this was the Lord's blessing on me as well as an answer to my prayers. There was no doubt in my mind that once Drewry Jr. had finished his flying courses and met his requirements, he would have been drafted into the U.S. Air Force for overseas flying.

However, he stayed at the Model Basin during the duration of the war and fumed and fumed over not wearing a uniform. He was always told at each bus station, "uniform men first!" I told him that many men were selected to carry a gun, but his engineering contribution was important. He tried in every way for a release to go to the front, but had to stay in Washington and see the sailors and soldiers go forth (many not to return). Drewry Jr.'s friends became officers and I know the anguish that he suffered. At the end of the war he was given a small service button. I remember one project he worked on was "airtight doors" for the Navy. His findings were written in reports and some

Drewry McRee Smith Jr. and his wife, Lt. Cmdr. Faith Samson Smith, USN, circa 1946 (Courtesy of Sharon Stuart McRee).

were sent to London, England. A good many reports were secretive and he did not talk about them. On one occasion, Drewry Jr. came for a week and asked me to invite his friend, Lt. Cmdr. Faith Samson of the WAVES,[13] who was very interesting. She was from Iowa and her people were originally from Vermont. She had a personnel position in Washington, D.C. and she expected to be in the Navy for another year. Drewry Jr. met her at a cocktail party, I believe. While they were at Drewmar they had a motorboat ride, a dance at the Surf Club, and a swim at Virginia Beach. I liked her ever so much and even then suspected that she would some day be my new daughter—and she eventually was.

A few years later, Drewry Jr., Faith, and their baby, Sharon, were visiting us at our Lynnhaven home. A beautiful day in November 1948 was moving to twilight and chill. An enlargement of our kitchen was in process, but the tools were put away and a blazing fire of cedar driftwood was adding an air of comfort, cheer, and aromatic fragrance. However, the family could not settle down for supper because the baby would not go to sleep in the upstairs room—all was suspense and waiting. Eight o'clock came and some of us had supper. Suddenly, the fire in the fireplace seemed to send up clouds of smoke and an offensive, sulfurous odor that we thought came from the salt-soaked driftwood. Meanwhile, a hidden electrical wire was smoldering. Drewry Jr. rushed outside and returned saying, "Mom, your house is on fire!" Faith came downstairs bringing the baby, whose little eyes were smarting from the smoke. Drewry Jr. set up a stepladder outside and called for water. I took bucket after bucket to him, climbing the ladder each time while Drewry Sr. drew the water in the kitchen as fast as the old pump would give it. Then I heard the fateful words, "bring an axe—it is beyond control—call the fire department!" However, the telephone line was dead or burned out, and the lights soon went out.

I started with baby Sharon lying on the front seat in my car for a point of safety and to a neighbor to call the volunteer fire company. As I drove I partly held the child with one hand and managed to blow the horn constantly and guide the wheel. The new neighbors, about one half mile from my home, had all their lights on but seemed unconcerned. The next place I sought help was closed, as that neighbor was on her vacation. So I drove to the Griffins and around the circular driveway and stalled my car in a group of trees. I left the baby on the Griffins' bed and returned to the burning house with Mr. Griffin in his car. Meanwhile, Mrs. Griffin asked two talkers on the telephone to please in the emergency let her call the fire department at London Bridge. Firemen came in twenty minutes with a tank of rusty water—and at their heels, cars and cars and cars-these blocked all roads and nearly made it impossible for our fire engine to get more water. Mr. Griffin said, "make up your mind to accept the fact that *your house is gone!*"

Cold chills passed over me—then a fireman forbade me to enter the house. He asked, "Is there anything you wish to save?" I answered, "Yes, my diamond engagement ring and my father's handsome old black walnut desk with inlaid holly and lovely brass Chippendale handles." However, I was unable to put into words just which secret drawer held my ring—so I was allowed to get that and went directly to it. Faith was saving my historical blue Staffordshire china by tossing it into bushel farm baskets. My son and husband were bringing down my paintings as fast as they could and putting them around on the ground. Strong men pulled out an old pewter cupboard and tripped over the raised door sill. I then heard the crash of Venetian glass and other choice pieces. I stood in a trance of grief and sorrow. Then, I saw people unknown to me stepping nearer and nearer to my disheveled treasures and looking over things on the ground. I immediately became a major general, shouting, "Will you please stand back! Will you please not come so near!" Fortunately, they heeded.

Meanwhile, strong men moved furniture outdoors, including the Hepplewhite mahogany dining table, the Frigidaire, and old chairs. Pillows and mattresses were hurled from the upstairs aflame, but not in time. Twin beds burned, along with my grandmother's old bookcase-writing desk that she had a cabinet-man make to suit her when she was at Stuart Hall. Five bookcases of treasured art books, an old walnut dresser, an old shaving mirror, chairs, curtains, paintings, and all of our clothes also burned. Axes chopped, water flowed, and flames leaped—then the fury of the fire abated and firemen faithfully stayed to see if it would revive. I learned that the Oceana Volunteer Fire Company came and brought an experienced Norfolk fireman who had been visiting to direct them. Thus, the lower floor was saved but was swimming in water. The crowd later left, and as I looked at the great charred beams pointing skyward I sighed deeply—and I saw the disorder surrounding this terrible catastrophe. Where would we sleep? Where would we live? Where would we start? The Griffins soon invited us to their home. I was touched but could not bring myself to walk away from an unlocked house and a yard brimming with our spared possessions. My son, his wife, and their baby accepted the thoughtful consideration for their comfort, while my husband and I tucked ourselves into our car and waited for the dawn. Then, the Griffins returned and brought us a tray with steaming coffee, rich cream, and delicious cake. Outside of this there was weariness, lost hope, cold wetness, desolation, and heartbreak.

At dawn I wiped the dew from our beautiful Hepplewhite table and was thankful to God that we had no human accidents. Then I went up the burned stairs and saw the ashes one foot deep over the damaged floor with no roof overhead. In the dwelling there was no water, no heat, no telephone, no

clock, no place to sleep, no place to fix a hot meal, and no clothes—just
cinders everywhere. Faith had packed her suitcase while I was getting help.
These suitcases were safe in her car at the entrance circle of our road. The
next morning they left for Washington, as it was our wish. Then came the
sifting and removing of the ashes and loading of paintings, Persian rugs, silver, and small objects in my car to take to Norfolk for storage in a friend's
home. We could not leave the unprotected wreck of our home, so we set up
life in the desolation and crumbled ruins and proceeded to comb the ashes.
A Northeaster came and rain poured while we mopped all night and moved
everything we could to one dry corner. The misery of these days is burned
in my memory. After this I prayed that I would always have a roof over my
head. One can live above material possessions, yet sometimes attachment for
such things through the years and their loss is like losing a dear one. However, time can soften all tragedy.

NOTES

1. Founded in 1930, the Norfolk Division of the College of William and Mary
was later renamed Old Dominion College in 1962. It gained university status in 1969,
and is now known as Old Dominion University.

2. Established in 1691, Princess Anne County was consolidated into the City of
Virginia Beach in 1963.

3. Adam Thoroughgood (1604–1640) was one of the first Englishmen to settle in
the area that later became Virginia Beach. A home in the area built by his descendants
in the 1720s, known as the Thoroughgood House, is now listed in the U.S. National
Register of Historic Places.

4. Robert Dinwiddie (1693–1770) served as lieutenant governor of Virginia from
1751 to 1758.

5. Established in 1937, the National Gallery of Art opened its doors to the public
in 1941.

6. This is likely the statue honoring Patrick County's Civil War soldiers (that
includes a plaque honoring General Stuart) located at the Patrick County Courthouse.

7. James H. Price (1878–1943) was later Virginia's 53rd governor, serving from
1938 to 1942.

8. First incorporated as the town of Taylorsville, Virginia in 1792, it was later
renamed Stuart, Virginia in 1884 in honor of General Stuart.

9. Granby High School was opened in 1939 and later renovated and expanded in
1996. It is named after General John Manners, Marquis of Granby (1721–1770), who
was a hero of the Seven Years War.

10. Built in 1939, the David Taylor Model Basin is one of the largest ship model
basins in the world. It serves as a test facility for the development of ship design.

11. Seth Thomas (1785–1859) of Connecticut was a famous American clock
maker.

12. *The Pilgrim's Progress from This World to That Which Is to Come* is a Christian Allegory written by John Bunyan that was first published in 1678. It is considered to be one of the most significant works of English literature and it has never been out of print.

13. The WAVES were a World War II-era division of the U.S. Navy. It stood for "Women Accepted for Volunteer Emergency Service." It was essentially a women's component of the U.S. Navy, where females held the same rank and ratings as male personnel.

Epilogue

Although the 1948 fire at Drewmar was a traumatic experience, Marrow and Drewry Sr. eventually recovered. They gradually restored their beloved home and had a new second floor constructed. Within a short period of time, life returned to normal for the couple, allowing them to focus their energies on other pursuits. In 1949, Marrow concluded her nineteen-year tenure as Director of Art Education for the Norfolk Public School System.[1] However, she was one year shy of thirty years of total service with the school division, and needed one more to qualify for full state retirement benefits. She therefore worked an additional year as a sixth grade art teacher with Virginia Beach Public Schools, retiring for good in 1950.[2] Drewry Sr. suffered from painful arthritis and other medical problems and had already retired several years before. Marrow enjoyed retirement immensely, as it allowed her more time to pursue her favorite activities such as painting.

The 1950s and 1960s were busy decades for Marrow. She offered art lectures regularly at the Chrysler Museum and was a founder of the Virginia Beach Boardwalk Art Show. Along with serving as president of the Tidewater Artists Association, Marrow was also an active member of the Norfolk Art Corner and the Virginia Beach Arts Center.[3] Even in Marrow's later years, people within the local art community considered her an expert with a wealth of knowledge about event coordination, art history, and art appreciation. Marrow was also active with her church, Eastern Shore Chapel Episcopal Church, off of Laskin Road in Virginia Beach. She enjoyed being around people and maintained an active presence in the community. However, Marrow also loved spending time at Drewmar, particularly outside where she could enjoy the vibrant colors of the water, flowers, birds, and trees. Never keen on television, she and Drewry Sr. enjoyed listening to operas on their vintage Victrola record player in the evenings. Visitors often marveled at Drewry Sr.'s singular talent for whistling, describing it as a unique gift. As he listened to the music, he could whistle note-for-note entire operas in perfect pitch![4]

Along with her other activities, Marrow loved spending time with children. For many years, Drewmar was a focal point for neighborhood youth, who would spend time there under her supervision painting, working on arts and crafts, or playing outside. With Marrow's extensive background in education and early childhood development, parents were delighted to have their children spend time with such a positive role model. One such child who was profoundly influenced by Marrow's mentoring was Stephanie Tucker Little, who is now a noted singer/songwriter. Stephanie first met Marrow when she was a young girl living only a short distance from Drewmar. Possessing her own artistic talent as a musician, Stephanie was drawn immediately to Marrow, and regarded her as a friend, advisor, counselor, and unofficial grandmother.[5] Many years later, Stephanie reflected on the important influence that Marrow had on her life:[6]

Marrow was the most remarkable person I have ever met! She really was a brilliant person in mind, spirit, and looks, and had a glow about her that I have never really seen in anyone else. Marrow had the most charming way about her. She always smiled at me and had the most beautiful twinkle in her eyes. I really loved to look at Marrow's face—it just beamed radiantly! We were like kindred spirits, as she had so much child left in her... she had never lost it. Her wonder in everything was amazing, and she and I shared our outlook in life in that way.

At Drewmar, we would sit together outside, overlooking the water in a grand view on a concrete bench that was lovely. Marrow would tell me her feelings about the water, the land, and their colors. As I grew older and drove to see her, she would want me to help her pick up sticks in her vast yard. It was a fruitless venture since there were millions of them, but I would do it anyway. I think she found it to be therapeutic. Afterwards, we would talk some more and eat together.

Following meals, Marrow had a lovely, quaint phrase she would always say when she was full, saying "I've had my sufficiency." She would not take a bite after that. Marrow always said it with so much grace! She was the epitome of a lovely, aristocratic, Southern lady. Marrow was such a wonderful hostess when we ate, too. Everything had to be just so and the setting of the tableware was exquisite. She used her china and expected proper manners, which thankfully I guess I had. Upon my departure, I always thanked Marrow for everything, and she always had a smile and a hug for me.

Meanwhile, my interests turned toward music at a very young age, and I give Marrow credit for nurturing my fragile self-esteem and facilitating my learning how to play the guitar. I brought my guitar to Marrow and Drewry's house, and being shy, would only play outside on the porch where they could only hear me. They both seemed so happy that I had my guitar with me and Marrow really appeared to enjoy hearing me play and sing. She was always sweet like that—never an unkind word. Marrow had a lot of patience as well. She moved easily through life and saw beauty in everything. In the end, it was Marrow who encouraged me with my music, giving me the confidence I needed at such a young and fragile time in my life.

Marrow lived a good life—a wonderful life. Her gifts to me, her spirit, smile, and charm will stay with me all of my days. I will always treasure her memory. Marrow shaped and molded my very spirit and helped me to become the person who I am now. Through the years, I have had several friends who also happened to be artists. However, none can compare to the splendor and magic of Marrow, or can see through her eyes the beauty in every living thing.

While Marrow and Drewry Sr. were enjoying their retirement years, Drewry Jr. was busy raising his own family and advancing his career. In the years following World War II, numerous job opportunities in the aerospace and defense industries became available on the West Coast, particularly in the Los Angeles area. As such, Drewry Jr., Faith, and their young daughter Sharon moved to California in 1952.[7] Over the next several years, he worked in the vanguard of the space age for companies such as Hughes, Douglas Aircraft, and Rockwell.[8] His last position was with the Naval Weapons Laboratory.[9] Along the way, Drewry Jr. and Faith had a son, Drewry McRee "Drew"

Marrow Stuart Smith, circa 1960 (Courtesy of Sharon Stuart McRee).

Smith III, who was born in August 1952. The couple later divorced in 1968 when Drew was in high school. With aging parents who needed his help, Drewry Jr. decided to move back to Virginia following his retirement in 1970.[10] Caring for his parents at Drewmar quickly became a full-time job, as Marrow and Drewry Sr. spent their final years in poor health, requiring constant attention. However, Drewry Jr. never complained about these responsibilities, even though they offered him few social or vacation opportunities.[11] His efforts allowed his parents to spend their last years in the comfort of their own home, surrounded by their flowers, trees, and an assortment of wild creatures. Drewry Sr. passed away in October 1974, at the age of eighty-four. Marrow followed eleven years later, passing away at the age of ninety-six in August 1985. Both were buried in the Eastern Shore Chapel cemetery in Virginia Beach.[12]

Following Marrow's death, Drewry Jr. remained at Drewmar until 1988, when he sold the property and returned to California to be near his family. He enjoyed his "second" retirement immensely and engaged in a multitude of interests, including the study of economics, political science, international affairs, and alternative medicine.[13] He was also active in writing and even cartooning. Along with his other hobbies, Drewry Jr. spent a great deal of

Drewry McRee Smith Jr., with his son and grandson, circa 1987. From left to right— Drewry McRee Smith IV, Drewry Jr., and Drewry McRee Smith III (Courtesy of the Smith Family).

time traveling. In 1991, he even moved briefly to Mexico in order to attend a language school and continue his studies in Spanish. In September 1994, Drewry Jr. suffered a fatal stroke while he was on vacation in New Zealand, passing away at the age of seventy-seven.[14] His memorial service and burial were held at the Eastern Shore Chapel Episcopal Church in Virginia Beach, where his mother had been a longtime member.[15]

Drewry Jr. and Faith's children, Sharon and Drew, continued to lead active and interesting lives following their father's death. Although they grew up in California, they spent a great deal of time at Drewmar during vacations and each lived there for extended periods as adults. They knew their grandparents and other Stuart relatives well. Sharon studied law and was one of a small number of women admitted to the California bar and U.S. District Court (federal bar) in 1976. She went on to specialize in international adoption law, maintaining staff in Costa Rica for several years. Sharon later took up the specialty of estate planning and has published extensively on the topic, including two books and numerous other publications. She married a fellow attorney, Galen Griepp, in 1979 and now has two daughters, Ravenna and Romy. Ravenna, born in 1982, studied photography at Burren College of Art in Ireland and at Brooks Institute[16] and is an avid traveler. Romy, born in 1990, is currently a college student studying art history and English. Sharon and Galen now operate the law firm of Griepp & McRee in Pasadena, California, which specializes in estate planning.

Following his graduation from San Francisco State University, Drew went on to pursue a successful career in computer programming and business consulting, serving nearly twenty years with Hewlett-Packard in Palo Alto, California. He also completed an MBA from UCLA in 1979. In 1983, he married Cathy Hodge, a University of San Diego graduate who has dedicated her career to volunteer work and philanthropic initiatives. In 1985, the couple had a son, Drewry McRee Smith IV. Along with their other activities, Drew and Cathy currently care for Drew's mother, Faith, who was blinded in a 2002 accident. After attending Saddleback College, Drewry IV went on to graduate in 2010 from California State University–Fullerton. He is now a hospitality specialist and supervisor at one of Southern California's premier resorts.[17]

Like Marrow, her siblings went on to eventful and productive lives after spending their childhood years together. Following a short career in teaching, Flora moved to New York after marrying George MacKenzie "Mac" Garmany on August 22, 1918. A native New Yorker, Mac had earned his bachelor's degree from Princeton in 1911, followed by a master's degree from the University of Virginia in 1918, where he and Flora likely met.[18] During World War I, Mac had served as a first lieutenant in the U.S. Army Engineering Corps.[19] Following the war, Mac and Flora settled in Port Washington, New York and had a daughter, Jane Jasper Garmany, in 1921. Fol-

The Griepp Family in 2010. From left to right—Romy Griepp, Sharon Stuart McRee, Ravenna Griepp, and Galen Griepp (Courtesy of the Griepp Family).

The Smith Family in 2010. From left to right—Drewry McRee Smith III, Cathy Hodge Smith, and Drewry McRee Smith IV (Courtesy of the Smith Family).

lowing Mac's death in December 1957, Flora spent lots of time visiting her sisters in Virginia while maintaining a residence in New York. She passed away in April 1975 and was buried with her husband at Arlington National Cemetery. After attending St. Margaret's School in Tappahannock, Virginia, Jane went on to graduate from Adelphi University in Garden City, New York. As a trained nurse and laboratory assistant, she spent her career working in various hospitals and laboratories.[20] Following a short marriage to a man she met during a trip to California, Jane had a son named Patrick Cavanaugh in 1947. Patrick went on to become a teacher and now lives on Long Island with his family.[21]

Marrow's other sister, Jo Stuart Grover, endured great personal hardship following the premature passing of her husband, Luther Prescott "L.P." Grover. A Massachusetts native and 1917 Harvard University graduate, L.P. had pursued a successful career as a New York City investment banker before his death from appendicitis on August 24, 1933.[22] Before his passing, L.P. and Jo had three children together—Charles Frederick (born in 1920, and nicknamed "Fred"), Stuart (born in 1921), and Josephine Prescott (born in 1926, and nicknamed "Jo Pres").[23] Following L.P.'s death, Jo concluded her employment with Texaco in New York City and moved along with her children to Nashville, Tennessee, followed by another move to Norfolk, Virginia. A few years later, they moved again to Alexandria, Virginia, where Jo worked for the Department of War in Washington D.C., and its successor, the Department of Defense, at the Pentagon. Following her retirement, Jo moved to Virginia Beach and spent her final years in Hampton, Virginia, where she passed away on September 5, 1966. She was buried with her husband at his family's plot in Mount Auburn Cemetery in Cambridge, Massachusetts.[24]

Jo and L.P.'s eldest child, Charles Frederick Grover, went on to work for a Norfolk shipyard before serving as an engineering officer with the U.S. Merchant Marine during World War II. With his wife, Melda Frazier Wright, he had two children, Jo Stuart (known as "Josie") and Charles Frederick Jr. (nicknamed "Fred" like his father).[25] Following the war, Fred Sr. worked as a plant superintendent, product engineer, and salesman. He is now retired and living in Pennsylvania. Following her marriage to Louis A. Pais, Josie moved to North Carolina and went into the ministry. She and Louis had three children—Angela, Joette, and Melissa, and now have five grandchildren and two great-grandchildren.[26] Fred Jr. went on to become a teacher and later had five children with his wife, Margaret Wood Grover. Now retired and also living in Pennsylvania, Fred Jr. and Margaret have three grandchildren.

Jo and L.P.'s second child, Stuart Grover, went on to earn a master's degree from the University of Virginia. He served in the U.S. Army during World War II and passed away on January 27, 1947. Stuart was later buried at

Arlington National Cemetery. Jo and L.P.'s youngest child, Jo Pres, attended Madison College (now known as James Madison University) in Harrison- burg, Virginia, and later graduated from the University of Maryland–College Park. She spent her early career as a teacher and guidance counselor. Around 1950, she married Hall T. Righter, who was a chief warrant officer in the U.S. Army.[27] They had four sons together (Stephan, Stuart, Grover, and George), and were stationed in Japan, Germany, and Fort Monroe, Virginia before their divorce.[28] Jo Pres later resumed her teaching career in Hampton, Virginia and was married a second time to a man named William Kidder in the late 1970s. Following her retirement, Jo Pres resided in Newport News, Virginia until her death in 1996.[29]

As General Stuart's namesake, perhaps the most public attention was placed on Marrow's brother, J.E.B. Stuart III, as he and his sisters grew older. Following his 1928 marriage to Mary Brittain Hurt, J.E.B. III resided in New York City, where he and Mary lived in an apartment in the Chelsea District, before moving to Long Island in 1930. Possessing degrees from the University of Virginia and the Massachusetts Institute of Technology, J.E.B. III found work prior to his marriage as an engineer on the Panama Canal Zone. In 1922, he began working for the Consolidated Edison Company of New York (known as "Con-Edison"). Specializing in the areas of construc- tion and engineering, J.E.B. III held a number of positions with the company, ranging from assistant engineer to superintendent to assistant vice president. Along the way, J.E.B. III and Mary had two children—Olivia (born in 1931) and J.E.B. IV (born in 1935).[30]

Following his retirement in 1965, J.E.B. III became active in preserving his grandfather's historical legacy and reputation. An active member of the New York City Civil War Roundtable, he spoke regularly about General Stuart, defending his actions during the Gettysburg Campaign, and became well known among Civil War history enthusiasts.[31] J.E.B. III and Mary continued to live on Manhasset, Long Island until the late 1980s, when they moved to Richmond, Virginia to be closer to their son. J.E.B. III passed away on April 11, 1990, at the age of ninety-two. Mary passed away two years later, on January 4, 1992. The couple was buried in the Stuart plot at Richmond's Hol- lywood Cemetery, right next to General Stuart and his wife, Flora.[32]

Their daughter, Olivia, went on to pursue an active career in advertising and journalism. A Stuart Hall alumna, she went on to attend Mary Wash- ington College (now the University of Mary Washington) before graduating from West Virginia's Bethany College in 1953. Olivia held several jobs with advertising firms in New York City before marrying Keith McFadden, a Cali- fornia native and World War II veteran.[33] They had four daughters together, including Laurie (born in 1957), Pamela (born in 1961), Barbara (born in

1962), and Gayle (born in 1966). Pamela later passed away in June 1981. Following their long residence in New York, Olivia and Keith later retired and moved to the Phoenix, Arizona area, where Keith passed away in 2006. Today, Barbara and her family live near their mother in Arizona, while Laurie and Gayle live in Connecticut.[34]

Like many of his ancestors, J.E.B. Stuart IV pursued a military career. Following his 1958 graduation from the University of Virginia, he was commissioned a second lieutenant in the U.S. Army. Later that year, he married Richmond, Virginia native Mary Louise McNiel (known as "Weasie"), who had attended Mary Washington College. J.E.B. IV and Weasie went on to have three children—Elizabeth Pelham (born in 1960 and known as "Betsy"), J.E.B. V (born in 1962), and John Alexander (born in 1963). During his army career, J.E.B. IV served two tours in Vietnam during the late 1960s and early 1970s. After completing a master's degree from North Carolina State University in 1972, J.E.B. IV also graduated from the U.S. Army War College in 1973. He later retired from the army in 1985 with the rank of colonel.[35] Following his army retirement, J.E.B. IV and Weasie moved to Richmond, Virginia, where he currently works in the financial services industry. Along with his job duties, J.E.B. IV has been active in a number of clubs, societies, and civic organizations in the Richmond area. Most notably, he is a past president of the Sons of the Revolution's Virginia Society as well as a former chairman of the board of trustees for the Museum of the Confederacy.[36]

J.E.B. IV and Weasie's children, all of whom live in Virginia, have also led active lives. Following her graduation from Mary Washington College, Betsy married Scott Hoehne and became a homemaker. J.E.B. V completed degrees at Randolph-Macon College and Eastern Virginia Medical School, and is now a respected orthopedic surgeon. He also followed in his father's footsteps by serving in the U.S. Army, reaching the rank of lieutenant colonel. J.E.B. V is married to Kelly Curry Stuart and has three children, including J.E.B. Stuart VI, who is currently a college student. J.E.B. IV and Weasie's youngest son, John, graduated from Virginia Military Institute in 1985 and served for two years as a U.S. Army officer, where he was stationed in Germany. Married to Dona Mauny Stuart with two children, he now works for an engineering consulting firm. Notably, these descendants of Marrow's brother have been successful in carrying the name "J.E.B. Stuart" into the twenty-first century.[37]

Marrow's youngest sister, Elizabeth (known as "Lib"), experienced many highs and lows over the course of her long life. Following her divorce from Rorer A. "Buddie" James Jr. in the early 1930s, Lib took custody of their youngest daughter Anne (born in 1925), while her other daughter Elizabeth (born in 1920 and known as "Stuart") lived with Buddie.[38] The scion of a prominent Danville, Virginia family, Buddie was president of Register Pub-

Col. J.E.B. Stuart IV, U.S. Army (ret.) in 2009.

lishing as well as publisher of *The Danville Register & Bee* newspaper. He had inherited both companies from his father, Congressman Rorer A. James Sr., who had passed away in 1921. However, Buddie died unexpectedly in 1937 at the age of forty, leaving his ex-wife to care for both daughters. A few years later, Lib married a U.S. Army officer named Forstal Adams, but divorced shortly thereafter.[39] A shrewd investor, Lib later amassed a small fortune by buying and selling land for profit. In the 1950s and 1960s, she owned an expansive property in Virginia Beach near 57th Street and lived in one of the several houses on that site.[40] Lib made the other houses available to family members, making the property a home base for multiple family gatherings over the years. Such events gave Lib and her siblings a chance to spend time together, along with their children and grandchildren. Marrow was a regular visitor there and enjoyed taking her younger family members on hunts for crabs and oysters. As Lib got older, she enjoyed playing cards, sunbathing, and spending time with her grandchildren. She passed away in Newport News, Virginia in 1982 at the age of eighty-one.[41]

Lib's daughters, Stuart and Anne, went on to lead busy and active lives. Upon her father's passing, Stuart inherited ownership of the *The Danville*

Register & Bee at the age of seventeen.[42] After graduating from Stratford College,[43] she became president and sole owner of Register Publishing in 1941. In 1942, Stuart married Richmond native Walter L. Grant. A businessman and civic leader, he had served as a pilot in the U.S. Army Air Corps during World War II.[44] The couple eventually had four children, including Walter Jr. (known as "Lawson"), Helen, Elizabeth (known as "Betty"), and Rorer (known as "Buddy"). Walter ran the newspaper and publishing company from 1945 until 1972, when he died of a heart attack. In the years following his death, Stuart had a long succession of managers run the day-to-day operations of her businesses, including some of her children.[45]

While she continued as owner and publisher of her family's newspaper, Stuart spent much of her time engaged in philanthropic initiatives and civic engagement. She had a lifelong interest in historic preservation and served for many years on Danville's architectural review board. Stuart was also considered a pioneer in the preservation of Danville's unique Victorian architecture.[46] Further, she spearheaded the restoration of the birthplace of Lady Nancy Witcher Langhorne Astor,[47] the Danville native who married a British peer and eventually became the first woman to sit in the House of Commons. While Stuart was recognized for some of her philanthropic work, most of it was done in anonymity. Following her death in August 1990, both Register Publishing and *The Danville Register & Bee* were sold to fund the E. Stuart James Grant Charitable Trust, which has supported a variety of philanthropic causes throughout the state.[48] As recently as 2008, it was listed among the top fifty Virginia foundations in total giving.[49]

Lib's younger daughter, Anne, attended Chevy Chase Junior College[50] before marrying Robert W. Hundt in 1954 and moving to Connecticut. A New York native who attended the U.S. Merchant Marine Academy and Lehigh University, Robert served in the U.S. Navy during World War II. He later worked with Luria Brothers Company in New York.[51] Robert and Anne had two children, Elizabeth (known as "Bonnie") and William (known as "Brae"). In 1962, the family moved to Millbrook, New York, where they operated a sheep and dairy farm. Following her divorce from Robert in 1982, Anne returned to Virginia and purchased property on the Piankatank River in Middlesex County. She later passed away in September 1994 at the age of sixty-nine.[52] A graduate of Johnson State College in Vermont, Bonnie went on to marry Thomas C. "Tim" Moorhead Jr. in 1984. A native of Pittsburgh, Pennsylvania, Tim graduated from the University of Pennsylvania and later earned his law degree at Widener University.[53] Like Bonnie, he has a distinguished ancestry and is a direct descendant of Martha Washington, as well as Sir George Calvert, the 1st Baron Baltimore.[54] Bonnie and Tim eventually had twin sons, John Appleton and James Custis (born in May 1990), who are now college students. Brae went on to marry Karen Luongo in June 1995 and establish a pool installation business. He and Karen now live near the Piankatank River in Virginia with their family.[55]

Along with her siblings, Marrow was also close with her aunt, Virginia Stuart Waller, as well as her three Waller cousins, Flora (born in 1892), Matthew (born in 1894), and Virginia (born in 1896). As noted in her original memoirs, Marrow spent a lot of time with them in Norfolk following her Aunt Virginia's death in 1898. Her uncle, Robert Page Waller, passed away in 1923, shortly after the death of Marrow's grandmother, Flora Cooke Stuart. Despite losing their parents at relatively young ages, Marrow's Waller cousins went on to live active and productive lives. On September 17, 1923, Flora married Jonathan W. "J.W." Old, a Norfolk native who had studied law under an attorney in Petersburg. The couple eventually had two children—Jonathan W. "Johnny" Old Jr. (born in 1924), and Flora (born in 1926). J.W. went on to a distinguished career in municipal law, serving as Norfolk city attorney for twenty-eight years, before his retirement in 1957.[56] He was also a consultant to the Norfolk City Council and played a vital role in securing financial support for the construction of the Hampton Roads Bridge Tunnel in the 1950s. J.W. passed away in 1979, at the age of ninety-two. Flora was also ninety-two when she passed away in 1984. The couple is now buried in Elmwood Cemetery in Norfolk.[57]

Their two children eventually built lives for themselves outside of the Norfolk area. Following his graduation from the University of Virginia, Johnny enjoyed an accomplished career as a New York City tobacco company executive before retiring to Connecticut. Married to Mary Graham Hull, the couple had two children, Jonathan III and Elizabeth, who attended Dartmouth and Middlebury College respectively. Each went on to careers in business and finance in Connecticut.[58] Flora later married North Carolina native Erle H. Austin Jr., with whom she had three children—Erle III (born in 1948), and twin daughters Stuart and Claudia (born in 1955). Following their divorce, Flora remarried before retiring to Florida, where she currently resides. A 1970 graduate of Dartmouth College, Erle III earned his M.D. from Harvard Medical School and completed his residency at Duke University Hospital. He is now a respected cardiac surgeon affiliated with both the University of Louisville and Jewish Hospital.[59] Married to Lucie "Scott" Dabney Austin, Erle has four sons: Christopher, Hunter, Waller, and Jonathan.

An Old Dominion University alumna, Stuart went on to pursue a career in teaching and eventually relocated to Summerville, South Carolina. She married South Carolina native Drury "Chip" Nimmich, a 1976 Citadel graduate who served nearly 23 years in the U.S. Navy, rising to the rank of commander. He now works for the admissions office at the Citadel. The couple

has a son and daughter named Dru and Claudia. Both recent college gradu-
ates, they are currently pursuing careers in business and law enforcement.[60]
Following her graduation from Old Dominion University, Stuart's twin sister,
Claudia, earned her C.P.A. and became an accountant. After moving to Florida in 1979, she worked for the McDonald's Corporation before becoming a
managing partner with the firm of Foelgner, Ronz, & Straw, P.A., based in
St. Petersburg. From 2002 to 2004, she was vice-president of the National
Franchise Consultants Alliance, and later served as chairman from 2004 to
2006.[61] Married to Michael Straw, a successful businessman and avid history
enthusiast, Claudia has a son named Wesley (known as "Wes"), who was
born in 1973. Married with three children, Wes is an attorney who recently
co-founded the Florida law firm, Emerson Straw PL.[62]

Relatively little is known about Marrow's cousin, Matthew Page Waller,
the middle child and only son of Robert and Virginia Waller. Following
his graduation from Virginia Tech, he married Norfolk native Helen Baker
around 1918. The couple had one daughter, Theodosia "Theo" Page Waller,
who was born in January 1920. During World War I, Matthew also served
as an ensign in the U.S. Navy, which sparked his lifelong interest in boats.
Sometime following the war, he divorced Helen and moved to the Chicago
area. Around 1928, he married his second wife, Helen Robinson. Matthew
passed away in February 1967 in Fox Lake, a small community in Lake
County, Illinois.[63] His daughter Theo later moved to Colorado to pursue a
career in nursing.[64] She never married and now lives in a retirement home in
Northern Virginia.[65]

Marrow's most colorful Waller cousin was without a doubt Virginia Stuart
Waller, the youngest child of Robert and Virginia Waller. While her sister
Flora enjoyed life as a homemaker, Virginia pursued a successful career in
government and media relations. A graduate of Stuart Hall, she attended the
Peabody Conservatory of Music and later studied journalism at the Norfolk
Division of the College of William and Mary, now known as Old Dominion
University. Around 1924, she married Andrew J. Davis, who was a Norfolk
investment banker. The couple later moved to Alexandria, Virginia, where
Andrew served as a manager with the Reconstruction Finance Cooperation
during the 1930s.[66] Meanwhile, Virginia covered the General Assembly for
the *Virginian-Pilot* and later served as press secretary to Gov. Colgate W.
Darden, Jr. from 1942 through 1946. In the late 1940s, Gov. William M. Tuck
selected her to head publicity for the celebrated historical drama, *The Common Glory*, based near the College of William and Mary in Williamsburg,
Virginia.[67]

Throughout her life, Virginia idolized her grandfather, General Stuart,
and was fiercely devoted to him. She guarded his reputation and legacy

closely and was quick to react whenever anyone questioned them. In one famous incident, President Dwight D. Eisenhower learned this lesson all too well. On May 12, 1957, President Eisenhower escorted British Field Marshal Bernard Law Montgomery on a tour of the Gettysburg Battlefield. During the tour, Montgomery criticized the commanding Confederate generals for their actions during the battle. Focusing on General Stuart, Eisenhower joined in, reportedly saying that Stuart's "forays had kept him out of touch with the Army of Northern Virginia and had thus deprived General Robert E. Lee of knowledge of the enemy's movements."[68] The comments were later leaked to the local press, and quickly made their way into national newspapers. Shocked by this criticism of her grandfather, Virginia wrote a sharply worded letter to the president on May 15th demanding an apology. She also included copies of various historical documents that supported Stuart's efforts at Gettysburg.

In his response a few days later, Eisenhower quickly apologized to Virginia, and wrote "let me assure you that no conversation of mine–in spite of piecemeal remarks obviously overheard by reporters–was ever meant to disparage the reputation of General Stuart for gallantry, courage, and resourcefulness."[69] The exchange speaks volumes about Virginia's fierce dedication to her grandfather. She did not hesitate to take on even the most powerful man in the world when General Stuart's reputation was brought into question! Following her government service, Virginia engaged in freelance writing. In her later years, she even had a successful second career as a real estate agent in Alexandria. Along with her career obligations, Virginia was quite active in civic affairs. A former president of the Junior League of Norfolk, she was also a longtime member of Stuart Hall's Board of Trustees, retiring in 1985.[70] With no children of her own, Virginia's nephew, Johnny Old, looked after her in her final years.[71] The last surviving grandchild of General Stuart, she passed away on May 22, 1995 in Alexandria and was buried in Norfolk's Elmwood Cemetery.[72]

Like so many of her relatives, Marrow lived a long, productive, and meaningful life. When it comes to her own legacy, Marrow will be remembered for her untiring efforts in preserving her family's history as well as her accomplishments in the fields of art and education. Known by relatives as the Stuart family's official historian, Marrow spent years accumulating books, letters, and other important documents outlining her family's contributions to the American story. Moreover, by writing so extensively about her childhood experiences, she generated what can be considered today the best primary source available chronicling the life and times of General Stuart's children and grandchildren. Without Marrow's efforts, this fascinating chapter of the Stuart family's history would have likely been lost forever.

Marrow will also be remembered for her leadership and work in the field of art. Many of her paintings are still owned and admired today by Stuart family members across the country. Others have made their way into the open market, and have been purchased by fans of Marrow's unique artistic style. Beyond her paintings, Marrow left a permanent mark on the artistic community in southeastern Virginia. Her efforts in founding or cultivating a number of fine arts organizations across the region have ensured that future generations will have the opportunity to learn about and enjoy art. Marrow was quite unique and there will likely never be another like her. In 1930, *The Virginian Pilot* editor Louis I. Jaffe summarized Marrow best when he wrote that she "belongs to [a] valiant band of adventurers…. who with [little] encouragement are pursuing beauty in a day given over to the exaltation of ugliness."[73] Despite living in a world sometimes overshadowed by human-generated ugliness, Marrow always saw beauty in everything around her. She loved life and always took time to "smell the roses." It is a life philosophy that is simple yet profound, and it provides a powerful lesson for those who are immersed in the frenzied pace of the modern world.

In sum, Mary Marrow Stuart Smith had a long-lasting influence in Tidewater Virginia and beyond through her achievements in art, education, and civic engagement. Descending from a prominent Virginia family known for its soldiers, lawyers, businessmen, and politicians, Marrow forged her own destiny in the realm of fine arts. Along the way, she touched the lives of many people and enjoyed a meaningful career doing what she loved. Now, after decades of silence, her life and art can inspire a whole new generation of Americans. For that, Marrow would be pleased.

NOTES

1. MSS Resume, MSS Papers (Private Collection).
2. Sharon Stuart McRee, email message to editor, June 11, 2010.
3. MSS Obituary, *The Virginian Pilot*, August 9, 1985, MSS Papers (Private Collection).
4. Stephanie Tucker Little, email message to editor, August 4, 2010.
5. *Ibid.*
6. *Ibid.*
7. DMS Jr. Funeral Program, October 16, 1994, MSS Papers (Private Collection).
8. *Ibid.*
9. *Ibid.*
10. *Ibid.*
11. *Ibid.*
12. Sharon Stuart McRee, email message to editor, August 9, 2010.

13. DMS Jr. Funeral Program, October 16, 1994.

14. *Ibid.*

15. *Ibid.*

16. Brooks Institute is a visual arts school with campuses in Santa Barbara and Ventura, California.

17. DMS IV, email message to editor, August 12, 2010.

18. JEBS III, "Genealogical Notes: Descendants of Major General J.E.B. Stuart, CSA," (N.p.: JEBS III Papers, Private Collection, 1981), p. 3.

19. Margaret W. Grover, email message to editor, July 19, 2010.

20. JEBS III, "Genealogical Notes," p. 7.

21. Margaret W. Grover, email message to editor, July 19, 2010.

22. *Ibid.*

23. *Ibid.*

24. JEBS III, "Genealogical Notes," p. 4.

25. JEBS III, "Genealogical Notes," p. 7.

26. Margaret W. Grover, email message to editor, July 19, 2010.

27. *Ibid.*

28. Jo Pres eventually had ten grandchildren.

29. Margaret W. Grover, email message to editor, July 19, 2010.

30. JEBS III, "Genealogical Notes," pp. 4–5.

31. *Ibid.*

32. Olivia Stuart McFadden, personal communication to editor, July 24, 2010.

33. JEBS III, "Genealogical Notes," p. 7.

34. Olivia Stuart McFadden, personal communication to editor, July 24, 2010.

35. JEBS III, "Genealogical Notes," p. 9.

36. JEBS IV membership application, The Society of the Cincinnati in the State of Virginia, 2004, JEBS IV Papers (Private Collection).

37. JEBS IV, personal communication to editor, August 11, 2010.

38. JEBS III, "Genealogical Notes," pp. 5–6.

39. *Ibid.*

40. Elizabeth H. Moorhead, email message to editor, August 4, 2010.

41. *Ibid.*

42. "Danville 'Register' publisher dies at 70," *The Richmond News Leader*, August 8, 1990, Helen L. Grant Papers (Private Collection).

43. Stratford College closed in 1974.

44. "Walter L. Grant Dies From Heart Attack," *The Danville Register & Bee*, June 3, 1972, Helen L. Grant Papers (Private Collection).

45. Helen L. Grant, personal communication with editor, August 4, 2010.

46. "Danville 'Register' publisher dies at 70," *The Richmond News Leader*, August 8, 1990, Helen L. Grant Papers (Private Collection).

47. Lady Astor (1879-1964), who was married to Waldorf Astor (1906-1952), the 2nd Viscount Astor, served in the House of Commons from 1919 until 1945.

48. Helen L. Grant, personal communication with editor, August 4, 2010.

49. See http://www.virginiabusiness.com/index.php/news/JUNE_top_50_VA_found/.

50. Located near Washington, D.C., the Chevy Chase Junior College was purchased by the National 4-H Club Foundation in 1951 and turned into a conference center.

51. Frances Stansbury, "Anne Wilson James to Become Bride of Robert Hundt; Wedding in Spring," *The Virginian Pilot*, March 7, 1954, Anne Wilson James Hundt Papers (Private Collection).

52. Elizabeth H. Moorhead, email message to editor, August 4, 2010.

53. "Elizabeth Hundt to Wed Lawyer," *The New York Times*, May 13, 1984, Anne Wilson James Hundt Papers (Private Collection).

54. Thomas C. Moorhead Jr., email message to editor, June 10, 2010; Sir George Calvert (1579–1632) was a Member of Parliament and Secretary of State under King James I. Many historians recognize him as the founder of Maryland.

55. Elizabeth H. Moorhead, email message to editor, July 13, 2010.

56. Jonathan W. Old Obituary, *The Virginian-Pilot*, undated, Jonathan W. Old Jr. Papers (Private Collection).

57. Jonathan W. Old Jr., personal communication with editor, August 11, 2010.

58. *Ibid.*

59. CTS*Net*, "Member Homepage: Erle H. Austin, III, M.D." The Cardiac Surgery Network, http://www.ctsnet.org/home/eaustin.

60. Stuart A. Nimmich, email message to editor, August 12, 2010.

61. Firm Profile, "Partner Profiles: Claudia A. Straw, CPA," Foelgner, Ronz, & Straw, P.A., http://www.frscpa.com/profile.html.

62. Claudia A. Straw, email message to editor, August 13, 2010.

63. JEBS III, "Genealogical Notes," p. 6.

64. Jonathan W. Old Jr., personal communication with editor, August 11, 2010.

65. Claudia A. Straw, personal communication with editor, July 15, 2010.

66. JEBS III, "Genealogical Notes," p. 6.

67. Virginia Stuart Waller Davis Obituary, *The Virginian Pilot*, May 24, 1995, Jonathan W. Old Jr. Papers (Private Collection).

68. Glenn W. LaFantasie, "Monty and Ike Take Gettysburg," *MHQ: The Quarterly Journal of Military History, 8* (Autumn, 1995), p. 71.

69. Dwight D. Eisenhower to Virginia Stuart Waller Davis, June 5, 1957, *The Papers of Dwight David Eisenhower,* ed. L. Galambos and D. van Ee, doc. 184. World Wide Web facsimile by The Dwight D. Eisenhower Memorial Commission of the print edition; Baltimore, MD: The Johns Hopkins University Press, 1996, http://www.eisenhowermemorial.org/presidentialpapers/second-term/documents/184.cfm.

70. Virginia Stuart Waller Davis Obituary, May 24, 1995.

71. Jonathan W. Old Jr., personal communication with editor, August 11, 2010.

72. Virginia Stuart Waller Davis Obituary, May 24, 1995.

73. Louis I. Jaffe to MSS, February 4, 1930, MSS Papers (Private Collection).

Index

CPSIA information can be obtained
at www.ICGtesting.com
Printed in the USA
LVHW091327180223
739842LV00033B/1455

9 780761 854630